Fields White
Unto
Harvest

Fields White
Unto
Harvest

Charles F. Parham
and
the Missionary Origins of Pentecostalism

James R. Goff, Jr.

The University of Arkansas Press

Fayetteville • London

1988

DESIGNER: *Nancy Burris*
TYPEFACE: *Linotron 202 Sabon*
TYPESETTER: *G & S Typesetters, Inc.*
PRINTER: *Thomson-Shore, Inc.*
BINDER: *John H. Dekker & Sons, Inc.*

The paper used in this publication meets the minimum
requirements of the American National Standard for
Permanence of Paper for Printed Library Materials
Z39.48-1984. ∞

LIBRARY OF CONGRESS CATALOGING-IN-PUBLICATION DATA
Goff, James R., 1957–
  Fields white unto harvest.
  Bibliography: p.
  Includes index.
  1. Pentecostalism—History. 2. Pentecostal
churches—History. 3. Parham, Charles F. I. Title.
BR1644.G64 1988   289.9 [B]   88-14375
ISBN 1-55728-025-8 (alk. paper)
ISBN 1-55728-026-6 (pbk. : alk. paper)

For Granny and Granddaddy

Acknowledgments

This work grew out of research and writing begun during my doctoral program at the University of Arkansas. It stresses the importance of Pentecostalism in the twentieth century and Charles Parham's role in the development of the movement. As my research unfolded, it became apparent that only a biography of Parham could uncover the origins of twentieth century Pentecostal theology. The uniqueness of his experience and theological evaluation hold the mystery of Pentecostal development and growth. My own background provided valuable insight into the Pentecostal milieu; nevertheless, I struggled to distance myself from any emotional association with my subject. The struggle grew out of not only my training as a historian, but also the simple belief that faith is never helped by sentimental history.

Many people contributed to the completion of this book. Four professors deserve special mention for nurturing my interest in Pentecostalism. Dr. Vinson Synan first inspired me with a freshman course in the intellectual origins of the movement. Years later Dr. Grant Wacker challenged me to think critically about the social and cultural roots. Through graduate study, Dr. David E. Harrell and Dr. Willard B. Gatewood offered invaluable direction and encouragement of the research which led to this study.

Part of the research was funded by grants received from the Mary Hudgins Scholarship Foundation and the Center for Arkansas and Regional Studies, Fayetteville, Arkansas. The following institutions and organizations also helped make this a successful project: The University of Arkansas' Mullins Library and especially its Inter-Library Loan Department, the Assemblies of God Archives, Oral Roberts University's Holy

Spirit Research Center, the Apostolic Faith Bible College and
the staff of the *Apostolic Faith Report,* the Pentecostal Holi-
ness Church Archives, the Kansas Historical Association, the
Bexar County Courthouse Archives, the Eugene Barker Texas
History Center at the University of Texas, the Southwestern
Assemblies of God College, the United Pentecostal Church
Archives, and Academic Computing Services at Appalachian
State University.

I would also like to thank my friends at the University of
Arkansas and my colleagues at both Watauga High School
and Appalachian State University for their encouragement
over the past few years of research and writing.

For special help and direction, I extend gratitude to Dr.
Timothy Donovan, Dr. Evan Bukey, Debra Cochran, Wayne
Warner, Karen Robinson, Margaret Muse Drum, Maxine
Benson, Dr. Pauline Parham, Rev. Bennie Stanberry, Marjorie
Haire, Geralean Harshfield, Rev. Jack Cornell, Rev. Naomi
Busch, Dr. Charles Chalfant, Dr. Wade Burnside, David Gar-
cia, Alma Nehrbass, Rev. Eddie Morris, Wiley and Jean
Clark, John Hendler, Chip and Lynne Woodward, Dr. George
Antone, and Ricky and Steve Weeks.

A separate word of thanks is necessary to all the members
of my family who have given so much of themselves to this
project in direct help, encouragement, and prayers. More
than anyone else, my wife Connie made the book possible by
her support, her help, and her love. My children, Gideon and
Kacy, gave much of their father to this work and, as an old
friend once advised me, they have made me a better writer.
I also thank my parents James and Kathryn Goff, my sister
Sheila Talton, and my parents-in-law Herman and Lucille
Crawford. In different ways, they have contributed much to
my life and the successful completion of this book.

Finally, I thank my maternal grandparents, Luther Gilbert
Forehand and Ella Gardner Forehand. Unwittingly, they
caused me to love the past as I grew to respect the era which
produced their character much more than the one which
produced my own. Granny taught me the power of personal

religious devotion; Granddaddy, that faith must be lived before it is spoken. Grateful for their quiet but profound contribution, I dedicate the book to his memory and in her honor.

James R. Goff, Jr.
April 1988
Boone, North Carolina

Table of Contents

Illustrations

In the mean while his disciples prayed him, saying, Master, eat. But he said unto them, I have meat to eat that ye know not of. Therefore said the disciples one to another, Hath any man brought him ought to eat? Jesus saith unto them, My meat is to do the will of him that sent me, and to finish his work. Say not ye, There are yet four months, and then cometh harvest? Behold, I say unto you, Lift up your eyes, and look on the fields; for they are white already to harvest.

John 4:31–35
King James Version

Fields White
Unto
Harvest

Introduction

Pentecostalism is arguably the single most important religious movement in modern times. Numbers alone are enough to give credence to this claim; Pentecostals boast phenomenal growth. In less than a century after its obscure origins in America in 1901, the movement now claims a worldwide total of some fifty-one million souls, which makes it the largest single element within Protestantism. An additional eleven million members of the Charismatic movement increase the figure given for practicing Pentecostals to sixty-two million, with as many as one hundred million under the regular influence of Pentecostal teaching.[1]

Pentecostals and Charismatics in the United States comprised nineteen percent of the adult population in 1980. The growth rate is most astounding when placed within the context of the last twenty-five years. When Henry Van Dusen first portrayed the phenomenon of a "third force" within Christendom in *Life* magazine in 1958, he estimated the entire movement of Pentecostals worldwide at eight and a half million.[2] Despite Van Dusen's optimistic assessment of the future of these Pentecostal sects, he could not have imagined the phenomenal growth of the sixties and seventies. By 1964 Pentecostal theology was invading the traditional Protestant camp; Episcopals, Presbyterians, Lutherans, Methodists, and

Baptists learned to pray in private cell groups for the onset of a spirit-filled life manifested by spiritual gifts. By 1970, the Roman Catholic Church was likewise infected. Seminary students and innovative priests sponsored the small—but rapidly growing—Charismatic renewal which, surprisingly for many observers, has remained within the church with the guarded approval of the Catholic hierarchy.

So much growth in so short a period of time has captured the interest of religious observers and historians. For the sake of clarification, the movement is here divided into three separate camps: the traditional (pre-1960) Pentecostals who formed distinct denominations are termed classical; the Protestant Pentecostals (i.e., those maintaining ties within their respective mainline denominations) are called the New or Neo-Pentecostals; the Catholic constituents are generally labeled Catholic Charismatics or the Catholic Renewal. Both Neo-Pentecostals and members of the Catholic Renewal are often linked together and are simply called Charismatics. Of the twenty-nine million adult Americans who claim ties to Pentecostalism, a full one-fourth are Catholic Charismatics. Another forty percent are Neo-Pentecostals. Thus only a third of the total, around ten million, of U.S. Pentecostals fall within the confines of the traditional Pentecostal denominations.[3]

The 1982 *World Christian Encyclopedia* defines Pentecostalism as "a Christian confession or ecclesiastical tradition holding the distinctive teaching that all Christians should seek a post-conversion religious experience called the Baptism with the Holy Spirit, and that a spirit-baptized believer may receive one or more of the supernatural gifts known in the early church: instantaneous sanctification, the ability to prophesy, practice divine healing, speak in tongues (glossolalia), or interpret tongues."[4] But is a Pentecostal a Charismatic? Is a Charismatic a Pentecostal? The most common answer is negative to the first question and affirmative to the second. But the theological diversity within the movement reasons that some tighter definition is warranted.

Important theological differences are recognized by participants on both sides of the fence. Traditional Pentecostals have called into question the lack of theological conformity on the part of the Neo-Pentecostals and Charismatics. Of chief importance is the doctrine of initial evidence which holds that reception of the Holy Spirit baptism carries with it a definable manifestation evident to all present at the time, namely, speaking in tongues, glossolalia. Charismatics have quite often objected to what they consider a singular emphasis on tongues and have accepted Holy Spirit reception evidenced by any of the nine spiritual gifts mentioned in I Corinthians 12:7–11.[5] The magnitude of the issue is demonstrated by the results of the *Christianity Today* Gallup Poll taken in 1980. While only seventeen percent of all U.S. Pentecostal-Charismatics reported having ever spoken in tongues, close to fifty percent of traditional Pentecostals claimed such an experience.[6] One prominent historian has tried to bridge the gap by using the image of "one river" (i.e., Pentecostalism) being fed by three different streams (traditional, Neo, and Charismatic). However, the ability to perform such a tightwire act is becoming increasingly difficult.[7]

Rather than continue to use Pentecostal as an umbrella term to cover all who argue for the validity of charismata in the church, it is more appropriate to reserve that term for the traditional Pentecostals. A historical perspective of the movement reveals more clearly than generally acknowledged by historians that Pentecostalism is a rather strict, definable movement within a larger phenomenon which has its origins in the late nineteenth century. The period since 1875 might be loosely termed a Pneumatic, or Spirit, age within which the stricter theological phenomenon of Pentecostalism arose. The Charistmatic movement (both the Neo-Pentecostal and Catholic Charismatic Renewals) should thus be viewed as a more recent manifestation of a century-old phenomenon. Pentecostalism is a more theologically defined movement which grew out of the Spirit age but succeeded in attaining an identity of its own.

Pentecostalism alone is an impressive enough historical phenomenon, as the ten million American and fifty-one million worldwide figures attest. That the worldwide figure is

five times that of the American—despite American roots—
emphasizes the importance and effectiveness of Pentecostal
missions. The bulk of worldwide growth has come in recent
decades within the so-called Third World nations and is to be
credited somewhat to the opening of the Charismatic age.
The message of Pentecostal missionaries has been captured by
local populations and transformed into a unique message of
religious liberation. The growth of the movement in certain
African, Latin American, and Asian countries suggests that
the movement there has achieved its own identity. Of the
fifty-one million Pentecostals worldwide, at least twenty-two
million were listed in a 1980 census as "non-white indige-
nous." The bulk of these Pentecostals are now far beyond the
tutorial arms of denominational missionaries, though they
often maintain an affiliated alliance with the smaller American organizations.[8]

The Pentecostal denominations in America had their origins in three separate stages. The earliest were organized in
the 1890s as radical holiness denominations breaking, in
large part, from the Methodist Church over the issue of entire
sanctification. The doctrine had been the cardinal plank in
the National Holiness Crusade, an interdenominational but
Methodist-dominated movement which spread the message
of an instantaneous second work of grace capable of cleansing individuals of the inbred sin-nature inherited from Adam.
By the 1890s a sizable number of holiness evangelists were
convinced that the mainline churches were concerned less
with holiness and more with social status and respectability.
The suspicion was enhanced by Methodist leaders who were
indeed embarrassed by the uneducated demeanor of many
of the holiness evangelists. The result was a host of "come-
outers" who launched their own small denominational units
in the interest of theological and ethical purity.[9] A portion of
these holiness denominations became Pentecostal during the
first decade of the twentieth century by virtue of accepting the
new Pentecostal doctrine of a separate experience of Holy
Spirit baptism evidenced by glossolalia. The Church of God
(Cleveland, Tennessee), the Church of God in Christ, and

the Pentecostal Holiness Church are representative of these denominations.

A second stage in denominational organization came after the spread of Pentecostal doctrine. The Apostolic Faith movement was a loosely organized body based in the Midwest by 1906. Their followers were, in effect, Wesleyan-holiness advocates who formulated the theological distinctions of Pentecostal baptism in 1901 and launched out with a new vision of apostolic purity. Others who came into contact with Pentecostal doctrine after 1906 did not share the Wesleyan definition of holiness. In addition to the National Holiness Crusade, the amorphous holiness movement of the late nineteenth century had drawn from at least two other sources of strength. One centered around a religious awakening at an annual retreat in Keswick, England; the other around an evangelically sponsored "higher-life" movement in the Reformed churches of America.

The Keswick constituents preached a message of holiness power, arguing that an experience subsequent to conversion served the utilitarian function of empowering the recipient for bolder Christian service. Similarly, the higher-life advocates noted the increased dedication and commitment available in the "second blessing." Those from both these traditions who accepted the Pentecostal message preferred to view it as the final fulfillment of this second experience for power rather than—as the Wesleyans had done—retain the older doctrine and create a new "third blessing." Unable to find medium ground on the sanctification issue and, no doubt, put off by the already established organization of the holiness Pentecostals, these Reformed Pentecostals merged in 1914 to form the largest of the classical Pentecostal denominations, the Assemblies of God.

The third avenue of denominational organization came via splits. From 1906 to 1908 the Apostolic Faith movement, rocked by the rapid growth of Pentecostal doctrine and weakened by its own loose organization, suffered a division into three distinct groups—each of which retained the original name. However, the issues involved in these divisions were largely personal conflicts between leaders and questions over worship style. A more important division struck during the second decade of the movement's existence when a trinitarian controversy within the Assemblies of God resulted in the formation of the Pentecostal Assemblies of the World, a Unitarian Pentecostal body. Subsequent splits solidified this third "oneness" division of Pentecostalism.[11]

Despite the schisms, Pentecostalism prospered. By 1930, the three divisions of the movement had organized their own distinct fellowships. Each began a pattern of steady growth and sponsored an increased program for foreign missions. William Warren Sweet's 1950 revision of his classic American religious survey was obliged to include the growing Pentecostals, noting that the depression decade had stimulated the public to an "otherworldly" message. The Assemblies of God jumped from 48,000 in 1926 to 175,000 in 1937. During the same period the Cleveland, Tennessee-based Church of God increased from 23,000 to 80,000.[12] Even more dramatic was the rise taking place while Sweet wrote. In 1950 the Assemblies of God reached 318,478; by 1960 they registered 508,602.[13] Over the next twenty years, the Assemblies tripled their American membership rolls. By 1983 the figure for U.S. membership totaled 1,788,394 and the Assemblies could herald the claim of fastest-growing denomination in America. The 1986 count continued to show an astounding growth rate with 2,135,104 Americans affiliated with the denomination.[14]

Along with the rise in numbers, American Pentecostals have enjoyed a not surprising rise in social status. Joining the "little brown church in the dell" are a host of new megachurches that boast fine physical plants, multistaffed ministerial leadership, and well-oiled programs for church growth and development. In addition to the traditional outreach to the poor and working classes of American society, Pentecostals have found a ministry among the middle and upper-middle income groups. Part of this has no doubt been the result of American prosperity in the decades since World War II. Some "birthright" Pentecostals have steadily climbed the social ladder and remained within their churches; but this alone is not sufficient to explain the change. Pentecostals have also begun a self-conscious middle-class appeal which displays their open worship style as a part of the "up and coming" religious fashion.

The social mobility of Pentecostals has created an interest in examining the roots of their development. Treatment by Pentecostals has too often romanticized the movement, though the better accounts have offered significant insight, particularly in ideological origins. Vinson Synan's *The Holiness-Pentecostal Movement in America* in 1971 traced Pentecostal roots through the Wesleyan-holiness movement, arguing that the later Reformed denominations represented theological division in the original ranks. Edith Lynn Waldvogel, in "The 'Overcoming Life': A Study in the Reformed Evangelical Origins of Pentecostalism," countered with the acknowledgment of the Keswickian and higher-life movements in the origins of Pentecostal thought. Thus it was not division which created the Reformed Pentecostals, Waldvogel argued, but the independent stream of Reformed theology which had roots in the movement's development equally as strong as that of the Wesleyans. Both Synan and Waldvogel defined Pentecostalism by its unique theological link with tongues as initial evidence. They credited a white Kansas healing evangelist, Charles Fox Parham, with directing the formation of this credo and a black Louisiana-born holiness preacher, William J. Seymour, with overseeing the spread of the doctrine through the international effect of the Azusa Street revival in Los Angeles during the three years from 1906 to 1909.[15]

Non-Pentecostal historians have also been much interested in Pentecostal origins. Spurred by the growth of the phenomenon, and particularly by the complexity of its current manifestations, Robert Anderson presented the most detailed study of the movement's origins in *Vision of the Disinherited*. Anderson's thesis was that Pentecostalism originated as a highly millenarian movement prompted by the social deprivation of generally poor and working class Americans. His

Marxist approach offered a simplistic analysis but his assessment of the social dynamics behind religious orientation forced historians of the movement to grapple with complex questions.[16]

A third historiographical vein warrants mention here. Douglas J. Nelson has suggested that Charles Parham's role in Pentecostal origins was overstated by historians in both the Synan-Waldvogel and Anderson scenarios. Developing a racial conspiracy theory, Nelson's "For Such a Time as This: The Story of Bishop William J. Seymour and the Azusa Street" Revival presents Seymour as the unqualified founder of a heroic religious movement whose origins are to be found, not in a glossolalia-evidenced Holy Spirit experience, but rather in a genuine breakdown of racial and class barriers. The interracial worship during the initial phase of the Azusa Street revival convinced Nelson that this phenomenon, more than tongues, recreated the spirit of the New Testament Pentecost experience described in Acts 2. Nelson's thesis suffers from an inability to support such a redefinition of Pentecostalism, given the admitted brief tenure of interracial worship and the subsequent failure of Pentecostals to prevent racial church segregation. In the final analysis, it is clear that racial equality was a doctrine of black Pentecostals at Azusa. In the same way, it permeated the mind-set of the black community in the early twentieth century; only whites consciously preached a message of white superiority. Nelson fails in his attempt to provide evidence that white Pentecostals at Azusa were significantly different from the public at large. The failure of an integrated movement by the midpoint of the Azusa revival proves the exact opposite.[17]

In the face of such conflicting research, it is imperative that a deeper study of Pentecostal origins be made. Anderson's sociological treatment is valuable but must be weighed against the Synan-Waldvogel ideological school. Nelson's work offers an in-depth look at one of the movement's crucial early leaders, but its overly romantic thesis has caused more problems than it has solved. As a part of the needed research, this

book proposes the first scholarly investigation of Charles Fox
Parham and his Apostolic Faith movement which originated
in the Midwest during the years that marked the turn of
the twentieth century. Parham, more than Seymour, must be
regarded the founder of the Pentecostal movement. It was
Parham who first formulated the theological definition of
Pentecostalism by linking tongues with the Holy Spirit baptism. Neither Parham nor contemporary Pentecostals would
declare tongues the "only" evidence of reception of the Pentecostal blessing. Rather it served as the "initial" evidence.
Despite the semantics, the phenomenon was crucial. As the
initial evidence, glossolalia becomes the *sine qua non* of the
experience and its importance is hard to overestimate.

Nelson's definition of glossolalia linked with interracial
equality is true only of the earliest months of the Pentecostal
movement and it is speculative whether whites ever accepted
such a premise. To redefine Pentecostalism as such would lead
to the ludicrous proposal that the movement ceased to exist
only months after it started. More correctly stated, Pentecostalism witnessed a temporary breakdown in the racial
mores of the Pentecostal community. Parham's wing of the
movement was similarly, though less dramatically, affected.
New religious movements have often portrayed such an idealistic quality. In the case of Pentecostalism, this idealistic
manifestation faded away as the movement met the harsh realities of life in the early twentieth century. What survived
was the central theological corpus which had always defined
the movement—the Baptism of the Holy Spirit evidenced by
speaking in tongues.

Parham's role is also significant because it symbolizes the
sociological origins of Pentecostalism. The themes expressed
in Pentecostal meetings—radical conversion, sanctification or
holiness in daily living, divine healing from all sickness, and
the premillennial rapture of the "Bride of Christ"—all contained a release within the individual's religious psyche which
portrayed a future release from the problems faced in the here
and now. More importantly, they provided comfort in this life

in dealing with disappointments and fears. Conversion absolved the guilt of past shortcomings; sanctification promised an assurance of one's rightness with God. Divine healing, perhaps more than all the others, symbolized God's approval of an individual and his power over the uncertainties of mortal life.[18] Premillennialism provided the knowledge that God's chosen people would hold a special place in the fulfillment of divine justice.

Pentecostalism differed little in the expression of these themes from evangelical Protestant religion in general, except that the emphasis on such divine intervention was unusually high. The one unique plank of the Pentecostal message demonstrated that intensity. The Baptism of the Holy Spirit offered divine approval in at least two ways. First of all, it identified the receiver with the saints of the early church, since the experience was understood to be a latter-day manifestation of the apostolic reception recorded in Acts 2. This experience then would serve as proof that one was fit to be in the "Bride of Christ"—the host of raptured saints who return at the end of time and, led by their triumphant Savior, defeat the forces of Satan in a series of final eschatological battles. In addition, the baptism experience itself signified the climax of human history as we know it. It served as a set of bookends marking the last of the eschatological ages—the Church age. Begun by the Acts 2 outpouring, this era would end with a similar manifestation. Thus the Pentecostal movement defined itself as the immediate signal of Christ's return and his triumphal victory over evil. All who participated in this outpouring were aiding the exciting conclusion of God's creative process.[19]

As Anderson has shown, this millenarian milieu was crucial in creating the revolutionary mind-set of early Pentecostalism. It explains why many aspiring but frustrated Americans, disillusioned by the failure of the Populist movement and unable to effectively change their status in society, turned to a developing religious movement which promised tangible changes in the imminence of the Second Coming. What Anderson's thesis fails to explain is why the movement affected some, but not all, Americans. That the movement drew its strength from the poor and working classes is certain. But it is equally true that the movement was vehemently rejected by considerable numbers within those social groupings. Most significant is the degree of opposition met within the radical holiness denominations that provided such an important seedbed for Pentecostal growth.[20] In short, a sociological explanation explains some but not all of the questions of origin. The theological interpretations did matter and carried great weight among the leaders of holiness denominations who, in turn, impressed such importance on their followers. In addition, the matter of religious motivation cannot be reduced to simple sociological models. In the end, what seemed sheer nonsense to some became an abiding assurance to others. Often the difference was tied to individual contacts with the converted and personal experience with the movement's evangelical exhorters. For the believers, acceptable doctrine merged with sociological needs to create fierce devotion. The earliest converts in this theological-sociological mix fell under the ministry of Charles F. Parham.

John Thomas Nichol's *Pentecostalism* placed Parham in a position of prominence two decades ago and listed at least five criteria for his claim as founder: (1) Parham was the recognized Pentecostal leader in the Midwest both before and during the Azusa Street beginnings, (2) His application of "Apostolic Faith" was the universal term used by the earliest members of the movement, (3) He published the first Pentecostal periodical, the *Apostolic Faith* (Topeka, Kansas), (4) He organized the first interstate Pentecostal meetings, and (5) He issued the first ministerial credentials within the loosely organized Pentecostal movement.[21]

Nichol's work underscored a revision in Parham's reputation as a Pentecostal pioneer. The earliest histories of the movement by Pentecostals failed to emphasize Parham's contribution; his evangelistic efforts were often noted without mention of his name. This oversight was corrected first by Frank J. Ewart in *The Phenomenon of Pentecost* and then by Klaude Kendrick in *The Promise Fulfilled: A History of the Modern Pentecostal Movement*. Kendrick, in particular, gave an in-depth portrait of Parham's part in the pioneering phase of Pentecostalism.[22] A non-Pentecostal writer, Charles William Shumway, noted Parham as an important part of the movement as early as 1914. Later non-Pentecostal writers, such as Anderson, gave increased prominence to Parham's role.[23]

Ironically, apologists for both Parham and Seymour have served to correct an older—though still recurring—notion that Pentecostalism had no human founder. The obscuring of Parham's place was due primarily to questions of personal morality centered around a homosexual scandal in Texas in 1907; Seymour's fall from prominence had mostly to do with the lack of unity at Azusa after 1906, as well as the failure of whites to take seriously the contributions of a black pioneer. The imagined void was thus filled by the romantic notion that the Holy Spirit alone had prompted this movement. That argument seemed to explain why early leaders had vanished from view and set well with Pentecostalism's vision of its own unique place within human history.[24]

The illusion that Pentecostalism had only spiritual origins is paralleled in the literature by assumptions that the movement sprang simultaneously into existence in a spirit of global revival. The conjecture breaks down because "tongues" used as evidence is traceable directly to Parham in the Topeka revival of 1901.[25] Similarly mistaken are the accounts which stress glossolalic outbreaks of the nineteenth century. Since tongue-speaking occurred, some Pentecostal writers have suggested that their movement began earlier than the Topeka revival. This assumes, however, glossolalia alone can link a wide variety of theological and historical settings. Glossolalic outbreaks prior to 1901 provide interesting comparisons but in no case do they provide an historical antecedent to Parham's contention that Holy Spirit baptism is initially evidenced by tongue speech.[26]

In addition to the Parham, Seymour, and "no-founder" schools, some Pentecostal writers have emphasized Parham's theological origins and Seymour's successful crusade in Los

Angeles. This school has argued that both men are founders in a kind of dual role which offered a merger of ideological roots and practical results.[27] The problem with this approach is that it obscures the primacy of theological formulation and overlooks the continuity of sociological factors present during the pre-Azusa Street period. While both men may properly be considered pioneers, only Parham can chronologically be labeled founder. His pre-Azusa contribution marked both the theological foundation of Pentecostalism and the emergence of a sociological message of liberation.

The dual thesis of this study is that Charles Parham founded the Pentecostal movement in Topeka, Kansas, early in 1901 and that the essential character of this new faith revolved around an intense millenarian-missions emphasis. The dynamics of this missionary thrust formed the identity of the movement through the early years of growth at Azusa Street and continued to influence Pentecostal thought even after the initial period of optimism faded.

When Anderson investigated the millenarian roots of Pentecostalism, he noted Parham's emphasis on xenoglossa. Distinguished from glossolalia, xenoglossa is speaking a known foreign language without having gained a prior knowledge of that tongue.[28] Since Parham and other premillennialists believed that the eschatological "last days" would witness a worldwide revival sparked by successful mission efforts in heathen lands, the importance of the new gift of tongues took on greater significance. Parham, and virtually all early Pentecostals, assumed tongue-speaking to be specifically xenoglossa. Taking a utilitarian approach, they theorized that this new gift from God signaled the dawn of a missionary explosion. Without the arduous task of learning foreign languages, almost anyone could now be christened a missionary. God gave the training and the message in the form of the tongues—all the recipient had to do was determine what language he had received and travel as an incogitant vessel of divine issue to the place that language was spoken. While Anderson was first to recognize the universality of this belief among early

Pentecostals, its ideological importance in spawning the movement was lost amidst his larger thesis of sociological determination.[29]

Actually, this remarkable belief in the utility of tongues was crucial in distinguishing Pentecostals from the broader holiness movement. It provided an idealistic zeal that promised tangible results within their lifetimes. By 1909 many Pentecostals were becoming skeptical of missionary tongues, at least as a widespread phenomenon. Tongues—now primarily understood as glossolalia—served as proof of one's reception of Holy Spirit baptism and, with the assistance of a divinely inspired interpreter, carried a message of hope and assurance to individual congregations. However, the initial interpretation most clearly indicated the revolutionary claim with which Parham and the Pentecostals burst upon the American religious scene.

Parham, then, is the key to any interpretation of Pentecostal origins. He formulated the connection between Holy Spirit baptism and tongues, oversaw the initial growth and organization, and initiated the idyllic vision of xenoglossic missions. The story of his life and ministry reveals the sociological and ideological roots of Pentecostalism. Before the movement was a decade old, Parham's name had been besmirched by scandal and his leadership repudiated by the major Pentecostal factions. Underneath his failure to control the movement he started lay the dynamic force of religious zeal which, in time, created other charismatic personalities who challenged his leadership. More profoundly, Parham's decline signaled a fundamental shift in Pentecostalism from a revolution of socioreligious significance to a movement of organized denominations seeking respectability as a part of evangelical Protestantism. The ambitions and dreams of a religiously obscure Kansas evangelist form the foundation of the fifty-one million strong Pentecostal movement of the twentieth century. At its earliest stages, the story of that movement is the story of Charles Parham and the Apostolic Faith.

1

The Perils of Youth
1873–1892

Charles Fox Parham was a child of the American frontier. The hardy souls who traveled west in the nineteenth century took with them a varied assortment of religious beliefs and cultural distinctions. The experience of the frontier did not ameliorate these differences but it did bring about a necessary degree of tolerance and, therein, helped produce the inventive genius of religious prophets. This was especially true in the agricultural West where economic depressions and natural catastrophes followed boom years to create a highly unstable economic and social climate. Religion served a dual purpose in such surroundings. It offered hope for the future and an avenue to deal with the frustrations of the conditions of the present.[1]

The Parham name has a small but distinguished link with the American past. Relatively few in number, the Parham clan traces its genealogy back to the England of William the Conqueror and its American roots to 1624 in Charles City County, Virginia. Though most Parhams remained in the South, a few pressed northward into the middle colonies.[2] William M. Parham migrated West with his parents from his native Philadelphia in the 1850s and took up residence near the riverfront town of Muscatine, Iowa. There he met and married Ann Maria Eckel, another transplanted Pennsylvanian, whose

ancestral roots lay in the German immigrant stock of Schuyl-
kill County. On June 4, 1873 Charles Fox Parham became
the third of five sons born to the couple.[3]

Muscatine County, Iowa, was a bustling frontier community by 1870 with a population of 21,897. The county seat of
the same name was a town quickly making its mark as a commercial lumber center on a strategic stretch of the Mississippi
River. William Parham worked as a horse-collar maker and
house painter and had no doubt achieved an average income
by the date of his third son's birth. He not only supported his
family but was able to afford baby pictures of his son Charles
made by a Muscatine photographer, J. P. Phelps. In addition,
the elder Parham was able to pack up his family and, early in
1878, seek his fortunes in the agricultural wheat boom of
Kansas. Traveling some four hundred miles southwest across
Missouri and Kansas in a prairie schooner, the Parhams came
to settle in newly developed Sedgwick County in the south-
central part of the Jayhawk state. There the family's hope
for success was rewarded with a half-decade of exceptional
harvests.[4]

To say that the Parhams arrived at an opportune time
would be an understatement. In 1860 the land soon to be
Sedgwick County remained unorganized. A decade later it
was only a sparsely settled county of 1,095. But by 1875 the
rush was on. Over eight thousand now inhabited the county
with land values running at five to ten dollars an acre for wild
land and eight to ten dollars for improved. Pamphlets and
books lauding the opportunities of the newly found Kansan
paradise were eagerly distributed. And they were not without
merit. In 1878 Sedgwick ranked second in Kansas wheat production with 1,883,838 bushels. The county also ranked near
the top in the production of corn, oats, and Irish potatoes.[5]

By 1883 William Parham had achieved a respectable place
within the Anness community, ten miles south of Cheney,
Kansas. A contemporary history recorded that Parham's 160-
acre farm "contains sixty acres in cultivation. His outbuild-
ings are very large and commodious. He has every facility

for the care of stock, in which he largely deals." In addition, Parham had served on the district school board since his arrival in 1878 and as local postmaster since 1880. All in all, the Parham frontier experience had been a successful one.[6]

In one sense, Kansas as a short-term Garden of Eden was no different than any other part of the American frontier. For those who arrived early with sufficient capital to survive the initial lean years, hard work alone seemed enough to guarantee fulfillment of the American Dream. The violence between proslavery forces and Free-Soilers that had first thrust Kansas onto the national scene during the 1850s had ended by the outbreak of civil war in 1861. Following the war, U.S. forces under General Phil Sheridan increased the security of white settlers in Kansas by defeating the native Cheyenne who had fought an intermittent war since the Colorado gold rush of 1858. With safety less of a factor, settlers began pouring into the newly admitted state in the late 1860s. The lure of virgin lands was the biggest draw; around sixty percent of Kansas real estate was ultimately distributed under the government's Preemption Act of 1841 and Homestead Act of 1862.[7]

The initial boom of the late 1860s was dampened by a series of events early in the 1870s. The economic depression of 1873 lowered agricultural prices and impeded Kansans' search for an economic bonanza. Even more devastating for many were the swarms of grasshoppers that attacked crops in the summer of 1874 on top of difficulty already caused by persistent drought. 1875 proved the problems to be temporary ones; a new growth spurt began as prosperity returned amidst record yields. The farm crop reports for 1878 listed many Kansas farmers at thirty bushels per acre for wheat and seventy-five per acre for corn. This time prosperity continued into the 1880s and the numbers willing to gamble on Kansas grew. The growth during the last five years of the decade pushed the 1880 census figure to 996,096—a 173 percent increase over the 1870 census. The biggest influx came in central Kansas where the bountiful wheat harvest quickly earned the region the nickname Golden Belt.[8]

By 1887 the dream of a mid-American agricultural renaissance had faded once again. The prosperous, wet years of the early 1880s had given way to struggling, dry years. Kansas would have to wait almost two decades before agricultural boom years were common again and, even then, comparable yields could be reached only with irrigation and dry-farming methods. The Kansas "crash of '87" revealed an unhealthy speculation on the rate of western expansion that would drive the nation toward another general panic in 1893. More immediately, the crash spelled an end to the idealistic Kansas frontier. In this environment of insecurity and lost dreams, religion played a vital role in restoring hope for the future.[9]

The initial outgrowth of the agrarian collapse was political discontent. Populism portrayed the frustrations of farmers faced with declining prices, due in part to the prosperous years of overproduction and the current low yields of the agricultural downturn. In addition, the deflationary money policy of an eastern establishment determined to secure the fortunes of the growing American industrial magnates actually increased the value of outstanding mortgage notes and forced many desperate farmers out of business. There was no organized conspiracy against agriculture as Populists often assumed; nevertheless, agrarian groups were correct in their assessment that political clout through organization was essential if any plan of effective change in government policy was to be achieved.

Kansas stood at the forefront of this political effort. Populist orator Mary Elizabeth Lease in the 1890 Congressional campaigns urged her fellow Kansans "to raise less corn and more Hell."[10] In the same campaign, Populist candidate Jerry Simpson, after accusing his opponent of wearing "silk stockings," proudly accepted the newspapers' derisive reply that Simpson wore no socks at all. "Sockless Jerry" then went on to serve six years as congressman from Kansas' Seventh District.[11] In addition, Kansas sent Populist William A. Peffer to Washington for a single term in the U.S. Senate and elected two Populist governors during the decade of the 1890s. The highly publicized "Populist-Republican War" in 1893 involved a disputed election following which both political parties claimed victory and, for a brief period, physically occupied different parts of the state capital building in Topeka.[12]

Despite its impressive strength in agricultural states, Populism by 1900 was all but dead. The depression of the early nineties had given way to increased prosperity for much of the nation. The Spanish-American War had drawn attention to what seemed a more important issue and the dramatic victory within a span of two months had the settling effect of renewed nationalism. Most importantly, Populists had cashed in their chips in 1896 by supporting the Democratic nominee William Jennings Bryan. In an effort to defeat the dominant Republican party, Populists supported a Populist-Democratic "fusionist" ticket. With Bryan's loss, the fusionist effort was abandoned and Populism in both state and nation faded from the political scene. Though many Populist reforms would live on in the guise of an upwardly mobile Progressive movement in both of the traditional parties, the loss of an organized party meant for many the loss of any meaningful political voice.[13]

Behind the agrarian revolt of Populism lay the dynamic impact of change. By 1890 the agrarian world of the past was rapidly giving way to a new industrial society. The frontier era that had once seemed so enduring was quickly coming to an end. For a generation or so, Americans lived in the wake of the old world though they recognized, to their dismay, the rules of the game had changed. In what Robert Wiebe called "island communities," life continued as before. Local autonomy remained the bastion of the American Dream. The difference was in the ability of these communities to effectively control the increasingly complex economic and social forces in their midst. Ultimately progressivism would seek realistic answers to help control the national community created by modern technology and the "island communities" of the past would suffer a devastating demise.[14]

Religion sometimes offered a unique vehicle for self-

expression and consolation to Populists who discovered their
attempt to control life thwarted. For some the explanation
was undoubtedly that human efforts for justice are futile; only
God could restore order on behalf of the weak and oppressed.
Thus, psychologically, religion became a tremendous source
of power for the powerless. It was from this insecure world
that Charles Parham drew his formative thoughts and it was
among others like him that his ministry, and the message of
the Pentecostal movement, found an enthusiastic following.

The Kansas environment is also important in understanding how religion could come to be the appropriate avenue for
lost dreams. Even prior to the economic insecurity of the
nineteenth century, Kansans had known their share of religious prophets. From John Brown's abolition crusade in the
1850s to Carrie Nation's saloon-wrecking campaign on behalf of temperance in the 1890s, the state seemed to produce
an inordinate number of zealots.[15] In what Patricia Spillman
has described as a "Kansan ethos," residents in the late nineteenth century revealed a "tendency to legislate morality as a
substitution for tradition and custom."[16] Thus folk-dancing
was outlawed for kindergarten children and both tobacco
and liquor sales were made illegal.

Kansas' prohibition law was one of the earliest and most
comprehensive. The revision of the state constitution in 1881
included a provision forbidding the sale of alcohol "except
for medical, scientific, and mechanical purposes" and offered
strict regulation of the manufacturing and selling of the product under those guidelines. Nevertheless, Kansans were far
from creating a puritanical state. As Nation's crusade showed,
the prohibition law was openly ignored by flamboyant "joint-
ists" and was undercut by a notable increase in those exercis-
ing the "medicinal clause."[17] Kansas' experience with prohibition was not unlike that of the nation several decades
later except that the arguments and actions for both sides
were even more intense. During this generation of conflict,
Kansans no doubt felt a greater need for salvation than did
more settled, culturally secure Americans. Religion played

a more pivotal role precisely because it exercised so little control.

Charles Parham's childhood was influenced by more than the political and social turmoil around him. His was a life of intense personal drama as well. Born a "sick and weakly" child, he spent his earliest days under the constant supervision of his mother. At the age of six months, he contracted a fever which began a five year struggle for survival. He later recalled suffering from "dreadful spasms, and enlargement of the head, until my fore head [*sic*] became abnormally large." The five-year-old boy appeared to be outgrowing this infant disease when the family moved to Kansas in the spring of 1878. The new climate, however, would make no discernible difference in Parham's physical stamina. At the age of nine, he endured a life-threatening battle with rheumatic fever. The hard-hitting "inflammatory rheumatism" left him "virtually tied up in a knot" and, by the time the illness abated, his young body was so emaciated that he could count the bones in his hand by holding it up to the light. Following the attack of rheumatic fever came a bout with a tapeworm. Strong medicines taken to kill the parasite caused temporary stomach disorders and convinced Parham that he was thereafter "dwarfed" in physical size. He later recalled that he "did not grow any for three years."[18]

Parham's recollections of his medical problems covered almost every imaginable physical shortcoming. In addition to the childhood diseases, by the age of twenty-five he testified to having suffered "dyspepsia," "catarrh," "sick headaches," and "stigmatized eye." He also reported problems from an "abscess on my liver" and recalled four separate incidents when "I almost died from heart failure (Angina Pectoris)."[19]

Even allowing quite a bit of leeway for exaggeration and Parham's lack of medical sophistication, the list is remarkable. The ailments fall into three separate categories. A viral infection, most likely encephalitis, struck Parham as an infant. The infection causes a blockage of the spinal fluid which flows through the brain; the excessive fluid in the brain thus creates an enlarged head. Infants who survive the illness are typically left with prominent foreheads.[20]

The second and most significant of Parham's maladies was the boyhood attack of rheumatic fever. Extremely painful, the illness is usually a lifetime affliction though extended periods of remission are likely. In the short run, rheumatic fever often stunts growth as it seems to have in Parham's case. In the long run, it damages the heart valves and gradually creates an enlarged and weakened heart muscle. Typically, rheumatic fever contributes to premature death by heart failure.[21]

The third category in Parham's list of ailments would be temporary setbacks not related to any long-term medical condition. Tapeworms were common enough in the nineteenth century and medicines given as cures were certainly capable of causing indigestion (dyspepsia) and other "stomach disorders" (possibly confused with a liver condition). Catarrh refers to respiratory infections such as influenza and the common cold, viruses prevalent enough even among the physically robust. Parham's "sick headaches" were undoubtedly migraines, which along with blurred vision (stigmatized eye), were possibly brought on by the stress of his overall debilitating condition.[22]

Equally important with the physical results of Parham's medical problems were the psychological results of long-term illness in childhood. Unable to perform the demanding tasks often assigned to farm children, Parham was relegated to light household chores and occasionally allowed to herd cattle.[23] In the absence of female siblings, he was the child who identified closest with his mother. Parham became, in modern slang, a mamma's boy. What made that trait important was the religious commitment made by a young boy of extremely weak constitution. Later in life he was fond of noting the paucity of religious training in his youth. This seemed to justify his own religious study as "entirely unbiased" and "not warped by preconceived notions or interpretations." He recalled:

Our parents were not religious—we scarcely knew anything about church and Sunday School; preachers seeming to be as scarce in those parts as hen's teeth. . . . We don't remember to have ever heard but one or two preachers before reaching the age of thirteen years. . . .[24]

But a lack of formal church affiliation did not mean Parham was without religious guidance and influence. More than anyone, his mother engendered a sense of godly devotion in the sickly youth.

Studies of children with asthma have noted the peculiar psychological drama that is played out within the minds of chronically ill youth. Though much of that particular disease is thought to be psychosomatic, the dramatic impact from fear of death is recognized as a genuinely traumatic experience. While there is no evidence that Parham had asthma, his chronic condition indicates a similar psychological effect. Like asthma victims, he became especially attached to one parent, needing his mother's love and attention beyond that of the average child and of his siblings. He also came face to face at an early age with the fragility of life. As David McCullough explains, this experience marks an important moment in such a child's life.

He has learned at an early age what a precarious, unpredictable thing life is—and how very vulnerable *he* is. He must be prepared always for the worst. But the chief lesson is that life is quite literally a battle. And the test is how he responds, in essence whether he sees himself as a helpless victim or decides to fight back. . . .[25]

For Parham life began as a battle and it continued as one. His career as a faith healer was predicated upon his own experience with the enemy of disease.

Parham's first religious experience came at age nine; not coincidental was the terrible struggle with rheumatic fever that began that same year. Perhaps due to his survival of the deadly disease, Parham came to accept that God had "called" him to be a minister. Strikingly, this compulsion occurred years before he experienced his personal "conversion" to the Christian faith.[26] Following his recovery from the fever, Parham set about practicing for the future fulfillment of this vocational revelation.

The Bible was almost a constant companion; and though unconverted, time and again we used to round up the cattle upon an emi-
nence, and give them a rousing sermon upon the realities of a future
life; whether of the "minstrels of bliss" or "the wailing of the
damned." [27]

In addition to his "call" to the ministry, Parham's early religious commitment was forged by tragedy. In December 1885
his mother died during childbirth. Though only twelve at the
time, he felt a loss compounded by the many hours of extra
care his mother had given him during his precarious youth.
By her deathbed the as yet unconverted preacher "vowed that
he would meet her in heaven." True to his word, Parham
found his assurance of conversion during the next year. [28]

Parham's conversion is highlighted by two separate events.
At a schoolhouse meeting held by "Brother Lippard of the
Congregational Church," he formally stood and was counted
as a convert. This commitment was less than genuine. He
skeptically recalled the incident as a reaction to the minister's
threat to close the revival services unless more concrete results followed. Thus his public conversion was primarily "to
keep the meeting running, as it was quite an innovation and
enjoyable place to spend the long evenings." [29] "Real conversion" came on the drive home from the service. Feeling a deep
sense of conviction over personal sin, Parham tried to alleviate his guilt by singing a Gospel hymn. During the third verse,
his experience reached a climax as he sang with face upturned
toward the night sky.

There flashed from the Heaven, a light above the brightness of the
sun; like a stroke of lightning it penetrated, thrilling every tissue
and fibre of our being; knowing by experimental knowledge what
Peter knew of old that He was the Christ, the Son of the living God. [30]

Parham's commitment dramatically increased his already
strong drive toward a religious vocation and he promised God
that someday he would go to Africa as a missionary. He became a Sunday School teacher in the local Methodist Church

and, by the age of fifteen, had held his own evangelistic meetings. The services, by Parham's assessment, met "marked results." It seemed only natural that such promise be cultivated by formal training and, at seventeen, he entered Southwest Kansas College at Winfield to prepare for the Methodist ministry.[31]

Southwest Kansas College had been founded only four years prior to Parham's enrollment. Incorporated in 1886 as the Southern Kansas Normal School and Business College, the coeducational institution enjoyed rapid growth. During Parham's first academic year, 1890–91, 311 students registered for classes; by the 1892–93 school year, enrollment increased to over 600. The growth spurt paralleled the forging of a quasi-alliance with the Methodist Church. By the end of Parham's first academic term, interest in religious studies sparked the founding of a student ministerial association.[32]

The national panic of 1893 temporarily damaged Southwest Kansas' rise in academic prosperity. Hard times depleted the available pool of students. Matters worsened when the college dormitory burned in 1894. By the spring of 1895, enrollment had dropped to 209. One of the casualties of the economic crisis was the young preacher Charles Parham. His formal education came to an end when he failed to register for the 1893–94 school term.[33]

There was more to Parham's uncompleted degree than financial panic. His experience at college had been an ordeal comparable to his childhood struggles. Priorities were a problem at first as he "pursued the religious work with more vigor than the studies." He took the consequences personally, noting that such zeal caused him to be "severely reprimanded and graded down in the examination." What followed was an even greater crisis for Parham. During his freshman year he not only curtailed his ministerial schedule but gradually suffered a complete vocational relapse. He decided the Methodist ministry "with . . . its many starvation stations and 'hard scrabble' circuits, was not near so alluring as some other professions."[34] Of paramount concern was the matter of public opinion. Now in an environment of socially prominent young people, Parham worried about the popular image of ministers as less productive members of the economic community.

The ministry seemed generally to be considered a great burden on society, which they don't seem to be able to get rid of, and which they are unwilling to support. Of whom it is often said they demand more salary than the school teacher, and in return do the community little or no good; usually working about one sixth the time the teacher does. Having been a collecting steward and being thoroughly educated and trained in all the grafts and gambling schemes used to obtain money, until it seemed that it was absolutely necessary to put a poultice of oysters, strawberry short cake or ice cream on the people's stomachs to draw or burst open their purse strings [sic]. [35]

Money became more important to Parham as he contemplated leaving the financially comfortable nest of his father and stepmother. Still, he wanted to do something meaningful in light of the infirmities of his childhood and the "call" he had accepted as assurance that he would survive them. The answer seemed to lie in medicine. As a physician he could help alleviate human suffering and attain financial security as well. The distinction with the ministry was obvious. Although some ministers attained financial security, it was not appropriate for them to actively seek it; they were "hired" by a higher authority. Physicians, on the other hand, served the public and were expected to seek payment for their services. Thus, early in 1891, Parham recharted his studies in anticipation of a medical career. Only later did he realize the magnitude of this decision. His spiritual dedication waned as he focused on the new vocational path. He later recalled that "the devil tried to make us believe that we could be a physician and a Christian too." For Parham, at any rate, the two could not be reconciled and he soon found himself "backslidden." [36]

If Parham could not recognize his loss of divine favor from his own inward struggle, it was made clear to him by the outward effects on his physical health. In the spring of 1891 the rheumatic fever returned. The pain was so intense that he begged to die. Yet inwardly he knew he could not die. God had called him to preach during his first bout with the fever; this flare-up, he was convinced, was a forceful reminder of that call.

Still Parham fought the inevitable, spending months in intense pain though heavily sedated by morphine. After overhearing his personal physician predict that he would not recover, the young rebel finally surrendered. Recalling lessons of healings in the New Testament, Parham repented of his backslidden condition and trusted God to bring about his recovery. Miraculously, the healing touch came but, in his case, the healing was not complete. After months of inactivity, Parham's feet lacked the strength to support him; they were "as use less [*sic*] as though tin cans were tied to my ankles." During the summer he learned to walk again but remained noticeably handicapped. When he returned to college in the fall of 1891, Parham literally staggered around the campus. He later recalled that [I had] "to walk upon the sides of my feet, or rather upon my ankles with my feet thrown out to the side." [37] He continued to pray for his complete healing somewhat mystified that God had left him in this embarrassing state.

Finally, in December 1891, Parham found his answer. Under an old oak tree on the college lawn, he renewed his vow to preach the Gospel and promised to quit college if that was what God wanted. In that moment of dedication, he found his ankles "instantly healed." [38]

Parham's decision to quit school came a bit slower. He finished the current school year and then re-enrolled for the 1892–93 term. Nevertheless, his vow to resume the ministry remained firm. Once again he sought out and accepted preaching appointments. During May of 1892, he held evangelistic meetings at the Pleasant-Valley School House near Tonganoxie, Kansas—the first of nineteen services he would conduct there during the next two years. Prior to his first service, Parham climbed a nearby knoll and "with hands stretched out over the valley, prayed that the entire community might be taken for God."[39] The assurance and sincerity of this young man drew interested listeners and brought about religious revival in the small farming community. To those content with regular religious exercises and good moral ethics, Parham preached the message of radical conversion. In keeping with his own spiritual encounters, he explained that authentic salvation was not "a 'hope so', 'guess so' religion, but a real 'know so' experience and assurance of sins forgiven."[40] The success at Tonganoxie confirmed his belief that his was a life set apart by God for tremendous religious significance.

Parham's renewed spiritual devotion and evangelistic experience served to further alienate him from college life during the 1892–93 school year. It was not that he alone concerned himself with religious work; other students were similarly inclined. Rather, it was the level of commitment—at least within his own mind—that set him apart. He may have participated in the religious activities of the college ministerial association but, if so, the experience was not one he felt worth recalling. A fellow student remembered his own activity in the organization during the time of Parham's attendance.

It was about this time that some of us began to "preach." . . . The way it came about was this. We learned of a school house or two within walking distance of town, where we somehow gathered a congregation for Sunday mornings. At first three of us would go and enlighten the congregation on a text which had three or less logical divisions, each of us speaking about ten minutes. Then we would go two by two, taking a text which we would divide into two parts and each of us occupying about fifteen minutes.[41]

It is most probable that Parham considered himself beyond such elementary undertakings, given his own experience at public speaking and his dramatic interaction with the divine during the rheumatic fever attack of 1891.

Other aspects of college life no doubt disturbed Parham deeply and made him suspicious of the benefits of a formal education. Fraternities arrived at Southwest Kansas in 1890 when a new faculty member helped organize Gamma Sigma.

One brother reminisced "I do not recall that the meetings of Gamma Sigma that year were of any serious nature."[42] September 1892 witnessed the founding of a Sigma Nu chapter on the campus. Within five years the brotherhood established a notorious reputation for mischievous behavior and, in 1897, the trustees of Southwest Kansas College formally banned the fraternity from any association with future student bodies. For a young man of Parham's religious commitment this type of atmosphere seemed trivial at best.[43]

Even more disturbing was the degree of tolerance for new ideas. In the spring of 1892, the school newspaper, *S.W.K. College Round Table*, published a controversial series of articles under the heading "Origin of Man." Though Parham would later welcome innovative ideas within his own theological framework, he seldom allowed tolerance as a final solution. In his understanding, innovative ideas must be biblically based solutions that had been overlooked or disregarded by those unconcerned with finding God's full revelation. Ideas published in the school paper undercut Parham's own philosophy of absolute truth.[44]

Whether these conditions of college life played an important part in Parham's decision to leave school after three years of study is unknown. It is probable that they contributed to his decision but were subordinate to the larger problem of finances caused by the Panic of 1893. There is also the consideration that, with a renewed vow to preach, Parham wanted to pursue the ministry with greater vigor and felt additional schoolwork interfered with his important schedule. He was licensed as a local preacher in the Winfield District, Methodist Episcopal Church, North, at the annual meeting of the Southwest Kansas Conference in March 1893. The following June, he was appointed as a supply pastor for the Eudora church and entered actively into the Methodist pastorate.[45] It was a promising start for the young man who, two years earlier, had despaired of life itself in his battle with God's vocational plan. But God was not through with the sickly farm boy from the central Kansas plains; he would speak to Charles Parham again.

2

Holiness and Healing
1893–1900

Eudora, Kansas, was an exciting appointment for a twenty-year-old, unmarried Methodist preacher. Located just outside Lawrence, the small town lay in the midst of the state's most populous region. Topeka, the state capital, flourished only thirty miles to the west; twenty-five miles to the east lay the sprawling frontier mecca of Kansas City. More importantly for Parham, Tonganoxie, the site of his previous summer's evangelistic success, was just ten miles to the north.

The Methodist Church at Eudora made a promising appointment for a young minister as well. The most recent pastor had been the prominent Methodist clergyman Werter Renick Davis. In 1858 Davis had been named as the first president of Baker University, the influential Methodist school at nearby Baldwin City. Davis died unexpectedly in June 1893 and Parham—probably because of his promising evangelistic work at Tonganoxie—received the nod to serve the church for the remainder of the conference year.[1]

Parham made the most of his new opportunity. Energetically he continued his thrust for evangelism and, in addition to his pastoral duties, held revivals in the rural areas ouside Eudora. By the end of 1893 he had organized a new charge at nearby Linwood from the fruits of his revival in the Congrega-

tional Church there. He combined the charge to his appointment at Eudora and, in addition to the regular morning services for the parishioners in Eudora, conducted afternoon
services for his converts at Linwood. The "circuit-riding"
minister spent his Sunday lunch hour en route from one
preaching service to the next. It marked the beginning of a
way of life for Parham. Always restless, he worked best on the
stump—recruiting and encouraging congregations—rather
than building a strong organizational unit. In the short run,
his labors were rewarded. The Linwood congregation grew
and began plans for a new church building. The Methodist
hierarchy expressed a measure of confidence in the young
workhorse when, in March 1894, they reappointed him to
Eudora for another year.[2]

Despite his success, there were also storm clouds in sight.
There is no evidence that Parham actively sought ordination
as a regular member of the Southwest Kansas Conference,
but it is safe to assume his superiors were not yet sure he was
ready; his reappointment in 1894 still listed him as a "supply
appointment." While at Eudora, Parham's theology had become controversial. His strict religious devotion had led him
to be much impressed by the holiness movement. Though he
never accepted the more extreme ethical tenets of the holiness
evangelists such as "marital purity" (chastity within marriage) and a ban on neckties, he was enticed by their sense of
commitment.[3]

Wesleyan holiness advocates taught that "entire sanctification" was a work of grace that could cleanse already-
converted believers of the sin-nature that still prompted them
to commit sin.[4] This nature, inherited from Adam as a result
of his sin in the Garden of Eden, could be dealt with by an
individual's faith in the sacrifice of Christ. The logic was obvious. One act of faith eliminated overt sins of disobedience
to God's law; another eliminated the source of the conflict.
The result of the "second blessing" was thus a Christian who
best exemplified triumph over sin. He was not immune to sin
since the human state required a continued vulnerability, yet

holiness evangelists had no doubt that the "second work" gave the believer the power to overcome any temptation. The "old man" of sin was crucified and no longer held the human spirit captive. It was here that Parham saw a parallel with his own vocational struggle with God. It had been the sin-nature operating unconsciously within him. He became convinced that his own deliverance from rheumatic fever in 1891 had involved, at the initial step, a "cleansing" experience which demonstrated a crucifixion of his own ambitions and goals. Thus his healing had actually been preceded by the sanctification experience.[5]

By the 1890s, the holiness movement was well on its way to breaking the strong link it had enjoyed with the Methodist church. That Parham would remain holiness, despite his promising start in Methodism, was not all that remarkable. Opponents of the holiness crusade argued that the denunciation of church leaders and promotion of extreme ideas on the part of the more radical holiness advocates threatened the authority of the hierarchical system and the credibility of the advancing social status of the Methodist denomination. However, ministers with the dramatic conversion experience of Charles Parham concluded that the educated elite within the church hierarchy had settled for a religion of cold formalism. More importantly, antagonism toward holiness doctrine would doom Methodists to a loss of its founder's emphasis on "Christian perfection." In this controversy there could be no doubt where the independent-thinking Parham would find his allies. He would affirm what came to him as experiential drama and stand with those who best exhibited his own brand of religious zeal.[6]

While Parham's enthusiasm for holiness placed him among the suspect, it was not enough to alienate him completely from the Methodist hierarchy. His evangelistic success suggested that he could be a valuable part of the denomination.[7] More threatening, however, were several unique theological positions he adopted during his early years in the ministry. Since a life dominated by experiential devotion was the goal, Parham decided that water baptism was a meaningless ritual at best. The true baptism was a baptism in God's spirit that imparted a special level of divine power. This Baptism of the Holy Spirit was similar to, but not the same as, sanctification.[8] It involved a re-creation of the zeal and commitment of the early church as described in the book of Acts. Thus Parham neglected his pastoral duties of water baptism and centered on encouraging his members to accept their spiritual baptism. Only later did he come to accept water baptism as an important complement to this baptism in the Spirit.[9]

In similar fashion, Parham failed to emphasize church membership. Membership into God's family came by conversion; growth in that relationship came by sanctification and spirit baptism. Thus organizational matters seemed trivial. Not only did he actively preach in non-Methodist circles, as his experiences in Linwood and Tonganoxie show, but he also encouraged listeners to join other churches—or none at all—in an attempt to deemphasize denominational affiliation. For Methodist leaders, Parham was a firebrand whose energy could work ecclesiastical wonders if properly harnessed; unleashed in his present form, he might just as easily create organizational chaos.[10]

Parham also adopted an unorthodox position on eschatological rewards and punishment. During his first preaching engagement at Tonganoxie in May 1892, he befriended the Quaker family of David Baker. An elderly man, Baker took an exceptional interest in the young Methodist evangelist. In lengthy private Bible studies, he shared with Parham his own conviction that the traditional doctrine of eternal punishment for the wicked was unscriptural. Rather, Baker noted, immortality was a gift granted only to the righteous. The unredeemed would suffer, but it would be a punishment of total annihilation. Always given to literal interpretations of scriptural passages, Parham was deeply moved by this revelation. As he studied with the older man, he decided that Baker was right. Thereafter, he included the "destruction of the wicked" into his growing arsenal of theological weaponry.[11]

It is difficult to gauge precisely the impact that Parham's theological eccentricities had on his relationship with Methodism. Mrs. Parham's account of his life suggests that the church was most upset with her husband's "nonsectarian spirit" which prevented large numbers from automatically joining the Methodist rolls. Yet the accounts from Parham's revival efforts during those years indicate that a significant number of converts did join the denomination.[12] Nevertheless, Methodist leaders surely recognized other troublesome characteristics in the young preacher at Eudora. Inherent in his evangelical style was a disdaining of ecclesiastical authority. Still, while officials may have delayed steps to formally ordain Parham, there is no evidence that any action was ever taken to remove him from the Methodist Church. Rather, it was Parham himself who voluntarily took that step. He reported to the annual Conference representing his Eudora congregation in March 1895. While listening to the presiding bishop ordain the new Conference members, he reportedly was "horror-struck at the thought that the candidates were not left free to preach by direct inspiration." He immediately surrendered his local preacher's license and severed all connections with the denomination. A new pastor was then assigned to the Eudora-Linwood charge.[13]

Parham's resignation confirmed the rebellious streak that had been growing in him for two years. He later described his experience at Eudora as "the confines of a pastorate" and openly admitted to having been "often in conflict with the higher authorities." Finally he had simply endured enough and had "left denominationalism forever."[14] At the root of his anger lay the unwillingness of the church to ordain him. In typical Parham fashion he observed the ordination of other candidates and decided that their acceptance reflected a lack of true dedication. Approval by the hierarchy meant a loss of spiritual freedom. He could obey God or man, but he could no longer try to obey both. In resigning, he fashioned for himself a ministerial career that would be unhindered by human authority. Charles Parham received his orders directly from heaven.

Looking back on his years as a Methodist pastor, Parham later recalled the experience as a failure. His respectable salary reminded him of the fears he had entertained in college about a minister's value to the community. What troubled the young preacher most was the mechanics of it all; how could he be sure God was his employer when church parishioners provided him a steady income? Even worse was the fact that his salary came through community pressure, often "raised by suppers and worldly entertainments."[15] Once again, the trappings of organization seemed to him to preclude the work of God's spirit. Despite the success noted by others, he could remember only one conversion during the entire two years.[16] The discrepancy is significant. Not only does it indicate Parham's pessimism about this period of his life, but it also reveals a subtle shift in his expectations of conversion. As the nineties continued, he gradually tightened the salvation experience to include a total consecration similar to his own. It was not unusual for professing Christians with distinguished records of nominal church membership to find "real conversion" under Parham's direction. That this happened on occasion served to strengthen his conviction that he was specially annointed.[17]

Parham's decision to leave Methodism greatly disappointed his parents. Feeling unwelcome at home, he lived for a time with Mr. and Mrs. M. J. Tuttle of Lawrence, Kansas. Here, in the home of friends who supported his holiness convictions, he reached a major decision. After much time in prayer he decided that his true ministry was in interdenominational evangelism. The rejection he felt from those critical of his leaving the Methodist Church appeared analogous to the rejection of the human Jesus. Parham had suffered few insecurities about his own divine mission, but what little doubt did exist faded here. With the world as his parish, he charted a ministry without the liability of ecclesiastical supervision.[18]

The next five years were years of training for Parham as he learned the hardships of creating an independent religious work. Interspersed between the tangible results of "hundreds . . . converted, scores sanctified, and a few healed" were the oratorical experiences and theological decisions that would influence the remainder of his religious career.[19]

Significant in this respect was his marriage to David Baker's granddaughter. Sarah Eleanor Thistlethwaite spent most of her childhood in her grandfather's home in Tonganoxie. A certain amount of Baker's Quaker devotion no doubt rubbed off on her; she recalled that prior to Charles Parham's 1892 revival, "my folks were about the only Christians" in the neighborhood.[20] Thistlethwaite was a fourteen-year-old student at the Friends Academy in Leavenworth, Kansas when she first met Parham in Tonganoxie in June 1892. He maintained close contact with the family after launching his independent ministry in 1895 and proposed to her through the mail during the summer of 1896. Their wedding on December 31, 1896 was celebrated in Quaker fashion as bride and groom exchanged their own vows inside David Baker's home. Following a short honeymoon in Kansas City, Parham resumed his evangelistic schedule with Sarah Parham at his side. She was to become a valuable partner and his most loyal defender.[21]

The newlyweds set up housekeeping in Baldwin, Kansas. Parental responsibilities soon followed; in September 1897 their first son, Claude Wallace, was born. Soon after the birth of the new baby, Parham faced yet another spiritual crisis. It was one of God's "lessons" and proved invaluable to the young evangelist's career. Although he had been healed in college, he had not stressed divine healing as a part of his ministry. He had assumed his healing was special—a part of God's assurance that he was chosen for the ministry. But late in 1897 he faced another medical crisis and this time he would interpret healing as a normative event for those willing to live by faith. The logic followed the same line as that used in Parham's decision to leave Methodism; when God is in charge, there should be no human authority.[22]

The crisis began when Parham grew weak and had to curtail his evangelistic schedule. His physician diagnosed the ailment as "heart disease" and advised the young man to give up preaching. Compounding the problem was the sickness of Parham's son Claude. All medicines prescribed by the doctor seemed to have no positive effect on the infant. One day while praying for someone else who was sick, Parham recognized the irony of his act. He remembered the scripture "Physician, heal thyself" and immediately turned his attention to his own ailment. He reported that the power of God touched his body and made him "every whit whole."[23]

Parham had no doubt prayed for his condition earlier; the difference now was the degree of faith. He noted that his failure to secure permanent healing had been a result of inconsistency on his part—"sometimes up and sometimes down, getting sick and taking the Lord for our Healer and at other times taking medicine."[24] Now he would demonstrate total dependence on God for his own health and that of his family. Out the door went both medicines and doctors. In answer to this display of faith, Parham believed, his son was soon healed as well. Parham further demonstrated his new commitment by resigning from the local lodge where he held a membership life insurance policy. Those depending on God for life and health had no need of life insurance.[25]

The final stage of what endured as a two month bout with human frailty was the death of Parham's close friend Ralph Gowell. Gowell, a promising University of Kansas professor, had befriended Parham early during the 1892 Tongonoxie revival. His death came as Parham continued to struggle with the mechanics of divine healing. Afterward, Parham convinced himself that he was partly responsible for Gowell's death; he had the message of healing and had failed to exercise it for his friend. He determined in the wake of the tragedy that his would be a ministry of salvation from both sin and sickness.[26]

Armed with a new evangelistic message, Parham approached the year 1898 with renewed optimism. He relocated his family to Ottawa, Kansas, and, from there, launched a ministry which increasingly emphasized divine healing. Securing the local Salvation Army building, he informed his listeners that God did not intend for them to remain sick. Immediately he found success as his congregations became sprinkled with those who testified of dramatic healings through his prayer of faith. Consumption, heart disease, and even nearsightedness were conquered to the amazement of curious onlookers.[27] One of the earliest healed was Mrs. Ella Cook whose "dropsy" affliction had convinced the local doctors she could die at any time. Sarah Parham remembered the event as a moment of drama:

When prayer was offered the disease was instantly killed so that she fell to the floor as one dead, or like one from whom the fever had just left. The audience arose as a mob to punish us for her seeming death. Mr. Parham stepped beside her body and ordered the people to stand in their places as she was not dead, as a few minutes would prove. In a few moments she opened her eyes, smiled and we assisted her to her feet. She not only walked down the stairs alone, but walked for over a mile to her home, shouting and praising the Lord; people along the way followed to see what would take place. Neighbors came running in and until three o'clock in the morning people were getting to God and others were wonderfully healed. Her recovery was complete.[28]

The notoriety gained in the Ottawa revival led to Parham's demand in wider circles. Soon he was being called to pray for the sick as far away as the state capital. It was in Topeka, a bustling city of thirty thousand, that he recognized his new ministry's potential for growth. During the summer of 1898 Parham moved his family to the city and, by the fall, secured enough backing to rent a permanent building for his healing work. On the corner of Fourth and Jackson Streets in downtown Topeka, the Beth-el Healing Home became the center of Parham's growing ministry. For the next two years the home remained under his control and served a variety of religious and social functions in the city.[29]

Kansas was particularly fertile ground for a ministry of health. Local newspapers regularly ran ads for the latest in patent medicines. Kansans responded, purchasing a variety of the cures through direct mail.[30] Personal physicians were also increasing in number, though it is important to note that, as competition for Parham, they were barely more sophisticated than the mail-order syrups and ointments. A historian of American medical practice noted the uncertainty of late nineteenth century diagnosis and treatment.

The average physician had only a hazy notion of etiology, and he prescribed largely for such symptoms as fevers, coughs, diarrheas, consumptions, and sore throats. The treatment itself was often hit or miss. While dosage was moderating, quinine, aconite, opium, alcohol, mercury, strychnine, arsenic, and other potentially dangerous drugs still formed the basis of materia medica.[31]

Parham had several advantages that doctors and patent medicines did not enjoy. In the first place, his healing services came free. "Patients" often made contributions but there was no direct payment required or sought. Another advantage came in Parham's healing theology. Parham never claimed the power to heal; rather he proclaimed the message of healing. Healing came to the sick because the sick had faith in God to effect a cure. Parham repeatedly denounced the title "Divine Healer," explaining that he could only help patients have faith. The result was one which put Parham, and all other "healers," in a safe position. If a person was not healed, he had simply failed to apply enough faith; something was wrong with the patient, not the treatment. If a person was healed, however, notoriety tended to increase the prestige and following of the preacher involved. In that sense, it was a ministry without risk.[32]

Such explanations, however, underestimate the dynamics of the healing movement. What made faith healers like Parham popular was not their message but their results. Healing testimonies had to come regularly in order to sustain momentum. The adulation of the crowd could quickly turn to scorn if a healer had no results. Parham carefully controlled the explosive issue; while he was known for healing, he did not let that become the single criteria for continuing his ministry. Parham was generally called into homes to pray for the sick. Thus healings usually occurred in private quarters and could be reported after the fact to strengthen the faith of others.

When he prayed for the sick in public, it occurred only as a minor part of a service emphasizing evangelism. In this way, he avoided the carnival atmosphere linked with charlatanry, yet retained a dramatic visibility.[33]

Parham also built on a latent distrust of conventional medical practice among the lower class. By the 1890s, doctors were more educated and better qualified than they had ever been. Along with their rise in education came monetary incomes commensurate with their professional status. Throughout much of America, this launched the beginning of a period in which physicians typically became members of their town's financial and social elite. For most Americans this meant better health care and increased confidence in the local doctor. For a minority of Americans, most notably those least able to pay, it meant an estrangement from doctors. Parham championed the source of this discontent by proclaiming that "the principle relief from medical science is pocket book relief."[34]

That a faith healing preacher used the charge of quackery against doctors seems incredible in a world of widespread technical sophistication. But in an age suspicious of the advancement of medical science, Parham captured the attention of quite a few.

Today the principle drugs used are poisons. But people say that was in those days when science had not older grown and reached the heighth [sic] of proficiency they have today; but if any other science had developed so slowly with the advantages given, it would long ago have been driven from the stage of action. Sanitary and quarantine laws, coupled with cleanliness and nursing have done a great deal for humanity. The fact still remains however, that after 4000 years of practice—humanity willingly laying herself upon the altar to be doped, blistered, bled and dissected, medical science has gained little more than has the Bible recorded of her, that they have sought out many ways of relieving pain. While the fatal diseases that have existed are fatal still; and medical science stands with fettered hands in the presence of consumption, catarrh, cancers, fevers, and many other diseases.[35]

Parham's opposition to medical science went deeper than skepticism about the success of certain treatments. Parham believed that taking medicine was wrong. His own extensive encounter with disease confirmed that belief. Despite medical advice and prescriptions, he had never been made well; only when he trusted God enough to throw his medicine away had any real change been effected. He interpreted his experience as a universal one for God's people and offered scriptural "proof."

So many say, "Why don't you use medicine; does the Bible forbid its use?" We say yes, most emphatically YES. After stating in the Old Testament that "Thou hast no healing medicines," and "In vain shall thou use many medicines, for thou shalt not be cured"; then the New Testament is most positive in the construction of its denounciation [*sic*].[36]

Medicine revealed a lack of faith in God. Parham accepted God's deliverance from sin to include a parallel deliverance from illness. Christians then should always be well; that they were not was simply an indication that they failed to believe God's promises. He declared almost in desperation, "Friends, we will never get rid of the devil until we quit this everlasting nursing of our diseases."[37]

Parham's claim to authority on health matters rested in his firm conviction that the fight against disease was a spiritual war, not a medical-scientific one. In addition to inherited and naturally acquired diseases, he noted that a third and more common source of physical malignance was sin. In securing relief from this type of disease, ministers of faith played a particularly important role.

Parham estimated that half of all diseases were psychosomatic and recommended that once people "threw back their shoulders and faced the world with a smile and cheerful disposition . . . the afflictions would disappear." The remaining percentage was much more serious. Some were contagious diseases that could be cured through the prayer of faith. Others represented "demonized torments that feed upon the body in various diseases." Parham calculated that "all such diseases as cancers, tumors, consumption, catarrh, rheumatism, all fevers, epilepsy, fits and spasms, whooping cough, St. Vitus dance, insanity and all nervous disorders are the direct result of tormenting demons." [38] Doctors and religious "frauds," such as Christian Scientists, might be qualified to deal with the "imaginary" diseases and any minister willing to preach the message of faith healing could handle ordinary diseases. However, the advanced cases of "demon-inspired disease" required the "God given authority to cast out devils." Without that gift, even the prayer of faith would fail and the disease would actually grow worse. [39] Parham described disease demons to his audiences in graphic detail and reported that they even ate food. One healthy demon lived in a Chicago woman's cancer and "ate or absorbed over a pound of raw beef steak laid upon it each day." [40] In the face of such "evidence," many were convinced that their ailments needed a religious, rather than medical, diagnosis.

When Parham opened his healing home in Topeka late in 1898, he envisioned a ministry that would appeal to the city's extensive religious clientele. A full one-third of the citizens were church members spread among sixty-seven churches. Several years before Parham's arrival, the Congregational pastor, Charles M. Sheldon, had challenged his own congregation—and then the world—to live each experience with the simple admonition "What would Jesus do?" First published in 1897, *In His Steps* became the most widely read religious novel of all time. [41] Parham hoped to tap this religious circle with his message of healing and then work jointly at the job of converting the two-thirds of the city that remained unchurched. However, Topekan church members failed to flock to Parham's ecumenical call. They recognized him only as a bundle of youthful enthusiasm. A generation later, some residents recalled that their parents labeled the twenty-five year old as the "boy preacher." [42]

Nevertheless, his work in Topeka was impressive. Beth-el Healing Home offered a variety of religious services. Central

to the operation was the healing ministry with the home serving as a resort for the ill and disabled. Although Parham clearly
expected all diseases to be cured by faith, he recognized that
healing required the building of faith within the patient. Thus
the home provided an environment which, along with his
teaching, encouraged recipients of the healing ministry to exercise faith and claim their answer. Parham also recognized
that in the absence of strong faith, healing may come gradually. The home then served as an infirmary for those awaiting
the culmination of their faith cure. An early advertisement admonished readers of the advantages of the Beth-el home.

All modern conveniences; centrally located. . . . Guests can be
transferred at station and get off at entrance. The object of the home
is to provide home-like comforts to all who seek healing and a temporary stopping place for a friend while at the capital city. Terms to
guests, $4 to $7 a week, unless they are worthy poor, when other
arrangements will be made. No charges are made in this work but
for board to cover actual expense of the guest entertainment.[43]

The Parham ministry also included a Bible Institute, a temporary orphanage service, and an ad hoc employment bureau. The school featured lecture classes which Parham conducted during the week. Limited in scope, the curriculum was
envisioned as a kind of adult education program for those already engaged in religious work. A Tuesday afternoon "healing study," a Tuesday evening "School of Prophecy," and a
Friday evening class of varying topics made up the course
offerings of the institute. The orphanage was essentially a
placement service where orphans could be linked to Christian
families interested in adoption. Only temporary accommodations were provided for the actual care of orphans since
Parham considered the home a mediator in the adoption process. The employment service worked much the same way.
The healing home posted ads from both Christian employers
and workers in an effort to secure an amiable link.[44]

To publicize and coordinate the variety of religious services
at Beth-el, Parham edited the *Apostolic Faith*. The journal

was begun in March 1899 as a joint venture with James A. Staples, a local publisher who shared the editorial responsibilities.[45] At a subscription rate of one dollar a year, the weekly paper printed a variety of articles pertaining to the holiness movement and served as a forum for local testimonies and religious advertisements. Staples admonished readers of the moral virtues of such a paper:

We want this paper run for the glory of God, and intend that it shall be. We believe the great majority of papers and magazines of this day cannot be safely taken into the home, because of their vileness, displayed in various ways. If you subscribe for the *APOSSOLIC FAITH* [*sic*] you need not be afraid to let the children read it. They will not find any tobacco advertisements in it, nor anything that defiles. They will not find any vile and abominable jokes in it. If there are any they will be pure.[46]

For Parham the paper served an even more crucial purpose. The income from the subscriptions was to cover the expenses of the Beth-el ministry not paid by lodging fees. After initial costs of five hundred dollars, Parham estimated that the paper would need to generate a monthly profit of one hundred dollars to cover the expenses incurred by the home.[47]

The *Apostolic Faith* proved to be less of a financial bonanza than Parham hoped. By May, Staples decided the enterprise could survive only as a monthly; Parham remained adamant in his commitment to a weekly paper. The problem was solved when Staples relinquished his share of the fledgling periodical and Parham assumed full control as editor and publisher.[48] He tried to increase circulation by cutting the subscription rate to fifty cents per year. The ploy was only partially successful. The paper survived but, in August, Parham switched to a bimonthly format.[49] Regular subscribers probably numbered only a few hundred, though as many as five hundred additional copies were distributed free with each issue. While the subscription list was not extensive, the paper did travel as far away as New Orleans and was no doubt widely distributed within the holiness ranks of the Midwest.[50]

The addition of the paper handsomely complemented Parham's work at Beth-el. At its height, the healing home on Fourth and Jackson boasted a multifaceted ministry bustling with energy. In one of the earliest issues of the *Apostolic Faith*, coeditor Parham described the various activities conducted on the home's main floor.

. . . [O]ur office, where daily the sick and sinful may consult as to their spiritual and physical welfare . . . a reading room, where all kinds of helpful literature can be found, and where amidst the flowers a quiet hour or two can be spent . . . the printing room, where busy hands prepare the messages of "glad tidings and great joy" to send to the dear friends outside of the city. . . . Our chapel occupies the rest of the ground floor. It will seat about 200.[51]

Upstairs were the fourteen rooms which provided living space for both the Parhams and their "patients." The home even added a telephone in July 1899 as another of the "modern conveniences" offered to overnight guests.[52]

Divine healing remained the focal point of the entire operation. The *Apostolic Faith* ran testimonies as advertisements. Often including Parham's own connection to the healing, the testimonies told of remarkable cures from heart disease, appendicitis, cancer, spinal meningitis, and consumption. Most extraordinary was the account of a left arm lengthened by a full one and a half inches.[53] By June 1899, over thirty out-of-town guests, including one Roman Catholic, had visited to seek healing for themselves. Visits varied from a few days to a full month but, assuming an average stay of two weeks, Parham would have had two to three guests in the home at any given time.[54] During peak periods, the six bedrooms were full and guests were placed in temporary sleeping quarters in the parlors and attic.[55]

All this activity increased Parham's local reputation. During July, curious Topekans wandered about the home in hopes of witnessing a remarkable cure, or perhaps even the exorcism of some devil. The *Apostolic Faith* reported on July 19, that "doctors, lawyers, preachers, and infidels have come in this week to see the cancer we have in a bottle."[56] What seemed strange to some Topekans seemed quite marvelous to others. The success of Beth-el created an interest in other healing homes; by early 1900, healing homes at Emporia, Ottawa, and Eskridge had been established and maintained a loose affiliation with Parham's work in Topeka.[57]

Parham saw himself as minister to all the residents of Topeka. Although he held Sunday meetings in the home's chapel, he kept the work interdenominational. A series of four separate services offered Topekans the opportunity to participate without neglecting their own church ties. An eleven o'clock morning worship hour emphasized holiness, a two o'clock Sunday School provided Bible study, a three o'clock meeting discussed healing, and a seven-thirty evening service highlighted Parham's evangelistic talents. Frequently he tried to include guest speakers from the area churches.[58]

The extent of the Beth-el ministry was quite impressive. While Parham never reached the pews of the prominent Topekan churches, he did provide a needed service to the city's underprivileged. Increasingly, the work took the tone of the inner city ministries in the nation's larger cities.[59] As early as April 1899, he served as a trustee for Topeka's "Industrial League," a philanthropic organization that helped "deserving working people" secure vacant lots and seeds to plant vegetable gardens.[60] By July, he was planning a rescue mission to provide food and shelter for prostitutes and young working girls with low incomes. Supported by the local police matron, he organized a mission late that summer on the corner of Third and Harrison Streets. Optimistically, Parham predicted that a significant number of Topeka's five hundred "fallen women" would soon convert to Christ and fill constructive jobs in the economy. He noted that "plenty of places are open to these girls as soon as they repent." The rescue mission ceased to receive coverage in the *Apostolic Faith* after September 1899 and it is probable that the effort folded.[61]

Despite the disappointing results of the rescue mission campaign, Parham continued his efforts toward social welfare.

In November 1899, the *Apostolic Faith* expressed Parham's interest in establishing a mission named "Helping Hand" for the purpose of providing regular food and shelter to the poor. At a New Year's dinner held in the Beth-el mission, the young minister dramatized his plan by feeding three hundred of the city's needy. Once again, however, his efforts failed to rally enough support for success. In April, Parham lent his support to a state-wide effort to raise funds for famine-stricken India, but there was a notable lack of zeal for the project. His participation was essentially confined to a donation of space in the *Apostolic Faith*. Social causes were important but, in the wake of failure, they ceased to hold his interest.

Slowly, Parham was becoming disenchanted with the state of his ministry. Shortly after arriving in Topeka a daughter, Esther Marie, had been born into the Parham family. Then, in March 1900, Charles, Jr. increased the family size to five. With the added pressure of new responsibility and still stinging from the failure of his increased social ministry, Parham felt the need to seek God again. Somehow, he had missed something; his divine call had to include more than the modest success of Topeka's healing home and street social work.[62]

As in the past, Parham's spiritual crisis followed on the heels of a medical one. In late September 1899, he suffered a nervous breakdown. He already had a weakened heart as a result of his battle with rheumatic fever. In addition, he was working an exhausting schedule trying to keep his multi-leveled ministry afloat. A more direct cause of the breakdown was the pressure to meet a shoestring budget which kept him appealing for donations and increased subscriptions to his journal.

A silent voice also haunted him. Parham had come to Topeka optimistically expecting to win all social classes over to his revolutionary doctrine of divine health. He had made converts but he had also been ignored by the social class that could make his financial problems disappear. Compounding the problem, some of his early supporters had now deserted him. In an obvious vent of revenge, he noted in August that "several worldly people have withdrawn from the Mission because they could not stand the preaching against world-liness and the awful tendencies of the age."[63] In the midst of this personal crisis he delegated much of his responsibility to subordinates and spent extra time in private devotion. It gave him valuable time to reevaluate his goals and reinterpret the specifics of his divine mission.[64]

By 1900 Parham had encountered a wide variety of reli-gious influences. The *Apostolic Faith* borrowed extensively from the host of periodicals that fell under the umbrella of the amorphous holiness movement. John Alexander Dowie's unique brand of divine health theology appeared early under the heading "Do You Know God's Way of Healing?" The radical position emphasized human health as normative and explained that poor health for the Christian was simply the result of an individual's lack of faith in God's power to heal.[65]

Dowie, an Australian faith healer, came to America in 1888 and by 1890 had spread his doctrine into the Midwest. He achieved national attention at the 1893 Chicago World's Fair when, across the street from the tent of Buffalo Bill Cody, he derided doctors and their treatments as "medical bosh." Dowie demonstrated his own brand of medical research with what were by all accounts a remarkable string of healings. Crowds flocked to hear him and to witness the miracles. Fol-lowing the fair, Dowie established a string of divine healing homes throughout the city of Chicago and solidified the en-terprise with a maze of religious and financial investments. In 1900 he organized Zion City, a 6,600-acre complex on the shores of Lake Michigan, just forty miles north of the Windy City. Zion became the focal point of Dowie's Christian Catho-lic Church, a denominational agency of some twenty-five thousand adherants.[66]

Dowie's ministry undoubtedly influenced Charles Parham. In addition to the teaching on divine health and the concept of healing homes, Dowie stressed social work and sent out ar-mies of workers to clean, feed, and clothe the residents of Chicago's slums. His weekly periodical, *Leaves of Healing,* advertised a "Bureau of Labor and Relief of the Poor" to link Christian employers with the unemployed. And like Parham's *Apostolic Faith, Leaves of Healing* thrived on the personal testimonies of those who were healed. In all respects, Parham's Topeka experiment was a much smaller example of what Dowie had already established in Chicago.[67]

More respectable religious figures influenced Parham as well. Many of the leading evangelists of the day adopted key facets of the holiness movement and publicized them through an assortment of Bible colleges and periodicals. The most influential of these national figures was Dwight Lyman Moody, by far the premier evangelist of the nineteenth century. Moody combined Reformed theology and an emphasis on personal piety into an evangelical art. He attracted huge crowds to his urban crusades of the 1870s and 1880s. Included in his message of conversion and personal holiness was an emphasis on premillennialism.

The doctrine of the millennial reign of Christ had roots in American Protestantism as early as Jonathan Edwards and the Great Awakening of the 1740s. The concept accepted literally the one thousand years of peace described in Revelation 20 and proponents argued that one day the millennium would be a political and social reality. Following the American Revolution and the optimistic nationalism of the early nineteenth century, many American churchmen assumed the dream would come to pass as a part of their nation's unending progress. By reforming society and winning the lost to Christianity, Americans would thrust the world into a millennial era of peace and harmony during which the forces of righteousness would effectively repress evil. The success of the millennium would prove God's plan of redemption and, at the end of this glorious period, humanity would be rewarded by the return of Christ and his subsequent rule over a new age of sinless perfection. This optimistic assessment endured through the ideals of the Social Gospel in American Christianity in the late nineteenth and early twentieth centuries.[68]

By the latter decades of the century, however, this postmillennial (signifying Christ's return after the one thousand years) theory seemed increasingly untenable. Instead of getting better, America seemed to be drifting from traditional Christian belief. Darwinism, denominational "worldliness," technological advances in weaponry, and the rise of gilded-age capitalism all encouraged such a pessimistic assessment. In addition, a literal interpretation of the book of Revelation led many to believe that Christ would return before, rather than after, the millennium began. The offshoot of such dissension was premillennialism. In this scenario, the world worsens until God finally intervenes by sending Christ to free the oppressed remnant of true believers. After an apocalyptic conflict between good and evil, the victorious Savior binds Satan and locks him away for a thousand years. Thus begins the earthly millennial reign with Christ himself serving as theocratic ruler.

In an innovative addition to the scheme, John Nelson Darby, a disciple of the pietistic Plymouth Brethren sect, postulated that Christ's return would actually include two separate stages prior to the millennium. The first advent would "rapture" the saints, secretly taking them from the earth for their own protection. The event would also signal the beginning of seven years of tribulation for those left behind on the earth. Christ's second advent would follow the conclusion of those seven years when, along with the returned saints, he arrived to inaugurate the millennial age. Darby's distinction was crucial because it ensured believers that they could escape the terrible wrath described for the tribulation period. Darby also explained that the coming millennial age was the last of a whole series of dispensations that God had ordered throughout history. Now apparent through biblical revelation, each dispensation had marked a significant era in God's unfolding plan of salvation. By searching the scriptures carefully, Darby argued, Christians could see that the final dispensation was near. However, no one should fall into the trap of setting a specific timetable since the millennium could not occur until seven years after the undatable "rapture." The doctrine encouraged Christians to live at their best since this secret rapture could come at any time.[69]

Dwight L. Moody popularized Darby's dispensational premillennialism through the annual Bible conferences he sponsored in Northfield, Massachusetts. As the dean of American evangelists, he emphasized personal conversion above all else and continued to embrace postmillennial advocates in a show of ecumenical evangelism. His successors, however, were less successful at bridging the gap. Increasingly, the premillennial Reformed evangelists, alienated from denominational seminaries, established their own independent Bible schools and institutes. By the 1920s they represented an important component of American Fundamentalism.[70]

Among those following in Moody's wake were Reuben Archer Torrey, first superintendent of the Moody Bible Institute in Chicago; Adoniram Judson Gordon, founder of the Gordon Bible Institute in Boston; and Albert Benjamin Simpson, founder of the Christian and Missionary Alliance headquartered in Nyack, New York. These men continued Moody's evangelistic appeals but bolstered their messages with a new "higher-life" theology. Originating from annual camp meetings at Keswick, England—which had in turn been prompted by Moody's British campaign from 1873 to 1875—the higher-life philosophy championed an emphasis on the Holy Spirit within the life of the believer. Most important was the concept that the Holy Spirit would provide a special annointing which better prepared a convert for Christian service. Through what was often loosely termed as "Baptism with the Holy Spirit," Keswickian advocates understood that Christians received an endowment of power which solidified their commitment and emboldened their character. As the nineteenth century drew to a close, R. A. Torrey predicted that this move of God's spirit marked the beginning of a revival that would stretch literally around the globe.[71]

A. J. Gordon and A. B. Simpson were particularly important in stressing the power of God to heal. Avoiding the sensationalism of Dowie, they rooted the theology of divine healing in the atoning death of Christ. With a firm scriptural analysis, the doctrine survived and became an essential component of the evangelical creed. While they did not explicitly adopt the radical position of divine health, Gordon and Simpson affirmed nonetheless that healing was universally available. Impressed with their national reputations, Parham frequently included their writings in the *Apostolic Faith*.[72]

Parham knew about Keswick's emphasis on the Holy Spirit and incorporated Torrey's worldwide revival into his growing assortment of religious ideas. He also admired the work of Gordon and Simpson and was greatly impressed with the results of Dowie's healing campaigns. However, an eccentric Wesleyan from Lincoln, Nebraska, ultimately influenced him far more than any of the national holiness figures. Benjamin Hardin Irwin, originally a Baptist minister, accepted the Wesleyan style of sanctification through his contact with the Iowa Holiness Association sometime around 1890. An innovative Bible student, he subsequently discovered that his new experience foreshadowed other "baptisms" for the believer. Beyond conversion and sanctification lay the "Baptism with the Holy Ghost and fire" which Irwin sought and believed he received in the early 1890s. He incorporated the new doctrine into his evangelistic meetings and quickly won converts to his "baptism of fire." Quite often, seekers receiving this third Christian experience exhibited an emotional release and, flooded with religious joy, they would shout, scream, or experience the "jerks."

The old-line leaders of the holiness movement were shocked by Irwin's new theology and disparagingly labeled it the "third blessing heresy." They continued to affirm that Holy Spirit baptism occurred alongside entire sanctification and was thus an extended part of the second and final work of grace. Unable to work freely in holiness circles, Irwin withdrew in 1895 and formed his own Iowa Fire-Baptized Holiness Association in Olmitz, Iowa. From this base, he spread his baptism of fire doctrine throughout the Midwest and South, organizing new associations with each successful revival. By 1898, he incorporated the state organizations into the Fire-Baptized Holiness Church and named himself General Overseer for Life.[73]

One of the earliest state organizations created by Irwin was the Kansas Fire-Baptized Holiness Association. By the time Parham arrived in Topeka late in 1898, fire-baptized believers formed the most vocal and fanatical element of the local holiness movement. Their enthusiasm no doubt struck a responsive chord in Parham's own experience and he adopted their new doctrine. In its first month of publication the *Apostolic Faith* listed the holiness beliefs of the Beth-el Healing Home as "salvation by faith; healing by faith, laying on of hands, and prayer; sanctification by faith; coming (pre-millennium) [*sic*] of Christ; the baptism of Holy Ghost and Fire, which seals the Bride and bestows the gifts." [74]

Shortly after assuming full-time editorial duties of the paper in May 1899, Parham provided publication for the doctrine in an article by Charles H. Croft who described his own "fire experience." Croft wrote that he had been converted late in 1897 and entirely sanctified in March 1898. The baptism of fire came to him the following month in a meeting conducted near Dixie, Oklahoma Territory. Croft's description clearly supported the theological assessment that this experience was identical to that received by the apostles on the Day of Pentecost and recorded in Acts 2.

It came upon me as a rushing, mighty wind, and I was literally swept in the flames of divine fire, and I was melted to tenderness on account of the presence of God. It was brighter than the sun, the fire in the room, and every atom of my being was aglow and ablaze with the fire of God. It soon subsided, and my soul was left far out upon a sea of glass mingled with fire and perfectly resting in God—in the mighty Rock of Ages. Hallelujah.[75]

Although Parham gave credence to the baptism of fire during his years at Beth-el, he never personally stressed the doctrine nor testified to having received it. By 1901 he was no longer incorporating it into his doctrinal creed. Part of the problem may have been Irwin's difficulties in early 1900. Irwin was forced to resign in disgrace after confessing to charges of immorality levied against him within the Fire-Baptized Church. His successor, Joseph Hillery King, remembered Irwin's sin as "open and gross . . . such as could not be further hidden or palliated." Within weeks the Fire-Baptized movement, and the holiness movement in general, was alerted to Irwin's fall. King managed to salvage a portion of the denomination in the South but he recalled that "everything west of the Mississippi River went to pieces in the course of a few years."[76]

Despite Irwin's personal difficulties, Parham had nonetheless been alerted to a new concept. Fire-baptized doctrine had clearly distinguished between sanctification and spirit baptism with the cleansing experience serving as a preparatory step for a twofold "divine baptism of Jesus." For Irwin, the Baptism of the Holy Ghost and the baptism of fire were closely related acts of the Holy Spirit but they were not identical. A sanctified believer would receive the Holy Ghost baptism prior to the baptism of fire.[77] Remarkably, during his last year as Fire-Baptized overseer, Irwin extended his string of "baptisms" to include the experiences of "dynamite," "lyddite," and "oxidite," though, after his resignation, those innovative planks gradually died out.[78] Crucial for Parham, however, was the belief that an important experience existed beyond the second work of sanctification. He was especially enamored with the concept that this experience was the same as that given the apostles on the Day of Pentecost and, like the followers of Keswick, believed it offered the recipient increased power for service.[79] In the spring of 1900, depressed by his work in Topeka and anxious over the loss of divine favor that renewed physical weakness seemed to suggest, Parham turned his thoughts increasingly to ironing out the difficulties he saw in Irwin's "third blessing." He felt certain the concept had validity. But the experience as defined by the Fire-Baptized movement lacked something tangible to ensure that it was genuine. Somehow he had to find God's sign and, when he did, he would know he had found the true Baptism of the Holy Spirit.

Just as Irwin tumbled from his seat of ecclesiastical authority, Parham discovered yet another rising star in the holiness ranks. He learned of Frank W. Sandford of Durham, Maine, through two of Sandford's students, Edward Doughty and Victor Barton, who visited Topeka early in 1900.[80] What he learned clearly excited him. Sandford's work included many of the goals—and more of the tangible results—of Parham's own ministry. In 1893, he had abandoned a promising career among the Free Baptists to begin an independent ministry of the holiness variety. Like Parham, he was heavily influenced by Moody and the higher life movement and adopted both divine healing and premillennialism.

From Bible conferences and books on Bible prophecy, Sandford learned the Anglo-Israel theory which depicted all Anglo-Americans as descendants of the "ten lost tribes" of Israel. Linking this theory with the widely held concept that an elite group of Christians—the "bride of Christ"—would form the core of the millennium's new order, he concluded that American Christians had a special role to fill in evangelizing the world before the Second Coming. As God's "chosen people," they were naturally candidates for membership into the "bride." Therefore, they exercised great responsibility for winning the lost during the last generations before the dawn of the eschaton, God's final judgment. Sandford calculated that, with the Second Coming so near, the bridal Christians would receive a special gift from God to make their task more manageable. This gift was the Baptism of the Holy Ghost which would prepare missionaries and evangelists with extra power and eloquence. In 1894, Sandford actively sought the experience and, after an agonizing eight month self-evaluation, claimed it in an act of passive acceptance. Nonetheless, the experience provided a new model for his ministry.

By the fall of 1895, he had established Shiloh, a community north of Durham which featured the "Holy Ghost and Us Bible School" for training evangelists and missionaries and served as a base for his occasional evangelistic trips abroad. Most remarkable was Sandford's ability to operate completely debt-free. His growing army of followers supplied extensive labor to support a huge economic enterprise predicated solely on a program of freewill offerings. Sandford charged no tuition fees and set no prices on room and board; students and guests voluntarily donated as much or as little as they wanted and could afford. Within ten years, the residents of Shiloh numbered over six hundred. Remaining free of debt, they constructed a seven-story tabernacle, an orphanage, a huge brick "hospital" for the practice of divine healing, a community church, and a dormitory large enough to house five hundred students.[81]

Late in 1899 Sandford received national attention—and suspicion—over an incident in which he allegedly raised Olive Mills, a young woman in his congregation, from the dead. He interpreted the incident as an endorsement of his own apostleship and became even more zealous in his efforts at world evangelism.[82] During the early months of 1900 he gathered seventy of his Bible students and, following the biblical example, paired them into groups of two. Leaving Shiloh, they crisscrossed the nation preaching a message of total surrender to the spirit of God.[83]

After their groundwork, Sandford traveled across the country and met his workers at key locations for city-wide revival campaigns. Doughty and Barton probably arrived in Topeka during early February where they immediately sought out other holiness workers in the city. Parham, still searching for an answer to his discontent, gave total support to Sandford's campaign. In mid-February he told *Apostolic Faith* readers that "one of the strongest men on the apostolic line in the United States has promised to be with us the latter part of March" and, several issues later, printed a favorable report of the Olive Mills affair.[84]

Sandford decided to travel to the West Coast by a different route and did not arrive in Topeka until June on his way back to Maine. The delay did nothing to dampen the spirits of the proprietor of the Beth-el home; Parham had been infected with Sandford's religious vision since the contact with Doughty and Barton in March. The April first issue of the *Apostolic Faith* evidenced this influence. In the place formerly filled with details about subscription rates, Parham now printed: "For Subscription Price See Isaiah 55:1." For anyone confused by his instructions, the verse in question could leave no doubt.

Ho, every one that thirsteth, come ye to the waters, and he that hath no money; come ye, buy, and eat; yea, come, buy wine and milk without money and without price.[85]

Elsewhere, Parham noted that as of the March fifteenth issue, "our entire work passed upon a free-will basis." In typical Sandfordian fashion he explained that his Topeka operation was completely debt free, a fact he had not previously felt compelled to mention. He also advised readers that the healing home was expanding, with plans already underway on a new auditorium and extra rooms at an estimated expense of ten thousand dollars. That construction, along with a rejuvenated rescue mission, would be "dedicated to God, free of debt or taxes."[86]

Unfortunately for Parham, his dramatic show of confidence was not rewarded. Within the next four months the *Apostolic Faith* folded and construction efforts at Beth-el were halted. Still, Parham was sure he had stumbled upon the proper method of Christian work. When Sandford arrived in June, Parham attended his meetings and was duly impressed. Along with eight other Topekans, he decided to join the self-proclaimed prophet's entourage and enroll in the Bible school at Shiloh. Leaving his family with friends in Topeka and the healing home in the care of two local holiness preachers, Parham departed late in June 1900. On the train ride to Maine he passed through Chicago and took the opportunity to investigate Dowie's sprawling enterprise on Michigan Boulevard and the smaller "Eye-opener Work" conducted by "Evangelist Kelly." He also made short visits to "Malone's work" in Cincinnati and A. B. Simpson's Christian and Missionary Alliance school in Nyack, New York.[87]

Arriving at Shiloh around midsummer, he spent six weeks there observing the intense activity of Sandford's sprawling complex. Parham adapted well to the lifestyle at Shiloh and was himself permitted to give an occasional lecture. He came to share Sandford's conviction that a special Holy Ghost baptism was available for deeply consecrated believers and that the gift was given specifically for world evangelism in the last days before the Second Coming. As the summer neared an end, Parham accompanied Sandford to Winnipeg, Manitoba for a month-long revival campaign.

Leaving Winnipeg in late September, he returned to Topeka singing the praises of his Northern tour. He explained to Topeka reporters that his trip had been an example of how life by faith works. He had left home over two months earlier with barely enough money to reach Chicago, yet now he stood before them with more money in his pocket than he had had when he left. God had provided money whenever it was needed. Relating the missionary journey into Canada, Parham seemed to speak for his entire experience when he noted "Take it as a whole, I never enjoyed a trip so much as that one."[88]

When Parham reestablished contact with the Beth-el Healing Home, he found that the two holiness ministers who had conducted affairs in his absence were now entrenched and quite reluctant to surrender control of the facility. He later accused them of stealing both his building and his congregation "through underhanded scheming and falsehoods." Yet, at the time, Parham did very little to try and regain control of the home. Disenchanted with the work and emboldened by his examination of the larger operations in the North, Parham disassociated himself with the healing home and immediately took steps to begin a Bible school modeled after the one in Shiloh, Maine. With his family and a small core of friends, he began recruiting students and in mid-October opened the school in a fifteen-room mansion on the outskirts of Topeka.[89]

Here, with a student body of thirty-four, Parham began teaching his assortment of religious doctrines, placing special emphasis on the two ideas he had added most recently—life by faith and Holy Spirit baptism for the purpose of world evangelism. The events of the next four months would dramatically alter Charles Parham's ministerial career; the doctrinal conclusions he drew from these events would eventually alter the landscape of American religious history.

3

The Gospel of the Latter Rain 1901

Holiness enthusiasts of the late nineteenth century searched the scriptures for proof of the authenticity of their revival. One popular rationale was Matthew 24:14, "And this gospel of the kingdom shall be preached in all the world for a witness unto all nations; and then shall the end come."[1] Holiness was a movement that stressed greater commitment among the already converted. The concept of a global revival effort seemed to validate this increased devotion since it would require greater zeal to successfully win the masses to Christianity. Likewise, the verse made a powerful imprint upon the minds of premillennialists eagerly anticipating Christ's return. It reinforced their inclination toward world mission programs and strengthened their own conviction that they lived in the midst of humanity's last generations. Holiness served as a prelude to missions—both home and foreign—while missions proved the validity of the premillennial warning.

One popular description of this massive endtime event was "the latter rain." Bible students employed the term as a metaphor for Palestinian rainfall patterns. The "early rain" revival of Acts 2 had watered the infant Christian Church in the same way that spring rains watered a freshly planted field. The "latter rain," however, fell toward the end of the growing

season and allowed the plants to reach maturity before harvest. Thus, premillennialists argued, the current revival spirit
was a final ripening of Christian saints immediately prior to
the harvest of Christ's Second Coming.[2]

Charles Parham returned to Topeka in September 1900
convinced that he had witnessed manifestations of this latter
rain. He consciously modeled his school upon what he had
seen at Shiloh and desired to establish significant works like
those of the other holiness leaders he had visited. Yet he was
also convinced that his calling had been a unique one and
firmly expected the Topeka school to reach even greater
heights in manifesting this endtime revival of the Holy Spirit.
He remained assured that there was something lacking in the
overall movement; it had not yet reached its crescendo. A
year later he remembered his northern tour with a lot less optimism than he had expressed to Topeka reporters immediately upon his return.

Pursuing our studies, we visited institutions of deep religious
thought, which were reported as having the power of the Holy
Ghost; yet these all failed to tally with the account in Acts. After
careful study, we returned from an extended trip through the east
and Canada with profound conviction that no one in these days
was really enjoying the power of a personal Pentecost. . . .[3]

The change in Parham's assessment from the fall of 1900 to
the fall of 1901 mirrored his experience as head of the new
Bible school. The six months from October 1900 to April
1901 would sufficiently separate him from even the radical
holiness leaders like Sandford. Out of the rubble of his break
with dominant holiness theories of pneumatology came the
Pentecostal movement.

Parham was a brash, twenty-seven-year-old religious ideo-
logue when he established Bethel Bible College in mid-
October 1900.[4] Yet he had made important contributions to
Christian relief work in Topeka and no doubt seemed a harm-
less enough fanatic to most of the city's social elite. The small
band of thirty-four students and a congregation of no more

than a hundred others saw something more. For them, Parham was a young man with extraordinary spiritual insight and a Bible scholar with three years of college education.

To house the Bible school Parham rented a curiously elaborate structure owned by the American Bible Society of Philadelphia. Located two miles outside Topeka's business section in a sparsely settled residential district, the "Stone mansion" was described as late as 1951 as "the biggest and fanciest residence ever built in Topeka." Thanks to a style one modern commentator has labeled "early Disneyland," the house looked to most residents like a medieval European castle.[5]

Erastus R. Stone made a small fortune in the nursery business during the early 1880s. Streetcars promised to revolutionize the living patterns of urban Americans by making suburban households a practical reality and the Topekan businessman enjoyed the results of a brief real estate boom. New homes and speculative development caused a tremendous increase in Stone's tree and shrubbery trade. Things progressed so well that Stone even invested directly in the real estate boom and emerged from a thirty-acre deal on the western edge of the city limits with twenty thousand dollars profit and a ten-acre tract of land reserved for his own use. He planted a grove of shade and fruit trees on the property and began construction with two helpers in 1884.

After two years of work and over twenty thousand dollars of material expenses, Stone's dream house neared completion. Unfortunately, his residence in the new house would be short-lived. The real estate market collapsed in 1887—a sign of troubled times to come for Kansas and America. With his business in shambles and most of his capital tied up in the new house, Stone was forced to sell the property. He suffered an estimated loss of ten thousand dollars and moved his family to California where he lived until his death in 1917.[6]

During the decade of the 1890s, "Stone's Folly," as Topeka residents termed it, remained mostly vacant. A few occupants tried renting the place as a family dwelling, but the size of the structure proved impractical for families struggling through the depression years of the 1890s. It stood as a monument to the hopes of the previous decade when Kansas had seemed an oasis to a never-ending caravan of western expansionists.

The enormous dwelling languished in general disuse until it caught Parham's eye late in 1900. With spired towers, large balconies, and ornate trimwork, Stone's Folly reminded Parham of the complex at Shiloh where Sandford often drew crowds of tourists to view his architectural handiwork. There can be little doubt that Parham returned from Shiloh with the express plan of securing the building with the help of friends. His new facility far outstripped the building on Fourth and Jackson, and like Shiloh it offered him and his students privacy from the bustle of city traffic. Here he hoped to resume his home healing ministry and probably planned someday to buy the ten-acre estate ouright and expand his operation into a series of Shiloh-like ministries.[7]

The old Stone mansion certainly contained enough room for beginning Parham's religious enterprise. The forty by seventy-five foot structure stood sixty feet tall. The earliest description of the building outlined Parham's plans.

The house is a large one, containing fifteen rooms, each finished in a different kind of wood, and the hall and staircase are in cedars of Lebanon. The hall at the landing of the stair on each of the three floors is large and roomy and the halls on the second and third floors will be utilized as sitting rooms.[8]

In addition to its size, the lavishness of the home was spectacular, if grotesque. A later description explained the elaborate detail Stone had envisioned.

The interior was finished throughout, no two rooms being trimmed with the same variety of wood. Mahogany, rosewood, magnolia, walnut, black and white, curly pine, birds-eye maple, butternut, and oak from all parts of the country are said to have been used in the inside decorations. Outside, the house was striking in appearance. It was of three-stories, surmounted with towers and battlement. The walls were of heavy studding with a brick veneer and stone cornices.[9]

For the first couple of months, life at the Bethel Bible School attracted only limited notice among Topekan residents. There was no doubt some interest that the mansion, once considered "haunted," now brimmed with human activity. Newspapers reported in October that students had formed a twenty-four hour prayer chain in one of the building's lofty cupolas. There, in the designated "Prayer Tower," intercession specifically for world evangelism continued unabated as the participants took turns holding three-hour shifts. The exercise, once again modeled directly after a practice at Shiloh, bound the small Bethel community together in a symbolic ritual of open communication between the students and God.

Some Topeka residents were aware of the financial needs of the group as well. Continuing the concept he had adopted earlier in the spring, Parham operated the school on the faith principle. When food ran low or money was needed to pay the sixteen dollars monthly rent, he placed the school on a prayer alert and the community of believers waited to see how God would answer their request. Neighbors often contributed in these times of need, and the contributions were interpreted by the recipients as answers to prayer and proof of the validity of life by total faith.[10]

As Christmas neared, Parham completed his lecture surveys in standard holiness-premillennial doctrine and led his students into an intense study of the Holy Spirit. His recounting of the subsequent turn of events is one of the best known episodes in Pentecostal history:

In December of [1900] we had had our examination upon the subject of repentance, conversion, consecration, sanctification, healing and the soon coming of the Lord. We had reached in our studies a problem. What about the 2nd Chapter of Acts? . . . having heard so many different religious bodies claiming different proofs as the evidence of their having the Pentecostal Baptism, I set the students at work studying out dilligently [*sic*] what was the Bible evidence of the Baptism of the Holy Ghost. . . .

Leaving the school for three days at this task, I went to Kansas City for three days services [and returned] to the school on the morning preceeding [*sic*] Watch night services in the year 1900. At about 10 o'clock in the morning I rang the bell calling all the students into the Chapel to get their report on the matter in hand. To my astonishment they all had the same story, that while there were different things [which] occurred when the Pentecostal blessing fell, that the indisputable proof on each occasion was, that they spake with other tongues. About 75 people beside the school[,] which consisted of 40 students, had gathered for the watch night service. A mighty spiritual power filled the entire school. At 10:30 P.M. Sister Agnes N. Ozman, (now La Berge) asked that hands might be laid upon her to receive the Holy Spirit as she hoped to go to foreign fields. At first I refused, not having the experience myself. Then being further pressed to do it humbly in the name of Jesus, I laid my hands upon her head and prayed. I had scarcely repeated three dozen sentences when a glory fell upon her[,] a halo seemed to surround her head and face[,] and she began speaking in the Chinese language, and was unable to speak English for three days.[11]

Struck by the powerful force of such an experience and convinced that this was the crucial spiritual element other groups lacked, Parham and his students fasted and prayed for the next two days. Each hoped to receive a dramatic experience similar to that which they had witnessed. Yet no one but Ozman spoke in tongues during this intense waiting period. On the evening of January third, Parham left the group in prayer and, taking only one student with him, preached at the Free Methodist Church in downtown Topeka. There he related the strange incident to the outside world for the first time, telling the congregation that he expected the entire school to receive this Holy Spirit baptism with tongues. When Parham returned to Bethel later that night, he found that the second floor of the building resembled a veritable "Upper Room" with visual, as well as audible, evidences of an Acts 2 outpouring.

The door was slightly ajar, the room was lit with only coal oil lamps. As I pushed open the door I found the room was filled with a sheen of white light above the brightness of the lamps.

Twelve minsters, who were in the school of different denominations, were filled with the Holy Spirit and spoke with other tongues.

Some were sitting, some still kneeling, others standing with hands upraised. There was no violent physical manifestation, though some trembled under the power of the glory that filled them.

Sister Stanley, an elderly lady, came across the room as I entered, telling me that just before I entered tongues of fire were sitting above their heads. . . . I fell to my knees behind a table[,] unnoticed by those upon whom the power of Pentecost had fallen[,] to pour out my heart to God in thanksgiving. . . .

After praising God for some time, I asked Him for the same blessing. He distinctly made it clear to me that He raised me up and trained me to declare this mighty truth to the world, and if I was willing to stand for it, with all the persecutions, hardships, trials, slander, scandal that it would entail, He would give me the blessing. And I said "Lord I will, if You will just give me this blessing." Right then there came a slight twist in my throat, a glory fell over me and I began to worship God in the Sweedish [*sic*] tongue, which later changed to other languages and continued so until the morning.[12]

Following the January third outpouring, even more members of the Bethel community experienced spirit baptism and glossolalia. Along with the glossolalia came other related phenomena. Some students received the gift of interpretation, enabling them to translate the new tongues into English. Others repeated a practice Ozman had exhibited shortly after receiving her experience several days earlier; temporarily unable to communicate in English, they tried writing messages and found that they uncontrollably scribbled what appeared to be foreign languages.[13] Soon such amazing feats attracted the attention of the outside world. Newspapers ran full-length articles with elaborate descriptions of the strange happenings at the new Bible school. At the center of this attention lay glossolalia, the most common spirit manifestation. According to Parham, outsiders proved what the students already assumed: the tongues were miraculously authentic.

No sooner was this miraculous restoration of Pentecostal power noised abroad, when we were besieged with reporters from Topeka papers. Kansas City, St. Louis and many other cities sent reporters who brought with them professors of languages, foreigners, Government interpreters, and they gave the work the most crucial test. One Government interpreter claimed to have heard twenty Chinese dialects distinctly spoken in one night, but all agreed that the students of the college were speaking in the languages of the world, and that with proper foreign accent and intonation.[14]

There are several problems with Parham's account of the Topeka Pentecost. In the first place, Ozman's glossolalic "Chinese" seems to have come on the night of January 1, 1901 rather than at the watch-night service of the previous evening. The confusion of dates has caused a variety of narrative interpretations, including the romantic notion that Ozman spoke in tongues precisely during the hour that the old century passed into history and the new one dawned.[15] In addition, Parham's designation of twelve denominational ministers has given the mistaken impression that the outbreak was a true ecumenical event. On the contrary, the small band formed a select group on the radical fringe of the holiness movement. While there may have been some semblance of denominational diversity in their backgrounds, it would be erroneous to state that a dozen of the forty students held credentials and remained in good standing with long-established Protestant denominations. Since Parham does not specifically say that the ministers came from twelve different denominations, it is most probable that they simply were affiliated in some way with several churches loosely associated with the overall holiness movement. Parham's sister-in-law, Lilian Thistlethwaite, seems to have confirmed this assessment by noting that of those who received the baptism at Bethel, "some were Methodists, others Friends, and some Holiness, while many belonged to no denomination."[16]

A more important discrepancy is Parham's assessment of how the Pentecostal formula was derived. The fact that the students independently came to the same conclusion that tongues were the indisputable evidence of Holy Spirit baptism has served an important function for Pentecostal apologists. The sequence undercuts Parham's leadership by creating the illusion that the theological formula proceeded merely from a community response to God-inspired scripture. Pentecostals have often used the story as proof that theirs is a movement of the Holy Spirit with no human foundations. What is generally overlooked is the fact that the scenario appealed to Charles Parham for the same reasons. His ministry thrived on deep suspicions about the role of humans as religious authorities; if a new theological message should appear, it would of necessity come directly from God to all willing to hear and receive it. Thus it should be no surprise that Parham, writing years later, consciously exaggerated the input of the student body.[17]

Earlier accounts, however, painted a different picture. The other principal figure in the story was Agnes Nevada Ozman, a thirty-year-old, unmarried holiness enthusiast from Nebraska. Like Parham, Ozman grew up in a frontier family struggling with the unpredictable forecast of late nineteenth century agriculture. Also like Parham, she experienced personal healing when, at the age of nineteen, her Methodist minister successfully prayed that she be healed of "lagrippe and pneumonia."

Following that experience, Ozman immersed herself in the doctrines of the holiness movement including premillennialism. She attended "C. Horton's Bible School" during the 1892–93 school year and, two years later, enrolled for courses at A. B. Simpson's Bible Institute in Nyack, New York. Along the way, she found time for a brief stay in Chicago where she visited both Moody Bible College and Alexander Dowie's healing home. In 1896 she settled in a Kansas City mission where she engaged in evangelistic street activities and continued her own search for religious fulfillment. It was there that she met Parham in October 1900. Fresh from his northern travel, Parham held several meetings in the city's holiness missions to publicize the opening of Bethel Bible College. Ozman was obviously impressed by his sincere devotion and his commitment to live by faith. When her sister unexpectedly gave her a monetary gift sufficient to cover the costs of the trip to Topeka, Ozman took it as an omen of God's will and accompanied the young evangelist back to Bethel.[18]

Ozman recalled her experience at Bethel in quite a different fashion from that related by Parham. Consistent with most early news accounts, she dated the dramatic encounter with Holy Spirit baptism to precisely 11:00 P.M. on January 1, 1901. She also claimed to have had a brief glossolalic experience several weeks prior to her New Year's Day reception.

One night three of us girls were praying together, and I spoke three words in another tongue. This was a hallowed experience, and was held in my heart as sacred.[19]

More striking was Ozman's failure to corroborate Parham's student consensus story. As she remembered it, any talk of tongues as normative evidence of the experience came after, not before, her reception.

Before receiving the Comforter I did not know that I would speak in tongues when I received the Holy Ghost for I did not know it was Bible. But after I received the Holy Spirit speaking in tongues it was revealed to me that I had the promise of the Father as it is written and as Jesus said. . . . I did not know then that any one else would speak in tongues. For I did not know how the Holy Ghost would be manifest to others.[20]

Following her experience, Ozman began an in-depth Bible study and claimed to have been "greatly surprised to find so much written on the subject." Several months later she concluded independently that tongues were the initial evidence of spirit baptism after witnessing nine different recipients demonstrate the same phenomenon. Ozman not only denied her own role in any pre-New Year's student assignment, but she also cast doubt on such a study by any of the other students as well. In her scenario the students approached her about the manifestation and she directed them to the account in Acts 2, explaining that her experience was the same one received by the apostles on the Day of Pentecost. Consequently Ozman portrayed herself as the teacher of both the students and Parham.[21]

The incongruity of the two versions has cast some doubt upon Parham's true role in the development of Pentecostal theology. Since tongues as initial evidence defined the movement as a distinct element apart from the overall emphasis on the Holy Spirit, that doctrine provided later Pentecostals their ideological birth announcement.[22] In effect, both accounts downplayed the direct hand Parham had in formulating this crucial tongues-as-evidence position and passing it on to the Bethel community. In each case student—rather than teacher— seemingly stumbled upon the truth and then had it confirmed by physical manifestation of the Holy Spirit. In actuality, Parham pieced the theological puzzle of Pentecostalism together sometime during the fall of 1900 and then predicted the revival that would ultimately confirm his conjectures.

Parham, and all early Pentecostals, assumed that their glossolalia was actually xenoglossa—speaking real languages unknown to the speaker. The speculation seemed confirmed early on when, the day after her dramatic reception of Holy Spirit baptism, Ozman spoke in tongues at a local Topeka mission and was understood by a Bohemian. She reported that the encounter "encouraged all very much knowing it was a real language."[23]

The importance of xenoglossa over glossolalia was more than just concern over the phenomenon's authenticity. Both Parham and the students shared an intense interest in world evangelism. They were also convinced that Christ's Second Coming would occur within their lifetime, making theirs the last generation to bear such an awesome responsibility.[24] Parham lamented as early as June 1899 that "the statistics show that there are 1,500,000,000 people in the world. Another fact is, as the statistics also show, that more [than] 1,000,000,000 of the world's population are yet without the Bible, and without the church, and without any missionary ministry."[25] The overwhelming effort that a genuine stab at world evangelism would require ultimately convinced him that newer and more spiritual methods were necessary.

Parham first happened upon the concept of missionary tongues early in 1899 while reading a St. Louis-based holiness periodical entitled *Everlasting Gospel*. The paper ran a short article on Jennie Glassey, a young lady affiliated with Sandford's Shiloh community. Glassey had raised a few eyebrows when, after accepting the "call" to Africa as a missionary, she had suddenly received the remarkable ability to command certain native dialects. Parham enthusiastically informed his readers of her experience in the *Apostolic Faith*.

Glassy [*sic*] now in Jerusalem, received the African dialect in one night. . . . She received the gift while in the Spirit in 1895, but could read and write, translate and sing the language while out of the trance or in a normal condition, and can until now. Hundreds of people can testify to the fact, both saint and sinner, who heard her use the language. She was also tested in Liverpool and Jerusalem. Her Christian experience is that of a holy, consecrated woman, filled with the Holy Ghost. Glory to our God for the return of the apostolic faith.[26]

Parham's identification of Glassey's gift with "apostolic faith," the name he had chosen for his own emphasis on primitive Christianity, was significant. As Parham interpreted the apostles' experience in Acts 2, they too had had a dramatic encounter with xenoglossa. The languages spoken on the Day of Pentecost served a twofold function; they allowed foreign Jews to hear the gospel message in their own tongue and demonstrated the power of God to work miracles within the newly formed Christian community.[27] Parham speculated that Glassey's experience provided the key to world evangelism in the last days. By April 1900 he had wholeheartedly accepted the premise and reported to his *Apostolic Faith* readers that a "Brother and Sister Hamaker" were staying at Beth-el waiting for Jesus to "give them a heathen tongue, and then they will proceed to the missionary field."[28]

A fascination with this phenomenon probably deepened Parham's interest in Glassey's mentor, Frank Sandford. Sandford solidified Parham's expectations of a Holy Spirit outpouring that would facilitate the seemingly impossible task of world evangelism. During his summer at Shiloh, Parham personally witnessed tongue-speaking for the first time. He heard several students utter glossolalic phrases as they came down from the school's "prayer tower" following long periods of intercession. The observation made a profound impact on him and it afforded him the opportunity to go one better on Sandford's theme of spirit baptism for world evangelism.

Whether Parham discussed his speculations with Sandford is not known. At any rate, the two men came to quite different assumptions regarding the tongues phenomenon. Sandford saw tongues as an occasional manifestation of the revival; such was the case with Glassey's unique gift. Parham, however, came to view tongues in a utilitarian fashion. Xenoglossa on a massive scale would make world evangelism a practical reality in a fairly brief period of time. It would preclude years of study by missionaries and would make almost anyone a candidate for missions service anywhere around the globe. Best of all, the method assured one of his own calling. All spirit-filled Christians had to do was match their language with the proper region of the world and God's appointment was secured.[29]

Parham had already solidified the Holy Spirit baptism confirmed by "mission tongues" idea by the time he opened Bethel Bible College on October 15, 1900. The key to his new doctrine was found in the Bible school itself. Bethel was specifically a training school for missionaries. In the past his Bible institutes had been subordinate to his work in the healing home. But in opening Bethel College, Parham reversed the roles; the training center came first.[30] The reason for the change was his conviction that he had a new message for world evangelism. During the weeks prior to Christmas he worked to convince his students that they had not yet received the true Baptism of the Holy Spirit. Ozman remembered that she, along with other students, had already claimed the experience "at a time of consecration or in sanctification." She also recalled that Parham explained to the student body "with much assurance and with power that the Holy Spirit was yet to be poured out" and proclaimed to them "that it was our privilege to have it fulfilled to us here and now."[31]

Parham wanted to prove to his students that the Baptism of the Holy Spirit should have some tangible evidence—something unmistakably biblical and functional. He centered his course of instruction on the book of Acts and, although other charismatic gifts are recorded there as well, glossolalia would be the obvious utilitarian link between Holy Spirit power and evangelism. It was especially noteworthy that the first glossolalic outbreak in Acts included what appeared to be xenoglossic tongues. The biblical aftermath of the outpouring was three thousand conversions on that day alone, precisely the kind of evangelistic results Parham had been looking for.[32]

There can be little doubt that Parham was consciously motivating his students toward this mission tongues concept. Although Ozman failed to mention it, Parham recorded that prior to asking him to lay hands on her to receive Holy Spirit baptism, she expressed a desire to go to the foreign mission field. The story gains credence through Parham's own express purpose in establishing the school and Ozman's decision to leave her long-standing work in Kansas City and travel to Topeka to study with him.[33]

What Ozman and the other students discovered at Parham's training school was, in effect, a holistic approach to missions. In the urgency of the last days, Christian workers would be consumed with power from on high. The experience would both inspire and equip them for service. Parham later explained that this foreign missions training was simply a matter of total dedication to God.

I had felt for years that any missionary going to the foreign field should preach in the language of the natives. That if God had ever equipped His ministers in that way He could do it today. That if Balaam's mule could stop in the middle of the road and give the first preacher that went out for money a bawling out in Arabic that anyone today ought to be able to speak in any language of the world if they had horse sense enough to let God use their tongue and throat.[34]

After Ozman's glossolalia seemed to be confirmed as xenoglossa on January second by the local "Bohemian," the other students were more impressed than ever. They promptly

sought this foreign missions tool for themselves and were rewarded by the more general outpouring of the following
evening.[35]

Of course, Parham and his students experiencing actual
xenoglossa would be a remarkable, though quite improbable
event. Proof would be almost impossible to verify. None of
the participants were qualified to assess linguistic patterns.
Had they been, there would have been little need to receive
such languages by divine gift. In addition it would be extremely difficult to evaluate the varied reports of foreigners
who heard, or thought they heard, their native tongue. The
original facility of each witness with a particular language
and the length of his stay in the United States would require
intense scrutiny before such reports could be taken seriously.
The best chance of amassing any such evidence ended with
Charles Shumway's scholastic research in 1914. Shumway
made a thorough search for Parham's "professors of languages" and "Government interpreters," but invariably failed
to find anyone willing to corroborate the evangelist's claims.[36]

Newspaper reporters, immediately after the Topeka outbreak, were as unconvinced that the tongue-speakers spoke
clear languages as they were amazed that the phenomenon occurred at all. To most, the tongues sounded like "gibberish,"
though some allowed that they slightly resembled what they
derisively termed "laundry talk." Written tongues, or glossographia, prompted similar suspicions. Though the Bethel
community claimed that the written scripts were authentic
languages, one newspaper reported a less than satisfactory
analysis.

Some of Miss Auswin's writing, which she claimed to be inspired,
was submitted to a Chinaman here in Topeka with the honest intention of seeing if he could translate it. The Celestial threw up his
hand and said: "Me no understand. Takee to Jap."[37]

Despite the prevailing consensus that Pentecostals at the
turn of the century experienced glossolalia rather than xenoglossa, there is one piece of evidence which suggests an an-

swer to the many reported encounters with actual language. Non-Pentecostal scholars since Shumway have recognized the possibility of cryptomnesia among the early recipients. This remarkable phenomenon involves foreign language forms stored in the memory of an individual without any conscious effort at retention. At a moment of intense stress, the mind then furnishes these words automatically. The effect is a kind of "simulated xenoglossa" since the speaker knows—but doesn't think he knows—the foreign words. Pentecostal scholars have agreed that cases of actual foreign words inserted amidst the defined norm of non-language glossolalia are conceivable as a result of cryptomnesia. However, they have not recognized the magnitude of this possibility.[38]

From 1860 to 1900 Kansas developed quite a linguistic variety due to immigration. Nearly every county and township was affected as large numbers of non-English speaking peoples settled the state. Norwegians, Danes, Swedes, Bohemians, French, and Germans made the greatest impact. Lesser numbers of Poles, Yugoslavs, Hungarians, Bulgarians, and Austrians made their presence felt as well. In 1870 more than fifteen percent of the state was foreign born. Assimilation into American culture took quite a while on the Kansas frontier; as late as 1910, over twenty-one percent of the foreign born adults could not speak English.[39] The Kansas language mosaic differed little from those across the rest of America's heartland. Similar and even higher figures are available for other midwestern states. What is unique is that Charles Parham developed the idea that foreign tongues would be given to those people receiving the Baptism of the Holy Spirit. Both he and his students had had exposure to actual foreign languages in their past. They also prayed intently for God to bestow his special endtime blessing on them. Thus they were prime candidates for cryptomnesia, and the phenomenon was no doubt widely responsible for the verification of certain words and the language-like structure easily mistaken for a foreign tongue.[40]

After speaking in tongues proved difficult for recipients

themselves to understand—at least without the separate gift of interpretation—Parham altered his original views slightly. Spirit-filled Christians were obedient servants dependent on God for both language and sermon. The experience was thus even more miraculous since the missionary spoke a message that came directly from God.[41] A few, however, could receive the gift of tongues in the same way Glassey had several years earlier. As late as 1919, Parham claimed that such language gifts continued to operate effectively in foreign lands.

We have several missionaries in the field who have the gift of tongues, who not only speak the language and understand the natives, but can use the language intelligently; it has become a gift to them.[42]

Tongues remained mission oriented even when they functioned among groups speaking the same language. They served as a dramatic sign of God's presence and encouraged nonbelievers to accept the gospel message.[43]

Missions explained the utilitarian function of tongues, but Parham concluded that the experience of Holy Spirit baptism brought an important internal distinction for the Christian faith as well. That distinction was the "sealing of the bride." Those who received Spirit baptism and became the triumphant missionaries of humanity's last generation would achieve recognition as members of Christ's bride upon the occasion of the Second Coming.[44] This elite band of Christians consisted of those to be snatched away in the rapture and spared the awful trials of the seven-year tribulation period. Upon returning with Christ during the second stage of his appearing, they would serve important positions in the administration of the millennial government. Pentecostal baptizing then was a special seal of God's approval and an assurance of one's place in the new age. Three weeks after the Bethel outbreak, Parham proclaimed that the new revival signaled the imminent return of Christ and, with it, the selection of his bride. By explaining that the special experience was for this unique generation, he could logically account for prominent religious divines of preceding centuries who had never received it.

Do you mean to say that John Wesley and others since, did not have this Baptism? Exactly; he and many since have enjoyed a mighty anointing that abideth, and spoke like the holy men of old as they were moved by the Holy Ghost but the power of this Pentecostal Baptism of the Holy Spirit is a different thing entirely. The Baptism of the Holy Spirit is especially given now as the sealing. Therefore the sureness of the last days.[45]

Glossolalia confirmed this sealing process and thus was an incontrovertible part of the new doctrine. Parham championed it in both the utilitarian and spiritual manifestations as the "Bible evidence" of Holy Spirit baptism.[46]

Despite Parham's success at convincing most of his students that theirs was an age destined to receive remarkable gifts and signs, a few remained skeptical. Following the Thursday night outpouring on January third, the religious atmosphere at Stone's Folly reached a fever pitch. Altogether about half of the student body received the new experience amidst prayer and shouts of praise that could be heard well into the early morning hours. On Saturday morning, January fifth, the spirit of ecstasy was temporarily broken as the Bethel community suffered its first defection. Samuel J. Riggins, a young student from Kansas City, left Bethel and secured lodging at Parham's old healing home in Topeka. The local press was alerted, and, the next day, Riggins' assessment of his classmates appeared on page two of the *Topeka Daily Capital*.

I believe the whole of them are crazy. . . . I never saw anything like it. They were racing about the room talking and gesticulating and using this strange and senseless language which they claim is the word from the Most High.[47]

Riggins' disclosure prompted a rash of reporters to descend upon the unique campus and form their own impressions of the strange affair. The following day, the *Topeka State Journal* ran an article headlined "Row At Bethel," detailing Riggins' defection and painting a similarly unflattering description of the religious environment he had left behind.

About fifteen members of the colony have now been given the gift of tongue [*sic*], and when a State Journal reporter called at the school this morning each of the favored ones were called up and spoke a few sentences in [a] strange and unnatural way, outlandish words which they neither knew the meaning of nor the language to which they belonged. . . . It is a peculiar sight to see a whole room full of the men and women of the school sitting around, occasionally breaking out with brief outbursts of talk in one of the many languages which they claim to speak, and writing the quaint and indistinguishable hieroglyphics which they believe to be the characters for words in the Syrian, Chinese, Japanese, Arabic and other languages.[48]

For the next several days, the media coverage continued. Reporters noted that the Bethel community practiced a primitive form of communism since all residents contributed their money and goods to a common treasury and trusted God for their future needs. They also detailed the regimen of activity in the twenty-four hour prayer tower. More significantly, news reporters accurately gauged the new theological formula for world evangelism that Parham had instilled in his students and acknowledged the role that the strange tongues played in the plan. Glossolalia, then, captured their attention above all else. One reporter even ventured to offer a transliteration of what he heard one of the students say.

"Euossa, Euossa use, rela sema calah mala kanah leulla sage nalan. Ligle logle lazle logle. Ene mine mo, sah rah el me sah rah me." These sentences were translated as meaning, "Jesus is mighty to save," "Jesus is ready to hear," and "God is love."[49]

One week after the initial wave of publicity, another student thrust the school into the Topeka papers. Ralph Herrill, spirited away from Bethel College with the aid of former student Riggins, became the community's second voluntary exile. Herrill's parents in Kansas City wired money and instructed Riggins to accompany their son safely back into the city of Topeka. Though no effort was made to prevent the young men from leaving, Riggins reported that the other students "protested" the removal of Herrill and "claimed that I was possessed of a devil." Herrill seemed more reluctant to criticize the school though he also doubted the authenticity of the new mission tongues. As might be expected, neither Riggins nor Herrill had received the Pentecostal baptism. In fact Riggins had had problems at the school before. Soon after arriving on campus in late October, he had returned to Kansas City following a disagreement with some of the students and had been back at Bethel for only a few weeks when the Pentecostal revival began. Strikingly, both men criticized their fellow students but were unwilling to publicly attack Parham. Herrill even intimated that Parham's tongue speech was authentic.[50]

Following the somewhat shaky start, the Bethel community hardened. No additional students defected; those remaining without the Spirit baptism apparently continued their search convinced that the experience of their classmates had been a valid one. At any rate, they waited to see the fulfillment of their teacher's dramatic plan of evangelism. After evaluating the nonenthusiastic reception of Pentecost in Topeka, Parham prepared to shake the dust from his feet and take his message to a larger market. Topeka papers reported on January twenty-first that Parham and seven spirit-filled followers had set out on a missionary tour of the United States and Canada. Leaving the bulk of the community behind to pray for results, this band of eight headed first to Kansas City. Beginning with a good reception there, they hoped to retrace Parham's trip of the previous summer and spread the new light of Pentecost throughout the network of holiness associations in the Midwest and Northeast. J. Nelson, one of the holiness ministers who succeeded Parham at the healing home in downtown Topeka and subsequently harbored the two student defectors, predicted the end of his former associate's young career.

I have expected this. I have seen schools before where it has been claimed that the gift of tongues was received. It always ends in breaking the school up. I expected to hear of some of them leaving on a little missionary trip, and I never look for them to come back.[51]

With true evangelistic zeal Parham and his wife left their children in the care of the Bethel community and set off to conquer the religious world. Highlighting their small band was Ozman, Lilian Thistlethwaite—Parham's sister-in-law and a recipient of both tongues and the gift of interpretation—and Albert Horr, a fourteen-year-old boy who now exhibited an amazing facility for foreign language. The group secured a small building at 1675 Madison Avenue in downtown Kansas City and began holding services. They encountered an initial measure of success, drawing nightly crowds of seventy-five to a hundred participants and interested spectators. A series of dramatic healings, most notably that of Mrs. Jennie Caine who had been crippled since childhood, drew even wider attention and prompted Parham to occasionally schedule larger meetings at the local Academy of Music. The success also brought a new horde of curious newspapermen.[52]

The Kansas City press first published Parham's exploits in mid-January when news from Topeka had warranted several visits from investigative journalists. Now the reporters came to see if he would have any impact on their own city's population. They described the young minister with great detail and much skepticism.

In person, Mr. Parham is below medium height, pleasant looking, has a fierce reddish-faddish beard, a voice like a pirate and a manner as brusque as a janitor in a flat. He is a native of Kansas and talks at the rate of 250 words a minute, and if it is a matter of doubt about his having the gift of tongues, he has at least the gift of one, for in his flights of rhetoric . . . he never stumbles for a word.[53]

Parham kept the press at his doorstep with frequent harangues that isolated him from the more respectable members of the religious clergy. He defended the communitarian lifestyle employed at Bethel by proclaiming the nearness of the millennial age. Christians should now concentrate on restoring the conditions of the "apostolic faith" since "private ownership of land and of all other things will be done away with and all Christian people will pour their money and their all into the coffers of Christ."[54]

Parham also drew quite a bit of attention for his unique stand on prohibition. Though he had once been a staunch advocate of organized temperance societies, he now argued that the saloon-wrecking tactics of Carry Nation were useless. Prohibition laws only immersed the liquor traffic deeper into the hands of big business operatives by driving up prices. Parham humorously noted that liquor was readily available in every town in Kansas to the man with a "red nose" to light the way to the nearest underground bar. The only solution capable of handling the problem was a spirit-moved revival that could "not only save men's bodies from the liquor traffic, but also their souls from the devil."[55]

In an even greater demonstration of his antiestablishment bent, Parham refused vaccination in the midst of a local smallpox epidemic. He publicly defied Kansas City authorities to try and vaccinate any member of his family with their "miserable vaccine." Life by total faith precluded any confidence in man-made cures.[56]

Followers of the new Pentecostal faith received their share of publicity as well; most of it was even less flattering than that received by their leader. Dismissing Parham as "a sincere and extremely optimistic fanatic," one reporter decided that the preacher's flock was "about as tacky a looking outfit as one would see in a trip around the world."[57] A few others, however, took a more sympathetic view. A graduating senior from Kansas State University, intrigued by the news stories, visited the Bethel community later that spring. He reported that although Parham's followers practiced some unusual religious beliefs, they did so voluntarily and without any noticeable loss of individual health or family welfare.[58]

Despite the generous amount of publicity, Parham never received the crowd support he hoped for. Congregations remained just under a hundred, enough to establish a small mission but not the financial support required for the proposed northern tour. In mid-February, the band of eight missionaries and a handful of the new converts returned to the Bible school in Topeka. Parham explained to reporters that he had been forced to return to clear up a problem at the school.

While that may have been true, the poor turnout in Kansas City had rendered any plan of continuing north financially impossible. In addition, other problems plagued the effort. Winter snowstorms were particularly fierce, dumping eight inches of snow on Kansas City in early February. Worse storms further north made travel difficult under the best of circumstances.[59]

Even had Parham made his journey, there is little likelihood that he would have encountered the overwhelming response he hoped for. Holiness groups around the nation responded indifferently to the initial reports of his Pentecostal restoration. Some accused the new movement of undue emotionalism and regarded the claim to missionary tongues with suspicion.[60] Stalemated after several weeks, Parham decided to regroup in the familiar surroundings of Bethel. The initial attempt to revolutionize the world had ended in failure.[61]

Parham was not one to fall with the first punch. He acknowledged that the group had encountered some "financial difficulties," but insisted that he had never lacked funds to do what God directed him to do. He reassured reporters that during the spring and summer months the student body would proceed with their missionary conquest throughout the country and that many with the gift of tongues would be going to foreign lands.[62] In late February Parham took a group of twenty students to nearby Lawrence. There he met some success but, once again, failed to inaugurate any sweeping changes in the city's religious convictions. Nevertheless, he remained undaunted.

From Lawrence, he returned to Kansas City where he told reporters that he expected the next few months to prove a time of tremendous growth for his new Apostolic Faith movement. Explaining that he had received many applications from ministers interested in attending the Bible school to receive languages for the mission field, Parham unfolded an extensive plan to build a big auditorium in Topeka. Trusting that God would supply the needed capital, he hoped to complete the building during the next few months and conduct a summer camp meeting there. The additional number of students coming for their "training" would reinvigorate the movement and launch a worldwide mission campaign from the headquarters in Topeka.[63]

Less than a week after revealing these optimistic plans, Parham faced a genuine tragedy. On March 16 his year-old son, Charles F. Parham, Jr., died suddenly. Some students maintained a hope that God would raise the toddler from the dead as a miraculous sign of apostolic restoration, but Parham understood that this was a time of trial, not triumph.[64] More than any other event, this tragedy spelled doom for any resurgence of world evangelism in the immediate future.

Parham tried desperately to salvage his floundering optimism. Two months after his son's death, he led a small band of travelers on a return mission to Kansas City. He announced the summer camp meeting but replaced the plans for a new auditorium with the simple acknowledgement that the event would be held on the campus of Bethel College. As if in an effort to convince himself, Parham issued wild projections about the "thousands" who would be attending the Topeka meeting from all over the United States. In similar fashion, he told the press that he now enjoyed five-hundred followers in Topeka and several thousand others around the country and world.[65]

The immense Topeka camp meeting never began. The spirit of desperation that gripped the Bethel community after the tragedy proved too large an obstacle to overcome. Many students simply could not rationalize the event with the optimism foreshadowed two months earlier by the dawn of Holy Spirit baptism. Agnes Ozman later recalled that, during the period after the initial revival, "a voice was followed which was not the Lord's."[66] Almost anticlimactic was the fact that Stone's Folly was sold to a new owner in July 1901 and Parham and the students were forced to vacate the property. Harry Croft, a local businessman, bought the building and promptly turned it into a local resort cottage. Rumors abounded that the exquisite old mansion now served as a private "joint" for the purposes of Croft's secret bootlegging operation.[67]

Parham secured a smaller building in Topeka to continue the school but only a faithful remnant of students remained with him. Most took the loss of Stone's Folly as a final omen of the work in Topeka and fanned out to new places of service, though they were inclined to carry their new Pentecostal doctrine with them.[68] By the fall, Parham had closed the school and moved his family to Kansas City. There he began a period of deep introspection. He solidified his experience of the previous year into a theological unit and published his first book in January 1902. *Kol Kare Bomidbar,* Hebrew for "A Voice Crying in the Wilderness," symbolized Parham's belief that, like John the Baptist, he had announced a new dispensation.[69] Also like the Baptist, he had found his road full of difficulties and trials. Nevertheless, the book affirmed his optimism that Holy Spirit baptism marked the dawn of a new era in world evangelism and Christian living.

Ironically, the completion of Parham's volume coincided with the destruction of the Stone mansion. The stately structure burned to the ground under somewhat mysterious circumstances early on the morning of December 6, 1901. Parham believed the fire was a fulfillment of God's wrath for the immoral activity conducted in the building since his departure—a feeling shared by many Topeka residents as well.[70] The irony of the event, however, escaped Parham's notice. The physical structure most closely identified with the new Pentecostal movement had been destroyed. In its place a more enduring monument had been erected; Parham's book marked the first published example of Pentecostal theology in history.

4

The Latter Rain Spreads
1902–1905

Times were tough for Charles Parham in 1902. He had spent most of the previous year predicting success. To his satisfaction, God had fulfilled a prophecy about endtime world evangelism and had charged him with the task of enlightening the Christian community as to its benefits. Within the confines of the holiness movement he had considered himself a rising star. Newspaper coverage, though patronizing, gave him a sense of importance.[1] The immaculate-looking Bible school at Stone's Folly and the troop of several dozen Christian soldiers had promised recognition within the Christian community and a leading role in the eschatological climax of the present age. Somehow, all of this had been lost. He opened 1902 without a Bible school, without sizable crowd response, and without the optimism that had been his forte during 1901.

Parham refused to roll over and play dead. He forged on, proclaiming the new Pentecostal doctrine. His determination, however, brought few tangible results, and he later recalled the period as a time when "my wife, her sister and myself seemed to stand alone." The birth of another son, Philip Arlington, in June seemed to lift Parham's spirits, and soon afterward he opened a new Bible school downtown on the corner of Eleventh and Oak. The Kansas City version of Bethel

College lasted all of four months. Late in the fall of 1902 he abandoned the city and moved the family to Lawrence, Kansas, where he launched a series of area-wide evangelistic revivals. The effort generated the same lethargic response. Mrs. Parham remembered that "the people seemed slow to accept the truth," and noted that many "declared it was not the power of God which enabled us to speak in other tongues." Early in 1903 Parham packed again and headed to Nevada, Missouri, at the invitation of a female minister who had accepted his Pentecostal message during the early months of 1901.[2]

The accusation in Lawrence of demonic ties apparently struck a raw nerve. Parham had not criticized emotional displays at Bethel, though news reports and local citizens had portrayed the worship as a rather wild affair. In Nevada, he now suddenly discerned the presence of "fleshly manifestations" and "fanaticism" directed by unholy spirits. Certain that this was detrimental to the work of the "true Pentecost," Parham made his stay in Nevada a short one as well. During the summer he suddenly felt that God desired him to go to El Dorado Springs, Missouri. With the move to the nearby health resort he rejuvenated his ministry with an emphasis that had brought him success in the past. It turned out to be a most propitious decision; the healing ministry once again brought Charles Parham local notoriety.[3]

El Dorado Springs had an unimpressive population of just under sixteen hundred at the turn of the century. During the summer months, however, the town swelled to more than twice that size as an annual flood of visitors came to bathe in the local array of mineral springs. In 1881, Mrs. Joshua Hightower discovered the "curative powers" of the springs when she stopped overnight en route to a health resort in Arkansas; her health rapidly improved after drinking the iron-hardened water. Local developers advertised the phenomenon and a new health facility quickly emerged.[4] Parham's choice of El Dorado Springs is indicative of his desire to rekindle his former ministry of divine healing. With a small band of workers, he stood and sang gospel hymns at the entrance to the healing springs. After gathering a crowd, he introduced himself with a short sermon and invited those interested in healing to visit the daily prayer meetings held in his home a block north of the springs. Soon, those unsatisfied with the results of the iron water came to give Parham a second hearing.[5]

One of those desperate for healing was Mary A. Arthur. Arthur, a resident of Galena, Kansas, was a frequent visitor to the healing springs. Now in her fourth summer of attendance, she had yet to find any relief for a myriad of debilitating conditions. She reported that she suffered from "dyspepsia for fourteen years also with prolapsis, hemorrhoids and paralysis of the bowels." Even more distressing was her failing eyesight. Born blind in the right eye, she now suffered from vision loss in the left eye as well. In the summer of 1898 she had undergone an operation but with dismal results. The sight in her left eye grew worse and she spent the next five years in pain vainly searching for a cure.[6]

Arthur visited the Parham home, heard the sermon, and observed others receiving prayer for divine healing. On the morning of August 17 she attended the services again and informed the congregation that she believed God would heal her eyes. After receiving "the laying on of hands" and prayer, she demonstrated her faith by removing the two pairs of eyeglasses she normally wore—prescription spectacles and the sunglasses she wore over them to relieve the pain caused by intense light. On the way back to her room, she experienced a sudden and miraculous recovery.

I stepped outside the door and wondered how I could get to my room. I folded my handkerchief and held it over my eyes, took the hand of my young daughter, who led me to the spring. There a young man filled my cup and while I was drinking, he said, "Sister do not get discouraged if you do not get your healing instantly, for I was healed by prayer here and I believe you will be too." My daughter led me out on the main street, and asked for tomatoes and cookies. . . . We went two blocks to get them, and on returning, about six blocks from the place where I was prayed for, she let go of my hand to eat the cookies. Soon I spoke to her, but had no answer.

I spoke again and still no answer. Then alarmed for her, I lifted my handkerchief off one eye. . . . she was a half block behind me. I could open my eyes in the light, and no pain. . . . I said, "Praise God, the work is done." He answered me, "You are every whit whole." . . . Then his mighty healing power surged through my body from my head to my feet, making me feel like a new person. . . . I gained 29 pounds in a very short time and could eat four meals a day. No more starving dyspepsia, the glasses and all remedies were all cast away.[7]

The Arthur healing proved to be a major turning point in Charles Parham's career. Upon returning home to Galena, Mary Arthur promptly amazed her friends and neighbors with the account of her dramatic healing in El Dorado Springs. Soon the whole town knew the story. The response was so overwhelming that local businessmen—Christian and non-Christian alike—invited Parham to Galena for a series of meetings. Arrangements were made through Mrs. Arthur, and on October 18 Parham began preaching in the Arthur home. The turnout exceeded all expectations, and within two days services moved to a tent pitched outside the residence. By Thanksgiving, Parham was enjoying the most sustained meeting of his career. The combination of cold weather and continued interest forced still another move. The "Grand Leader Building on Main Street," a fifty by one-hundred-foot structure, housed the two-meetings-a-day revival until its completion on January 15, 1904. Crowds of up to two thousand overflowed the building at the crowded night services.[8]

Galena, Kansas, held an important position in the precarious economy of the tri-state mining region of Kansas, Missouri, and Oklahoma. Lead, zinc, and coal mining operations began in Missouri in the early nineteenth century. By the 1870s the activity spilled into Cherokee County, Kansas where vast deposits of lead and zinc provided a new source of income for the region for the next three generations. In the early 1900s eighty-one mining camps dotted the landscape as the tri-state area became, "for the half century, the richest lead and zinc producing center in the world."[9]

The new economy meant a change in lifestyle as well. Galena became a booming frontier mining town of over ten thousand during the half decade before the dawn of the twentieth century. Saloons were commonplace, despite Kansas prohibition laws, and violence frequent among the hardworking transient population. A miner trying to work his way up the ladder of administration remembered the environment of Galena's economic heyday.

Rough men came from every direction, riding or driving through the deep mud or dust, whichever for the moment made up the newly laid-out streets. They drank, gambled, shot, fought or killed each other as they pleased. Largely making their own laws, they went their own ways, and worked in the mines when they felt like it, or when they ran out of money and were compelled to. In the business section almost every other building housed a saloon with brothels sandwiched in between.

Few were the mornings when I went to work that I did not see at least one dead man lying between the tent shacks where he had been thrown during the night to get him out of the way. After some nights there would be several bodies in evidence.[10]

The savage lifestyle created a starkly irreligious environment. In nearby Joplin, Missouri, the hub of the tri-state district, a local poet humorously described the lack of religion in everyday life.

Suez was still east of us and there were no Ten Commandments, for way down yonder in Southwest Missouri, where women drink and curse like fury; where the barkeepers sell the meanest liquor which makes a white man sick and sicker, where the tinhorns rob you a little quicker, that's where Joplin is.[11]

When Charles Parham arrived in Galena in the fall of 1903, he found a town ripe for repentance. The entire population suffered from the instability of the town's sudden growth. Most residents had arrived during the boom years of the previous decade and were not yet secure in their new surroundings. The few who enjoyed deep roots in the community had witnessed the shocking changes that converted their peaceful farming village into a seedy mining town. Almost all depended on the continued output of the local mines for their livelihood. Yet despite considerable supplies of iron and coal, the promise of great mining wealth proved elusive. Missouri never achieved the stability of the larger mineral states of the North. Local strikes created boom towns but frequent layoffs destroyed them. Galena was, in effect, on an economic roller coaster. The uncertainty of its situation is reflected in population figures: Shortly before Parham's arrival, the town peaked at 10,155; by the end of the decade, barely 6,000 souls were present.[12]

Parham's healing message struck a responsive chord in many of Galena's transients. His was a message of power— power demonstrated by spiritual gifts and remarkable episodes of healing. Healings reaffirmed that, despite the uncertain surroundings of life, God cared and personally intervened in the ordinary lives of human beings. In short, Parham encountered large numbers of Galenans who were ready to believe. Their faith created the kind of atmosphere he had sought all along to initiate his Apostolic Faith crusade.

Parham's results at Galena were no less than amazing. Over eight hundred new converts joined his interdenominational alliance; over one thousand worshippers claimed healing from some physical ailment. Baptismal services for the newly converted attracted widespread attention as groups of one hundred or more were immersed in the icy, winter waters of the local Spring River. Howard A. Goss, one of those baptized that winter, remembered that despite record low temperatures none of the converts contracted so much as a cold from the experience.[13] The highlight of the revival was a watchnight service on New Year's Eve which attracted close to twenty-five hundred. A thousand of the faithful remained until after midnight and over four hundred were still present when the prayer meeting finally ended at daybreak.[14] Included in the success at Galena were several hundred who received the Holy Spirit baptism evidenced by glossolalia. The experience of Pentecost was slowly gaining a foothold.[15]

The religious impact of the Galena revival spread through the tri-state mining region. Denominational churches found the atmosphere conducive to impromptu revival efforts of their own.[16] For Parham the success meant that the mining district would be his new ministerial center. In February 1904 he followed his success at Galena with a three-week revival in nearby Baxter Springs. The population of 1,000 yielded 250 new converts.[17] Heartened by the response and concerned about the birth of his newest son, Wilfred Charles, Parham moved his family to a more permanent home in Baxter Springs in April. For the first time since 1901, their household furniture was taken from storage and the Parhams settled into a comfortable home provided by area followers. Using Baxter Springs as a base, Parham continued to evangelize the mining district. A successful meeting at Melrose, a small town twelve miles west of Baxter Springs, prompted the construction of the first Pentecostal church building. At the rural crossroads of Keelville, Kansas, Parham supporters built a small meeting hall and organized their own local Apostolic Faith congregation.[18]

In the fall of 1904, Parham held a seven-week revival campaign in Joplin, Missouri, the commercial center of the lead and zinc district. He continued to command a significant following and occasional healings attracted quite a bit of attention to the man known locally as "The Divine Healer." But damaging publicity spelled a sudden end to his dramatic rise in popularity.

Most of the newspaper accounts of the Galena revival had been favorable. The good press had prompted not only continued success at Parham's meetings but also attention from others within the holiness movement.[19] Now a story hit which threatened to damage Parham's credibility throughout the mining region. On October 23, nine-year-old Nettie Smith of Baxter Springs died after a brief illness. Her father, Bert Smith, refused medical assistance throughout the ordeal. An avid Parham disciple, he preferred to practice the Apostolic Faith method of no doctors and no drugs. When the young girl died

from what most in the community considered a treatable illness, public opinion of Parham shifted from respect and awe
to disgust and anger. To many, he now seemed more of a
menace than a prophet. For the short term, at least, Parham's
movement was stymied.[20]

Coincidentally, Parham suffered a physical relapse during
the Joplin revival. In what was probably a recurrence of the
childhood rheumatic fever, he became ill and "went down
even to the valley of the shadow of death."[21] The sickness
forced him to return to Baxter Springs where he spent the
winter months recuperating. A few of the faithful visited his
home regularly where Parham, propped up in bed, delivered
Bible lectures. But the intensity of the previous year had been
lost in his own physical collapse and in the damaging reper-
cussions of the Nettie Smith affair. Not surprisingly, he felt a
new call during that winter of recuperation. The unmistak-
able divine voice that had spoken so often in the past seemed to
tug at his heart and say "Go to the southland!" In early April
1905, still in weak health, he traveled by train to Orchard,
Texas.[22]

Parham's invitation to Orchard, a small crossroads forty-
five miles west of Houston, came not only from God but also
from Mr. and Mrs. Walter Oyler. Residents of Orchard, the
Oylers had visited Kansas during Parham's phenomenal success of the previous year. Both attended the Galena revival
and received the Baptism of the Holy Spirit. At the Joplin revival, they persuaded one of Parham's workers, Mrs. Anna
Hall, to return to Orchard with them and help spread the
Apostolic Faith message. After little success, they decided a
meeting by Parham might be the added ingredient that would
bring Pentecostal revival to Texas. Recognizing Parham's
weakened condition, they convinced him that the warmer
southern climate would aid his recovery; at the same time, he
could offer invaluable advice and encouragement to the small
band of believers in Orchard. One of the new converts, a
wealthy rancher named Henry H. Aylor, even offered the
evangelist lodging in his home.

Parham accepted the invitation as a three-week recuperative vacation; but, once there, the enthusiasm in Orchard sparked a rapid recovery. Three days after arriving, he reported that "a great revival broke out and I was instantly strengthened for the campaign."[23] Preaching his first sermon on Easter Sunday, Parham quickly reaped an evangelical harvest. In early May, he wrote home that "there were only five or six Christians here but, in two weeks, there were only about that many sinners." He closed by noting: "They are bringing the sick twenty miles in wagons for healing and I am as well and strong as ever."[24]

Parham's recovery in Orchard is not at all amazing in hindsight. He had always intimately associated his health and his relationship with God. More precisely, he had come to expect divine guidance through the occasional flareups and setbacks of rheumatic fever. As a small boy, the initial attack had preceded his call to preach. In college, a frightening encounter with the illness placed him back on the right track after a period of backsliding. As a young minister, the weakness caused by the lifelong affliction had led to his acceptance of divine healing and a life without modern medicine. And, most recently, an attack in Topeka in September 1899 had led to disillusionment with the state of his work at Beth-el and the subsequent belief that he was specially chosen to lead the Christian faith in an endtime Pentecostal missionary effort. The present recovery, then, would follow the same pattern.

Parham discovered that the Lone Star State provided an excellent training ground for his young missionary movement. He explained to his family that the revival spirit in Orchard "was the grandest scene I have witnessed since the outpouring of the Holy Spirit in the Bible School in Topeka." Encouraged by the results, Parham returned to southeast Kansas in mid-May and held a series of spirited revival meetings. Reawakened to the dream of worldwide evangelistic conquest, he actively recruited workers to help in an apostolic assault on the state of Texas.[25]

Parham targeted the Houston-Galveston area to begin his

campaign. Like Galena, they were boom towns. Rising quickly in the wake of the Spindletop oil strike just outside Beaumont in 1901, they evoked much the same type environment and were peopled by large numbers of transients. Unlike Galena, they remained bustling centers of commerce for decades to come.[26] On July 4, Parham and fifteen workers from the Midwest arrived in Orchard. After recruiting another ten associates from among the faithful there, they headed off, in Mrs. Parham's words, "to lay seige to the city of Houston in the name of the Lord." With the financial help of the Pentecostal faithful, especially Henry Aylor, Parham rented Bryan Hall for fifty dollars a week and on July 10 began a revival that lasted for over a month.[27]

Assisting in the Houston campaign was the independent Holiness Church from the suburb of Brunner. The pastor, W. Faye Carothers, learned of Parham's effort during the Orchard revival of the previous month. A member of his congregation, Mrs. John C. Calhoun, attended the meetings, received Holy Spirit baptism, and returned to tell her fellow church members of the wondrous latter rain outpouring. Soon the entire congregation accepted the new Pentecostal doctrine. The Brunner flock added enthusiastic support to the midwestern missionary corps and W. Faye Carothers became Parham's right-hand man.[28]

As usual, dramatic healings set the stage for local press coverage and increased attendance by attracting curious spectators. By early August the *Houston Chronicle* reported marvelous cures from epilepsy, consumption, and an assortment of other ailments and diseases. One five-year-old boy claimed a dramatic encounter in which he was "straightened" from curvature of the spine. His weak legs suddenly gained strength, enabling him to walk. The miracle continued to impress the community as gradually "the shorter of the two limbs lengthened to the normal."[29]

Even more graphic was the experience of Mrs. J. M. Dulaney. The wife of a prominent Houston attorney, Dulaney suffered complete paralysis on the left side of her body as a result of a November 1902 street car accident, and despite over twenty-three hundred dollars in medical bills, she remained unable to walk. A subsequent lawsuit had publicized her condition throughout the city. Dulaney told reporters that in May 1905, she received a vision ensuring her of healing; included in the vision was the image of a man she had never met. Early in August she happened upon Parham during a Houston street-corner service and recognized him as the man in her vision. Accompanied by her husband, Dulaney attended the revival service at Bryan Hall a couple of nights later and received prayer for healing.[30] A local newspaper described the scene.

Two of the women placed their hands upon her and others prayed and sang. In a short time Mrs. Dulaney arose from her chair and walked about the hall in a state of ecstatic joy shouting, clapping her hands, and praising the Lord for restoration. The incident created much excitement. Mrs. Dulaney walked down the stairs from the hall and went home. She has attended their meetings daily since, but not in the chair, and is still rejoicing and praising God for her recovery.[31]

The Houston campaign also enjoyed the publicity provided by Parham's energetic band of workers. Early in 1905 Parham had purchased a set of fifteen Palestinian robes depicting the lifestyle of the social classes of Bible times. An old friend, Thomas J. Alley, sold him the authentic costumes after retiring from a career as an independent Bible lecturer.[32] Realizing their public appeal, Parham often wore one of the robes in the pulpit. During the daylight street meetings in Houston, he organized impromptu fashion shows by parading his workers in the Palestinian splendor. He also borrowed from Frank Sandford the stratagem of using large, colorful flags and banners. Bearing inscriptions of "unity" and "victory," the Pentecostal robe-clad army marched down the street proclaiming a revolution of apostolic Christianity. The purpose of such displays was twofold: to publicize the nightly meetings and to evangelize Houston's lost. After service, the faithful would hit the streets again, visiting the "red light district" and witnessing individually to the scores of "fallen" men and women they encountered there.[33]

Another attention-getter was glossolalia. One reporter, intrigued by the phenomenon, transcribed what he heard as "Leever a honsie, monsella ma hosta." Amazed by the missionary claims of the band, he noted further that when under the direction of the Spirit, at least, the faithful "may command the classics of a Homer or talk the jargon of the lowest savage of the African jungle."[34] Reporters also repeated Parham's claims of validation by "Government interpreters" and "professors of languages," though none of the authorities were ever named. One of the participants in the revival later claimed to know several college language professors who attended the meetings out of curiosity. She reported their reaction with obvious delight:

One of them spoke five languages. He said that to him the most marvelous thing about the use of these languages was the original accent they (the workers) gave. They demonstrated that under instruction, it was impossible for an American to learn. They gave the *real foreign accent so perfectly,* that when he closed his eyes, it seemed to him as though he were listening to utterances from his native masters in the Old World.[35]

Despite this positive assessment, Charles Shumway's search a decade later failed to produce any conclusive evidence of xenoglossa. In his 1919 Ph.D. dissertation Shumway censured the local *Houston Chronicle* for credulous reporting and stated that "letters are on hand from several men who were government interpreters in or near Houston at the time, and they are unanimous is [sic] denying all knowledge of the alleged facts."[36]

Yet the claims are too widespread to be categorically cast aside. An unnamed Latin scholar told reporters that he heard a participant speaking lines from Virgil. W. F. Carothers adopted the new Pentecostal message after he recognized German words spoken in the services.[37] Even more credible was the experience of a German sailor whose merchant vessel had docked overnight in Galveston. Coming ashore, he happened by a hall where some of Parham's students were conducting a meeting. After hearing the unlearned provincials utter words in his native language, the young man converted to the new faith. When he sailed for Germany the following night, he took with him a copy of Parham's *Kol Kare Bomidbar*.[38]

As with the Topeka outbreak, cryptomnesia provides the most plausible explanation for the large number of reported instances of xenoglossa. Latin would have been readily accessible to anyone attending high school or college. Parham himself studied the language at Southwest Kansas back in the early 1890s.[39] German was even more accessible. Large numbers of German immigrants carved out a new life in the bustling towns and communities of East Texas. Likewise, Parham promoted quite an extensive ministry within the Texas German community; his immigrant friend Franz Muenzner published a parallel *Apostolic Faith* with sermons printed in the German vernacular.[40] Language forms unknowingly retained within the mind and then uttered during moments of religious stress would easily have given the impression of actual xenoglossa. Given the lack of substantial documentation by authorities, it is safe to assume that this "simulated xenoglossa" was generally uttered in only words and phrases. Still the phenomenon was enough to create excitement among the faithful and a certain amount of awe among the spectators.

Late in August 1905 Parham closed the Houston campaign and returned to Kansas for several meetings. He took only a handful of workers with him; most remained behind to continue the work in Texas. Evangelistic teams fanned out from Houston holding street meetings and revival campaigns in Richmond, Katy, Alvin, Angelton, Needleville, and a host of other small Texas towns. Encouraged by the success in Houston, Parham regrouped his following along the Kansas-Missouri border for a new thrust of Pentecostal evangelism.[41]

In June 1905 he had moved his family from Baxter Springs to nearby Melrose, Kansas, where he launched a new edition of the *Apostolic Faith*. Bolstered by individual chapters from *Kol Kare Bomidbar* and occasional repeat testimonies from the Topeka editions, the new paper now gave Parham a means of advertising his success and coordinating his movement. The July and August issues included details for the first annual Baxter Springs Camp Meeting to be held for a week beginning August 28. The camp meeting was an effort to draw from the disparate support groups Parham had created throughout the tri-state region. Informal as it was, it marked the first regional gathering of Pentecostals in history.[42]

The camp meeting was also designed to recruit new converts. When Parham advertised that "thousands upon thousands will attend," he was not exaggerating. He planned the meeting to concur with the annual "Old Soldier's Reunion" held on the site of the Union fort, Camp Logan, on the banks of Spring river in Baxter Springs. Reunion sponsors invited Civil War veterans and their families from throughout the Midwest; included on the 1905 agenda were two lectures on the battle of Gettysburg delivered by the widow of Confederate General George Edward Pickett.

The gathering attracted five to fifteen thousand people each year and Parham recognized it as a golden opportunity to peddle his religious wares.[43] With the approval of reunion organizers he pitched his tent adjacent to the campgrounds and held preaching and song services from six in the morning until midnight. Parham competed with a host of entertainment activities, yet he held his own. On one occasion the religious service held a crowd of four hundred in captive attention despite the fun and frolic of an "Indian barbecue" a mere one hundred yards away.[44]

Parham's ability to draw crowds included more than curiosity about tongues and divine healings. By 1905 he had established himself as an entertaining speaker. Howard Goss remembered Parham's prowess during this period with obvious awe:

I remember well Brother Parham's preaching. Himself a personable, gifted, accomplished, original and forceful thinker and a vivid, magnetic personality with superb, versatile platform ability, he always held his audience in the curve of his hand.

People sat spellbound, one moment weeping, the next rocking with laughter, as the words flowed from his lips like water gushing from a fountain. But through it all he was sending home with clean, incisive, powerful strokes, the unadulterated Word of God.[45]

Parham bombarded his audience with an array of interesting biblical and social topics. One of his most popular sermons featured an optimistic appraisal of Zionism. In February 1896 Theodor Herzl published *The Jewish State*. With the publication of this memorable treatise, the political arm of Zionism was born. Herzl and his supporters argued that an independent Jewish state was the only pragmatic answer for the recent growth of anti-Semitism in the Western world.[46] Many evangelical Protestants greeted the Zionist call with extreme enthusiasm. For premillennialists, the young movement seemed a direct fulfillment of eschatological prophecy. Though Herzl argued strictly from political grounds, the premillennialists pointed out that in the last days God would restore the Bible lands to his chosen people. As early as 1878 the topic had been advanced as a sure sign that the millennium was at hand.[47]

Parham began proclaiming this Zionist gospel in the late 1890s. He publicized Herzl's efforts to buy Palestine from the Sultan of Turkey for ten million dollars and optimistically predicted that the dream of a Jewish homeland would soon be a reality. He also portrayed the horrors of anti-Semitism in Russia and defended the Jewish people from the popular stereotypes often prejudicially placed upon them.[48]

A parallel to the Zionist theme was featured in Parham's explanation of the Anglo-Israel theory. The United States owed the Jews a helping hand in restoring a national Israel because, with a predominance of English blood, American citizens were themselves descendants of the chosen tribes. Parham explained that remnants of the ten lost tribes migrated out of Palestine after their fall to Assyria in 722 B.C. Three separate companies of "Israelites" found their way respectively to India, Japan, and Western Europe where they ultimately influenced the development of sophisticated cultures. In Western Europe they became the Angles and Saxons—and subsequently the Anglo-Saxons. Parham drew as support for the Anglo-Israel position a wide assortment of racial theory. He assured his crowds that these ethnic questions were all a part of proper biblical analysis. Indeed, the world still fit a clear dichotomy of chosen people versus the ungodly.

The Old Testament distinction of the peoples of the earth remain almost the same today. The Hebrews, Jews and the various descendants of the ten tribes—the Anglo-Saxons, High Germans, Danes (Dan), Swedes, Hindoos, Japanese and the Hindoo-Japanese of Hawaii, and these possess about all the spiritual power of the world. The Gentiles—French, Spanish, Italian, Greek, Russian and Turkish. These are formalistic, and so are their descendants in all parts of the world. Heathen are mostly heathen still—the Negro, Malay, Mongolian and Indian.[49]

Particularly novel in Parham's lecture on Zionism was his explanation of archeological efforts underway to recover the ancient Ark of the Covenant. Parham explained that the Ark alone held the power to create a massive migration of Jews back to their homeland. The original Ten Commandments of Moses stored there would serve as a signal to the Jewish race that God's nation should be restored in all its splendor. Parham announced that he had discovered a secret tip about the Ark's whereabouts in an old Jewish document. He told his audiences that he hoped to visit Palestine in the near future and, with this fortuitous discovery, aid the completion of the Jewish homeland scheme. With these startling predictions and the striking beauty of the Palestinian robes, Parham made quite an impressive presentation to turn-of-the-century American audiences.[50]

Another favorite topic which drew crowds was "Where Cain Got His Wife." The *Houston Daily Post* even published the sermon in its Sunday morning edition. Parham began by explaining to his listeners that "long ago the theory that the seven days of creation were of twenty-four hours' duration began to lose its force upon the minds of the people, and today is found only in narrow intellects with a moss-covered growth."[51]

Parham rejected that "narrow" approach and adopted the fashionable practice of recognizing the evolutionary development of creation through the hand of God. The secret was found in 2 Peter 3:8 which clearly stated that "one day is with the Lord as a thousand years, and a thousand years as one day." Yet Adam and Eve were not a part of this gradual creation. Recognizing the two separate creation accounts in the first two chapters of Genesis, Parham explained that Adam was formed, rather than created, in a separate "eighth day" period and placed in the Garden of Eden apart from the rest of the world. Adam and Eve were inherently different from those human creatures that lived outside the garden. They received human souls; the first creatures were mere flesh and blood. In addition, a different class of animals was created to accompany the new race of human beings. Thus Parham garnered biblical support for the scientific discoveries of dinosaurs and cave men; they had been a part of the original creation.[52]

With an amazing mix of theology and pseudoscience, Parham spellbound his audience. He explained how Adam and Eve were cast out of Eden after their sin and made to live among the inferior race. Eden, located somewhere in the Caribbean, was taken from their view and became, Parham speculated, the legendary "lost continent of Atlantis." After rebelling and killing his brother Abel, their oldest son Cain left home and sought refuge among the first race. There the young man took a wife. Parham then described the awful wrath of God kindled against Cain and the inferior first creation for their despicable act of intermarriage. Since the first race faced no fear of natural death—that trait came only to the Adamic race as a direct result of sin in the garden—God sent the Flood which destroyed both the "unsouled people" and all who had mingled with them. In conclusion, Parham interjected a dose of racial ideology that many of his hearers no doubt instinctively applauded:

Thus began the woeful intermarriage of races for which cause the flood was sent in punishment, and has ever been followed by plagues and incurable diseases upon the third and fourth generation, the offspring of such marriages. Were time to last and intermarriage continue between the whites, the blacks and the reds of America, consumption and other diseases would soon wipe the mixed bloods off the face of the earth.[53]

The scenario provided Parham with an entertaining and provocative lecture. It also allowed him the luxury of agreeing with scientific discovery while holding to what seemed, to him at least, a staunchly literalist interpretation of scripture.[54]

Following the Baxter Springs Camp Meeting late in the summer of 1905, Parham held a revival campaign in nearby Columbus. Despite local hecklers he drew crowds as large as three thousand. During the course of the campaign, he received a telegram from Texas emphasizing the need for more evangelists to keep the missionary efforts there underway. Parham promptly dispatched Lilian Thistlethwaite and another disciple to Texas and began collecting funds for a renewed assault on the Lone Star State. On October 16 he boarded his entire family and twenty coworkers on a train bound for Orchard.[55]

Once again Parham enjoyed success. During his absence he had sent handkerchiefs which he had prayed upon as a substitute for those requesting his special touch of faith. Now he resumed a personal ministry to the crowds interested in divine healing.[56] More important for the spread of his movement, however, were those who received Holy Spirit baptism, by now several hundred in the Houston area alone.[57] From these recipients came the workers—the missionaries expected to capture both nation and globe within their lifetime. Recognizing the need to indoctrinate these workers and prepare them for their quest, Parham decided to open a ten-week Bible school in Houston. In December he moved his *Apostolic Faith* printing operation to the city, rented a large house on the corner of Rusk and Brazos streets, and advertised the opening of the school.[58]

With the opening of the Bible school, the spirit of Topeka began to reappear. Parham hoped that the training session would create a wave effect which would rapidly spread the Apostolic Faith message across the country. Like Topeka, however, the immediate results in Houston would be much more modest than he anticipated. But unlike Topeka the new faith would gain valuable allies who would, in time, effectively spread the message. Within a year the Pentecostal revival would erupt full force and spread to all parts of the nation and world. But somehow it did not come about exactly as Charles Parham had envisioned. The next two years would mark his climb to fame and, in many ways, the fulfillment of his life's ambition; they would also mark the period of his deepest disappointment and, ironically, his decline within the movement he had worked so hard to found.

5

The Projector of Pentecost
The Promise
1906

Charles Parham opened 1906 optimistic about his prospects for the new year. The work in Texas continued to grow and, with additional workers trained by the Bible school, expansion into new states seemed inevitable. Befitting his place in the Pentecostal outbreak, Parham began in December 1905 using the title "Projector of the Apostolic Faith Movement."[1] Though he pointed out that the renewal effort was for all churches and believers, he left no doubt where the voice of human authority lay.

As in Topeka, students at the Houston school learned the valuable lesson of life by total faith. With expenses that totaled seventy-five to one hundred dollars per week, the school operated on a shoestring budget dependent on periodic gifts from Pentecostal supporters. When donations arrived at strategic times of great need the students understood that God had answered prayer and their commitment to live by faith had been rewarded.[2] In response to such providential care the students concentrated on a rigorous program designed to transform them into obedient servants. Howard Goss attended the school and recalled the busy regimen laid down by Parham:

We were given a thorough workout and a rigid training in prayer, fastings, consecration, Bible study and evangelistic work. Our week day schedule consisted of Bible Study in the morning, shop and jail meetings at noon, house to house visitations in the afternoon, and a six o'clock street meeting followed by an evening evangelistic service at 7:30 or 8:00 o'clock.[3]

The most important decision at the Houston school, considering the later history of Pentecostalism, was Parham's decision to allow William Joseph Seymour, a black holiness evangelist, to attend the daily Bible classes. Seymour met Parham through Mrs. Lucy F. Farrow. Farrow, pastor of a local black holiness church, had been interested in Parham's doctrine of Holy Spirit baptism since the recent summer campaign. When Parham returned to Kansas in late August, she accompanied him and spent the next two months serving as the family governess. A benefit of her short-term employment was attending Parham's services and thoroughly indoctrinating herself in Pentecostal theology. While in Kansas she received Holy Spirit baptism evidenced by speaking in tongues.[4]

Before leaving Houston, Farrow had convinced her friend Seymour to pastor her church while she was away. When she returned in late October she intrigued him with her testimony of Pentecostal fulfillment. Seymour learned of Parham's plans to open a Bible school and inquired about admission. Parham, sensitive to the local Jim Crow statutes and yet sympathetic to the spread of Pentecostal doctrine among blacks, admitted Seymour to the Bible school but provided separate seating. Seymour attended daily and sat in an adjoining room where, through an open door, he absorbed Apostolic Faith theology. He enthusiastically accepted the new teaching of spirit baptism but failed to personally receive the experience at that time.[5]

Parham's ministry among black people was considerable. His well-known racial ideology did not prevent him from including everyone in God's endtime evangelistic drive. Essentially Parham used racial theories to explain the historic development of civilization but did not exclude any racial group from God's grace. In fact he felt a special obligation to those races he considered inferior. His concern was paternalistic but, in the context of the day, he could hardly be considered a "racist."

Despite enthusiastic emigration from the South following the Civil War, the percentage of blacks in Parham's native state was quite small. Overall, blacks enjoyed better living conditions in Kansas than in southern states, but economic problems and a limit to racial tolerance had proven that the state was no "Promised Land" of equality.[6] Although his encounters with blacks were limited, Parham had not neglected to offer his ministry to them. There were no black people at Bethel College but at least three had been filled with the Holy Spirit in February 1901 during the Lawrence campaign.[7]

In Houston, Parham first encountered large numbers of blacks. Though he obeyed the specifics of Jim Crow laws, he refused to abandon his efforts to evangelize the black community. Parham not only made provisions for Seymour to attend the school but also preached alongside the evangelist to the black people of the Houston area.[8] Consequently Seymour was not the only black minister to join Parham's movement. R. A. Hall was listed along with Seymour early in 1906 as an "able and faithful minister to the colored people".[9] Shortly thereafter, two other black affiliates, W. M. Viney and M. H. Robinson, were recognized in the *Apostolic Faith*. Reverend Viney even received the special title of "Director of the . . . Houston District among his people."[10]

Parham's openness on the racial issue was not shared by the Texas wing of the movement. In March 1906 W. F. Carothers outlined his own racial ideology. His ardent segregation policy extended far beyond Parham's explanation of superior and inferior races. Where Parham had simply abhorred racial intermarriage, Carothers severely restricted any form of social contact. Explaining that sinful greed had resulted in slavery and the "unnatural condition" of white and black races living alongside each other in the American South, he happened upon the novel interpretation that racial animosity was a corrective gift from God to ensure separation.

Now, to meet this unnatural, unheard of condition, God has resorted to the next best expedient, and through His Spirit has intensified the racial impulses between the white and black man as the only remaining possible barrier to the miscegenation of their respective races. This intensified racial impulse is mistaken by many outsiders for prejudice, or a work of the devil, when in truth it is the work of God's Holy Spirit, and as such is binding upon all Christians.[11]

Carothers' harsh views provide two important insights into Parham's efforts among the black race in Houston. First, Parham was on the level when he justified his own accommodation to Jim Crow; he bowed to local custom in providing the unique circumstances of Seymour's Pentecostal training classes. There is no evidence that any such adjustments had been included in his contacts with blacks prior to 1905. Second, Carothers' comments hint that despite those accommodations, Parham's Kansas evangelists—and thus presumably Parham—remained much too free in their racial contacts to suit the sensibilities of their fellow Texans. The Brunner pastor barely stopped short of publicly censuring them for flaunting Southern customs.

I trust, therefore, that our evangelists and workers from the North will not forget this condition of affairs and embarrass the work South by well means [sic] but mistaken efforts to disregard them. Take the word of a native Southerner, who through the sanctifying grace of Jesus Christ is incapable of prejudice, loving the colored man's soul equally as much as the white man's, and let the race question alone until you have been South long enough to know by experience what it seems impossible for our Northern brethren to learn through other sources.[12]

Carothers' ideal was a Pentecostal revival which spread from white to white and black to black. Inherent in the plan was the assumption that white leaders would train black leaders, a la Seymour, and that blacks would follow proper social etiquette when interacting with their white counterparts. It was a plan adopted almost uniformly by white Pentecostals even in the wake of a brief period of racial cooperation at Azusa Street. Douglas J. Nelson's conjecture that racial equality provided a cornerstone for Pentecostal origins overlooks the paternalistic attitude of Southern Pentecostals who felt it more than enough to be rid of racial hatred. To love the black man's soul did not, in the context of that day at least, mean that the broad dimensions of Jim Crow were any less sacred.[13]

Parham's position on the race question occupied moderate ground somewhere between Carothers' overt social segregation and the open racial policy of John Alexander Dowie in Zion City, Illinois. Dowie never accepted Parham's Pentecostal theology but, as the preeminent faith healer of the late nineteenth century, he helped forge one of the cardinal doctrines of the young movement. The Zion City reformer, however, had little impact in transferring his racial program to the budding Pentecostal pioneers. Dowie advocated genuine racial equality; his treatment of blacks and non-English immigrants illustrated a level of human concern far less paternalistic than most nineteenth-century reformers. Dowie insisted on an integrated seating arrangement for his religious services and filled his Zion City publications with indictments against American racial prejudice. He occasionally speculated that the only long-term solution to white-black relations was miscegenation, thereby ending the racial distinctions which he felt certain God did not recognize.[14]

It would be erroneous to suggest that Parham ever attained sufficient enlightenment to place him anywhere near Dowie's policy of racial equality. Nonetheless, it is equally erroneous to suggest, as Nelson has, that in 1905–06 Parham operated from the hard racial guidelines of W. F. Carothers. Parham's sensitivity to black people's needs would decrease with age and in response to his bitter break with Seymour and Azusa Street. Yet the Charles Parham who made provisions for Seymour in December 1905 was far from a ranting, card-carrying racist. Convinced that his race was superior, he was equally sure that his spiritual revelation superseded the constrictions of society. His outreach to blacks in Houston came from a firm conviction that the Pentecostal message was for all races and was bridged in spite of local opposition. Jim Crow legislation and public opinion forced Parham and his Kansas associates to proceed cautiously but they forged on nonetheless.

In the final analysis Parham was neither a racial reformer nor a champion of white supremacy. Rather, he occupied a paternalistic middle ground typical of many if not most white ministers from the Midwest. His goal was the radical salvation of Christianity in the twentieth century through the renewal of Pentecostal power. Missionaries would be endowed with the gift of language to ensure the glorious endtime revival. Such a revolutionary goal, of necessity, included all races.[15]

Toward the end of January, Seymour received an unexpected offer from Los Angeles to pastor a small holiness mission there. Despite Parham's concern that he was needed in the Texas work, Seymour felt confident that the call carried with it the direction of the Holy Spirit. Parham finally gave the determined disciple his blessing and even contributed toward his travel expenses to Los Angeles.[16] Seymour left Houston in early February after completing about five weeks of training in Parham's school. Though he had yet to receive the experience, he clearly accepted his teacher's central thesis that a third religious work evidenced by tongue-speaking would revolutionize the world through spiritual power and missionary zeal. The ministry Seymour forged in Los Angeles would ultimately change the course of Parham's movement; one year later the "city of angels" had become the largest center of Pentecostal expansion.[17]

Parham concluded the Houston school by mid-March and then began preparing for a first-anniversary celebration of the Texas campaign. In mid-April the religious gathering was held at the birthplace site in Orchard, where Parham triumphantly reported that "hundreds of people" had been converted to the new movement during the past year in Texas alone. He concluded the two-day meeting by publicly announcing an assignment schedule for the new Pentecostal apostles. Over fifty workers were dispatched throughout Texas. They joined the handful of pioneers still operating from the Kansas-Missouri base and Seymour, the lone figure in the far West.[18]

In late April the Parham family returned to Kansas and settled in a house at Keelville. The town was strategically located between the Pentecostal mining centers at Baxter Springs and Melrose. In addition to shoring up the work there, Parham returned to nearby Galena in May for a revival calculated to regain the following he had lost in the wake of the Nettie Smith tragedy. He continued to schedule local meetings and remained close to home during the final stages of his wife's sixth pregnancy. On June first, the last of Parham's children, Robert, was born.[19]

By August, Parham was back on the road again. He held a camp meeting in Houston to reestablish contact and assess the summer work of his young evangelists. Anna Hall, the pioneer of Pentecost at Orchard, requested that she be allowed to travel to California to aid Seymour. Parham consented and helped raise the fare for her travel expenses. Several weeks later, four additional workers were dispatched to California.[20]

Hall's sudden interest in going west was prompted by Seymour's success in Los Angeles. The black minister's original connection with the holiness mission there had ended shortly after his arrival when church leaders rejected his Apostolic Faith doctrine that glossolalia signified the initial reception of Holy Spirit baptism. Nevertheless, Seymour's devotion and earnest religious manner earned him a handful of converts. He began holding a Bible study in the home of friends at 214 North Bonnie Brae Street. Optimistic that he could eventually spread an Apostolic Faith work in Los Angeles, Seymour convinced two Houston friends affiliated with Parham's black ministry in the city to join him in California. Lucy Farrow and J. A. Warren arrived in March to join the small group praying for a Pentecostal descent.[21]

Seymour's prayer group was predominantly black though interested whites from allied holiness missions occasionally attended the highly emotional services. On April ninth, the little band finally received their expected spiritual sign. One of the black members, Edward S. Lee, experienced glossolalic tongues. Rapidly, the experience spread. By April twelfth, a number of the faithful, including Seymour, had "prayed their way through to Pentecost." Emotional displays, especially the glossolalia, attracted a great deal of local attention from both black and white holiness camps. Crowds swelled at the services at 214 North Bonnie Brae, and within a matter of days larger quarters were required.

On April fourteenth, Seymour began holding services in a rented old building at 312 Azusa Street. Spurred on by a report in the *Los Angeles Daily Times* which confounded readers with the headline "Weird Babel of Tongues," the Azusa mission slowly drew even larger crowds of the curious and the spiritually expectant. By Hall's arrival in August, interracial crowds of up to twelve hundred overflowed the mission doors during the evening services and smaller congregations met for both morning and afternoon worship. More importantly, the Azusa mission had attracted the attention of holiness leaders nationwide, many of whom attended and personally carried the new experience home to their churches. It became the overflowing well that Parham had expected since the Topeka revival of 1901, spreading the message of Pentecost to small holiness missions throughout the United States and, through the work of foreign missionaries, throughout the world.[22]

Unfortunately for Parham he failed in August 1906 to comprehend the dimensions of the Los Angeles revival. Seymour had written faithfully during the summer with glowing reports of the revival's progress and clearly anticipated that his own work would reach unparalleled heights when the leader of the Apostolic Faith arrived in Los Angeles for a mass citywide campaign.[23] Parham obviously cared about the outbreak since he dispatched five additional workers, though circumstances detained his own visit to the Azusa mission. With the work growing at an unprecedented pace, the Projector found himself in greater demand than ever and opportunities elsewhere seemed more immediate.

The size of the Azusa work did not begin to rival that of the midwestern Pentecostal centers until early in the fall of 1906. Although significant crowds sometimes attended the revival during the months of June and July, reception of the new glossolalic experience had been less than spectacular. The September issue of a new *Apostolic Faith*,[24] a religious paper emanating from Azusa Street, noted that "about 150 people in Los Angeles . . . have received the gift of the Holy Ghost and the Bible evidence."[25] Undoubtedly a larger number had been affected by the revival impact; still the number of committed followers remained small through the summer months. Following the initial press coverage in April detailing the novelty of glossolalia, Los Angeles dailies felt no obligation to report on the activities of Azusa Street. The inference is obvious; the phenomenon failed to attract enough attention to warrant continued coverage. Increased crowds in the late summer months reestablished Azusa as an item worthy of local news and, in September, the Pentecostals once again received visits from the news reporters.[26]

Azusa's growth was stimulated in large part through the publishing efforts of Frank Bartleman, a local white holiness evangelist who had been active in the Azusa circle since the prayer group days at 214 North Bonnie Brae. After the San Francisco earthquake in late April 1906, Bartleman distributed thousands of leaflets noting the significance of the nearby catastrophe and the "last days" outpouring at Azusa Street. To a population who had felt the tremors of the mammoth earthquake to the north, the message of an imminent end to human history seemed relevant indeed. The two events fitted nicely into the framework of the dozens of holiness missions intent on seeking God's special revelation to the endtime generation.

Bartleman followed his tract distribution with a series of glowing reports to the nation's leading holiness periodicals explaining the great outpouring of Holy Spirit power at Azusa.[27] By the end of the summer, the publicity began to pay dividends as curious ministers and holiness workers traveled west to investigate the strange work of God at the Azusa Street mission. By late August the work had spread to two other nearby missions—one led by Bartleman at the corner of Eighth and Maple and another under the direction of Elmer Fisher at 327 1/2 South Spring Street.[28]

The effect Azusa would have throughout the holiness movement could not be ascertained by Parham during the summer of 1906. Azusa seemed just one of several flourishing Pentecostal revivals—all of which he anticipated would contribute to the endtime evangelization campaign. Evidence appears contradictory; a reasonable assessment of the primary data on hand seems to indicate that by the summer of 1906 Parham had a movement of roughly eight to ten thousand persons. Of that total, Azusa Street encompassed no more than eight hundred to one thousand, or one-tenth of the movement, by August 1906.[29]

With the overwhelming bulk of his movement in the Midwest, it is little wonder that Parham preferred to remain there during the summer months in an effort to build support and consolidate his following. The overall picture looked bright indeed in the summer of 1906. Since the initial poor reception following the Topeka outbreak in January 1901, Parham had rebounded with a steady string of successful revival ventures. Particularly since the Galena revival in the waning months of 1903, his meetings had attracted a healthy amount of newspaper print and a steady stream of new evangelists to spread the Pentecostal message.

Parham had shown his concern over the increased numbers by providing, in early 1906, a form for converting the movement into a more structured organization. The move toward organization went against Parham's original goals and his expressed vows to remain interdenominational. As recently as December 1905, the *Apostolic Faith* had included a repeat of the chapter on "Unity" from *Kol Kare Bomidbar.* The selection left little doubt of Parham's aversion to organized religion. Yet it also demonstrated his concern over a total lack of religious authority. He concluded that true unity could only be reached through the successive experiences by all Christians of sanctification and the Baptism of the Holy Spirit. It was an overly optimistic advertisement for the future of his own movement though, incredible as it seems, Parham failed to recognize that his own prominence violated the spirit of his rather naive argument.

Unity is not to be accomplished by organization or non-organization. Unity by organization has been tried for 1900 years and failed. Unity by non-organization has been tried for several years and resulted in anarchy, or gathered together in small "clicks" [*sic*] with an unwritten creed and regulations which are often fraught with error and fanaticism. . . . To be brought into Bible unity we must as certainly lay all our creeds, doctrines and teachings at Jesus' feet, asking Him to cleanse them though it take them all, as we did our life in consecration, when we sought His sanctifying power; and very many of the things you have held the dearest will pass from your life forever. When you in your home, wherever that may be, and I in mine, seek and find the cleansing blood, purifying from all error and false teaching; it will bring us into unity, whether we ever see each other in this world or not; but if we should meet we should find that the cleansing of the blood, and the Holy Ghost our Teacher, had caused us indeed to see "eye to eye."[30]

Parham's simplistic philosophy of religious unity was rivaled by his similarly unstructured program of church finance. Every Christian was expected to give a tithe—one tenth of his total income—to God. Yet there was never to be any organized collection or coercion. Once again, church work was a matter of the Holy Spirit in direct action with God's people. Parham's audiences no doubt took great delight in this freestyle philosophy since it placed the operation of church finances firmly in their hands and at their discretion. Parham made significant mileage on the issue by drawing an unfavorable analogy with the organized churches of the day.

We do not believe the Bible to teach, or that God ever intended Christians to be taxed for the support of salaried preachers or the building up of any religious society, with some scheming charlatan at the head of it, but that the workman is worthy of his hire, and without having a stipulated salary every true minister called of God would receive exactly what he is worth. This would cut out the modern useless professional ministry. The Indian who got a dollar for six months preaching answered when some one remarked to him that it was very poor pay, "True, but it was heap poorer preaching."[31]

The end result was a kind of loose, freewheeling evangelism program which was ultimately tied to the charismatic
personality of Parham himself. Parham claimed the "biblical"
pattern worked wondrously, noting on one occasion in 1913
that the annual salary he received as a Methodist pastor in the
1890s had risen tenfold as a free-lance evangelist.[32] Yet the
faith system sometimes worked rather slowly. Parham's *Apostolic Faith* continued to operate without a subscription price
but occasional lapses in revenue meant a corresponding lapse
in regular editions. The March 1906 issue explained that
other expenses had prohibited the two previous monthly editions and gently reminded its readers of their vital role in
regular contributions.[33]

Of course Parham's movement was not nearly as unstructured as he thought. The vital element that brought unity of
action and financial support was Parham himself. He made
regular visits to the centers of his Apostolic Faith work and
thereby lent a sense of continuity to the disparate missions of
the midwest. By early 1906 the movement had grown so fast
that he felt some local semblance of authority was necessary.
Of primary concern was the training of Pentecostal evangelists and the retention of those followers who attended
churches hostile to his innovative endtime theology. Still he
kept the organization to a minimum and closely followed the
relatively unstructured model used by the writers of the New
Testament.

Parham retained his vision of worldwide conquest by organizing his followers into support groups for "Assembly meetings." Modeled after lay class meetings formerly used by the
Methodist church, Parham envisioned groups of twenty to
thirty Apostolic Faith workers meeting weekly at a regularly
scheduled time for prayer and discussion. The meetings were
not to be held on Sunday since that was a time for public
preaching. The ideal location, Parham suggested, was in individual homes. Preaching was not to be a regular part of
these services since their main objective was to encourage
each other and share individual burdens and problems. Like-

wise, "unsaved" visitors were to be kept to a minimum in light of the nonevangelical nature of the meetings. Each assembly was to have a leader, usually an appointed "elder," whose function was essentially pastoral. The assembly meetings provided an element of organization yet retained the openness required in a movement optimistically expecting to convert all of Christendom to a worldwide evangelistic effort within a generation.[34]

The March 1906 *Apostolic Faith* initially broadcast Parham's new organizational scheme. In addition to the rules and regulations of the support group assemblies, Parham announced the ordination of elders in each of the major towns claimed by the movement and the appointment of three state directors. W. F. Carothers was named director of the work in Texas with headquarters in Houston. Rilda Cole received charge of the Kansas work headquartered at Baxter Springs. Henry G. Tuthill accepted the appointment in Missouri and operated from headquarters in Carthage. Other state directors would be appointed as necessary. In addition Parham appointed his sister-in-law, Lilian Thistlethwaite, as General Secretary of the Apostolic Faith Movement. He personally retained the title Projector of the Apostolic Faith and assumed overseership of the general organization. Beginning in May 1906, all evangelists and full-time workers received official credentials signed by Projector Parham and their respective state directors.[35]

Parham's attempt to organize in the spring of 1906 ensured that he would spend the next six months in the midwest ironing out the problems of his growing work. The plan was not initially popular with all Apostolic Faith followers, some of whom considered it a retraction of the movement's avowed stance against organized Christianity. Much of the May 1906 *Apostolic Faith* was dedicated to emphasizing the advantages of the assembly system and the movement's continued determination to remain interdenominational in its outreach.[36]

As a result of the energetic efforts in the Midwest, Seymour and the budding Apostolic Faith group in Los Angeles received only marginal treatment from their movement's Projector during the formative period from April to September 1906. Seymour wrote State Director Carothers and received his credentials in July. Requesting a hundred "buttons" for street workers to wear in personal witnessing, he joyously reported that "people are getting saved [th]ree times a day, justified, sanctified, Baptized with the Holy Ghost and [th]e gift of tongues as a witness. Praise the Lord, Amen." Seymour also noted that a handful of workers had independently launched out to the foreign mission field.[37] Parham probably underestimated the reports from Seymour; at any rate, he clearly recognized the need to launch a smooth program in the Midwest before attempting to harness the newer wing in the far West.[38]

In August Seymour formed a "Board of Twelve" to serve as directors of the growing Azusa mission. Yet officially he remained an Apostolic Faith minister in the Texas state division under W. F. Carothers' jurisdiction. Though Seymour was thoroughly acquainted with Parham's new system and adopted the term "assembly" as a designation for the local church unit, he did not have the authority to appoint new elders. The incorporation of the Apostolic Faith system required a personal visit from Parham himself.[39]

By early September, Parham certainly could have justified a trip west to capitalize on Seymour's groundwork. On August 27 the black evangelist had written Parham to acknowledge the arrival of Anna Hall and to urge him to come to Los Angeles to consolidate the movement.

Dear Bro. Parham:—
Sister Hall has arrived, and is planning out a great revival in this city, that shall take place when you come. The revival is still going on here that has been going on since we came to this city. But we are expecting a general one to start again when you come, that these little revivals will all come together and make one great union revival.[40]

Parham returned correspondence telling Seymour that he planned to reach Los Angeles around September 15. The

Azusa-based *Apostolic Faith* promptly printed a segment of Parham's letter in its inaugural issue.

> Bro. Chas. Parham, who is God's leader in the Apostolic Faith Movement writes from Tonganoxie, Kansas, that he expects (D.V.) to be in Los Angeles Sept. 15. Hearing that Pentecost had come to Los Angeles, he writes, "I rejoice in God over you all, my children, though I have never seen you; but since you know the Holy Spirit's power, we are baptised by one Spirit into one body. Keep together in unity till I come, then in a grand meeting let all prepare for the outside fields I desire, unless God directs to the contrary, to meet and see all who have the full Gospel when I come.[41]

Yet the proposed September revival never unfolded. Parham suddenly shifted his plans in the midst of the Baxter Springs Camp Meeting in early September. During the services he reported a divine call to Zion City, Illinois.[42]

Zion City did not appear suddenly in Parham's mind in September 1906. He had carefully followed the career of Zion's prophet and founder, John Alexander Dowie, for over a decade now. Kansas newspapers, of which Parham was an avid reader, had recently run detailed accounts of Dowie's sudden loss of authority in Zion.[43] Since his height of power in 1903, Dowie had been accused of a series of irregularities, including polygamy and misappropriation of funds. The aging prophet, still suffering the effects of a stroke one year earlier, now faced a stiff battle for leadership with former disciple Wilbur Glenn Voliva. In late July a federal judge ruled that Zion's industries, previously owned and controlled by Dowie himself, fall under control of a receivership. Dowie's utopia was effectively ended. John Craig Hadley, a prominent member of the Chicago Board of Trade, was named as receiver and elections were scheduled for September eighteenth to determine the local overseer favored by a majority of Zion's population. Dowie suffered a humiliating defeat and, in declining health, faded from importance in Zion affairs.[44]

The vacuum created by Dowie's sudden fall offered Parham an unprecedented opportunity to advance the Apostolic Faith. Voliva's leadership was not yet secured and the history of religious devotion in Zion suggested to Parham that the site might serve as a launching pad for worldwide distribution of his new doctrine. Thanks to Dowie, Zion had enjoyed continued press coverage since its founding in 1901. With contacts around the world that numbered over twenty-five thousand, success in Zion could mean an almost instant start of the global Pentecostal revival. The prospect of personal success seemed promising as well; Parham's background as a faith healer made him a logical contender for Dowie's throne.

Sometime around 1904 Parham's Pentecostal theology had made a brief and unimpressive entrance into Zion's confines. A Mrs. Waldron, a recipient of spirit baptism at Parham's Lawrence campaign in 1901, moved with her family to Zion City. She began a short-lived prayer meeting during which at least one other person, Mrs. Hall, received the experience. When officials of Dowie's Christian Catholic Apostolic Church heard about the meetings, they quickly ruled them illegal religious gatherings and suspended the prayer band. Using economic pressure, Zion authorities succeeded in forcing both the Waldrons and the Halls to move away from Zion.[45]

Parham now recognized a chance to turn the tables on that inauspicious beginning. With the city in religious and political turmoil, he seized the opportunity to offer the seventy-five hundred residents a role in the Apostolic Faith's endtime mission. Timing was crucial; a delay of several months could mean that the opportunity to transform Zion into a Pentecostal powerhouse would be lost. Appropriately, Parham postponed his trip to Los Angeles and hurried north to challenge Voliva for the religious minds of Zion's faithful.[46]

Parham had expressed a specific desire to expand his movement north as early as April 1906 when he planned an assault on Iowa, Illinois, Minnesota, and Canada and sought to raise five thousand dollars for the campaign.[47] Probably due to insufficient funds, the northern campaign had not materialized during that summer. Now Parham envisioned a new effort begun by capturing the religious forces already in place in Zion. He and his small band of workers arrived in Zion on the heels of the well-publicized elections of September eighteenth. Refusing to accept the federal court decision, Dowie had urged his flagging supporters to boycott the election. As a result, Voliva had won a deceptively impressive decision. He was by far the most popular choice as Dowie's successor; yet his support was far from unanimous as the invader from Kansas would soon prove.[48]

Parham secured quarters at the Elijah Hospice and promptly began holding three services a day for anyone his workers could convince to attend. By September twenty-first he had attracted the attention of Overseer Voliva and of the local press as well. Though they initially spelled his name wrong, the reporters from nearby Waukegan were impressed with Parham's success and, more importantly, with his challenge to Voliva's spiritual leadership. They reported that when Voliva heard of Parham's meetings he arranged a personal meeting to try and convince the new prophet not to make trouble. Parham simply refused to show. Voliva, not to be outdone, called Parham on the telephone and demanded to know how long he planned to hold services in Zion. Parham's response was short and to the point: "Till Kingdom Come."[49]

By September twenty-sixth Parham had emerged as the darling of the Waukegan reporters. They almost immediately placed him as Voliva's chief opponent in a long list of Zion competitors that ranged from the Mormons to Miss Lucy Jane Crosby's "Free Love" cult.[50] They noted that Parham had attracted several hundred followers, including prominent elders of Voliva's own church, within a single week and had forced the Zion overseer to take specific actions to try to prevent any further defections. Sensing the drama that was building in another prophet's fall from power, they printed Parham's ambitious goals and his divine call to Zion's corporate limits. While Voliva denounced the newcomer in the auditorium at Zion's college, they noted that Parham scored points elsewhere.

Meanwhile Parham was holding an enthusiastic meeting at the residence of John Clarr not more than a block away from the college. The house was crowded and the congregation covered the lawn.

"I have come to save the people of Zion from the selfishness and bigotry of their leaders," said the evangelist boldly. "Four months ago I saw Zion City in a vision, and the troubles of its people were made clear to me. 'Arise and go to Zion and take up the burden of an oppressed people,' a voice said to me. I am here and will bring you out of all your difficulties if you will trust in me."

"We will!" shouted more than 300 people with the vim that formerly greeted the utterance of John Alexander Dowie.[51]

The Waukegan reporters had no tangible reason to favor Parham over Voliva. They simply wanted a good fight and recognized the feistiness of the underdog from Kansas. Religious turmoil in Zion made good news, and Parham stirred the waters. His initial success in Zion even propelled Parham's name into the nationally circulated *New York Times*.[52]

On September twenty-ninth the *Waukegan Daily Sun* featured an exclusive interview with the new evangelist as their lead story. Parham came off quite well, portraying himself as an apostle of unity and building credibility.

It is untrue that I have had "visions and dreams." Some time ago I was under a great strain of thought concerning Dowie and at the time came to the conclusion that he should renounce all his honors and step down in order to be healed of his disease and forgiven.

Later, when I had no idea of coming to Zion to preach, one night I prayed that God would direct me what next to do in my work as a preacher of the full gospel, and in the middle of the night it came to me that I should go to Zion City and unify the church.[53]

Parham argued that his trip to Zion in no way reflected a desire for money or personal fame and pledged to remain aloof from any business affairs in the city. He even claimed that his visit was necessary as self-defense for his own work, noting "I was obliged to come to Zion City, as through the fall of Dowie, people came to distrust divine healing, which is one of the tenets of the 'full gospel.'" The Waukegan reporter was favorably impressed and added his own description of Voliva's chief opponent.

Thus simply he explained his mission, accompanying his remarks with characteristic motions of the hand and arm. He is a slight, dark man of medium height, smooth shaven and with raven black hair that he wears rather long. His garments are clerical in cut. He is a ready and fluent talker who believes in himself and in what he preaches.[54]

By the end of September Parham had garnered well over three hundred followers in Zion City. Newspapers reported that "thousands" were attending his collection of home-style Bible meetings throughout the city. By all accounts Parham appeared headed toward a direct power struggle with Voliva for control of the city.[55]

Even more impressive than the numbers were the valuable converts made from among the leading citizens of the Zion community. George A. Rogers, manager of the Elijah Hospice and a deacon in Voliva's church, not only granted Parham use of his establishment's parlor for nightly services but soon joined in as an enthusiastic participant. More striking was the conversion of A. F. Lee who, after accepting the Apostolic Faith message, resigned his position as general ecclesiastical secretary of the Christian Catholic Apostolic Church. Another influential acquisition was W. H. Peckham, former manager of the Zion City bank.[56]

Voliva, disturbed by Parham's momentum, responded by publicly attacking the newcomer. Parham, Voliva maintained, was an intruder intent on destroying the city. Furthermore he was "full of the devil" and anyone who followed him was "a fool." There could be no middle ground. Acknowledging that "this man is winning some of our most faithful people from their allegiance at a crucial time," Voliva admonished Zion residents to "choose either me or this intruder who has stolen into our church. You can not serve two leaders." He then dismissed those who supported Parham as "a pack of contemptible hypocrites and a disgrace to Zion."[57] Merely attending a Parham meeting became grounds for dismissal from the church. Voliva also resorted to more tactical assaults. Using his leverage as church leader, he regularly rented and scheduled activities in all schoolhouses and public halls in the city. By tying up the large auditoriums, he hoped to prevent Parham from consolidating support.[58] Voliva determined to fight tooth and nail for his ascension to Dowie's throne.[59]

Despite Voliva's concern, events of the next few months would ensure that Parham would fail to unify Zion City for the Apostolic Faith. The first chink in his armor was, ironically, the outpouring of Pentecost in Zion. Incredible as it seems, Parham had neglected to explain his theory of xenoglossic missions in his interview on September twenty-ninth. In addition, none of the reporters attending his meetings had noticed anything out of the ordinary. Intent on building toward an emotional climax, Parham waited for the right moment to publicly preach the central theme of the Apostolic Faith movement. He preferred that the experience burst forth from the people themselves. Much like his role at Topeka five and a half years earlier, Parham deftly led his congregation toward an intense desire for spirit baptism.[60]

The silence broke on the night of October seventeenth when twenty-four Zionites erupted in the glossolalic manifestations of Pentecost. The *Waukegan Daily Sun* recorded the drama of the occasion.

Last night at a largely attended meeting Hubert Grant, formerly stenographer for Dowie and later stenographer for A. K. Stearns, Waukegan, was giving "testimony" before the people when he stopped, a pallor swept across his face and he commenced to talk in a strange language. After he had spoken some time it was declared that he was speaking Chinese. His friends say he has had no previous knowledge of the language.

Grant had barely taken his seat when another convert, James Lang, arose and talked in Chinese. . . . Of the twenty-four persons who are said to have been seized with the sudden ability to talk in other languages than their own, some have spoken German, French, Italian, Russian, Spanish and a few Norwegian.[61]

The publication of the glossolalic outbreak brought a noticeable decline in Parham's stature with the press. When details of Pentecostal theology reached reporters on October eighteenth, an immediate loss of credibility ensued. The honeymoon ended abruptly and no longer was the Projector of the Apostolic Faith presented as a serious contender for Zion leadership. Articles on the Apostolic Faith meetings now exclusively stressed the tongues phenomenon. The October nineteenth *Waukegan Daily Sun* featured a front page article in which the local reporter deadpanned on the possible ramifications of the new spiritual phenomenon.

CHANCE FOR HIGH SCHOOL STUDENTS BEHIND IN THEIR WORK
TO GET THE PENTECOSTAL SPIRIT
AND TAKE ADVANCED STANDING.

This is a tip to the students of the Waukegan high school, where Latin, German and French are taught.

Do you wish to learn either of these languages without any trouble at all?

Of course you do, even if you are the star pupil, the one favored by the teacher, the one who gets the high marks.

Wish to know how?

Whisper.

Consult Evangelist Parham at Zion City.

Get the gift of the tongues. Feel the pentecostal spirit. Let the tongue of fire descend upon you. That's how to get next to the language game, and Parham says so himself.[62]

Yet Parham's loss of credibility with the press hardly disturbed his own projections of the future of his Apostolic Faith movement. The power of Pentecost had fallen and Parham left no doubt as to the importance Zion City would play in the endtime mission campaign. He explained to his excited Zion followers that in the future millennial reign of Christ their city would rank second in significance only to Jerusalem itself.[63] As far as he was concerned, the Apostolic Faith continued down the road toward total victory. By early November, fifty Zion residents had prayed through to Pentecost and Parham felt sure that their example of spiritual power would ultimately deliver the bulk of the city into his hands. More important, the expansion of Pentecost would hasten the success of the endtime revival.[64]

Shortly after the outbreak of Pentecost in Zion, Parham decided to proceed on to Los Angeles to consolidate Seymour's growing work. Now that his Zion supporters were enjoying the fullness of his teaching, he reasoned that he should fulfill the obligation of several months' standing to lead a general revival campaign in the west. On October 23 he left the city in the hands of Texas director Carothers and headed for Los Angeles to consolidate Seymour's work into his growing network of Pentecostal enthusiasts.[65] Little did he know that his place in the movement would suffer a swift and catastrophic decline. Parham's prominence and optimism would never again rival that of the last few weeks in Zion City.

6

The Projector of Pentecost
The Fall
1907–1908

Exactly what Charles Parham expected to find in Los Angeles in October 1906 is not known. He obviously claimed the revival there as his own. Seymour's ordination credentials from the reorganization plan had been approved and forwarded to Los Angeles in July, and Parham had boasted to Waukegan reporters that he had followers in both the Midwest and on the West Coast.[1] Yet reports from the revival disturbed him as well. Earlier, in July, he had encountered negative publicity from the California Pentecostals while conducting an evangelistic campaign in Topeka, Kansas. West Coast dispatches picked up by Midwestern newspapers described the Los Angeles revival as a wild, fanatical affair which flaunted social custom and threatened public security. One account noted that the Azusa Street meeting "is composed of whites and Negroes in about equal proportions. Many of the worshipers are uneducated, and the 'jabbering' of those who profess 'to speak with tongues' is not often possible of interpretation." Less scrupulous newsmen created fantastic headlines by reporting rumors that the California sect practiced child sacrifice.[2]

Parham, concerned by the negative publicity, explained to the press that outside influences had infiltrated the Los Angeles wing and promised to visit the city "to eradicate any fanaticism." To ensure credibility, he favored reporters with his political views—restating his novel position against Prohibition, blasting the legislative and judicial branches of the federal government as "a set of unprincipled scoundrels," and predicting the results of the upcoming gubernatorial election in Kansas.[3] The inference was obvious. Parham billed himself as a public orator on a variety of political and social issues; only sane people could logically discuss such topics. To clearly disassociate himself with the disturbing reports, he offered a scathing denunciation of fanatical "Holy Rollers" and explained the differences between them and his own followers.

The Apostolic Faith movement . . . is a dignified movement, directed by the Almighty power, and has no connection with the sensational Holy Rollers. We have no sympathy with nor do we countenance the gymnastic contortions of the Holy Rollers, who throw fits, perform somersaults, roll and kick in the straw or dust or upon the floor of the meeting house.

I do believe, however, in throwing one's whole heart into the work and to show one's feeling in an enthusiastic manner. Our revival meetings are no dull affairs, but we do not countenance absurd exhibitions which a certain element seem disposed to display. When any of that class come to our meeting and begin throwing fits, we quietly have the attendants take them out.[4]

Though reporters no doubt marveled at Parham's ability to separate his "enthuasiastic" worship from the "gymnastic contortions" of others, Parham himself had made an important distinction. The original outpouring at Topeka had been, admittedly, an uncontrolled affair. But following the "fleshly manifestations" in Nevada, Missouri, early in 1903, Parham had guarded against excessive emotion.[5] He believed that valid spiritual manifestations could be distinguished from vain emotionalism by the person in harmony with the Holy Spirit. Though some may have had trouble distinguishing such differences, Parham's ability to discern between the two remained quite constant. Followers of the Apostolic Faith might occasionally get out of kilter with true spiritual manifestations but, when they did, their leader stood ready to correct them and keep them in line.[6]

It was this role as spiritual leader which Parham carried foremost in his mind as he traveled from Zion City to Los Angeles. Parham later claimed that Seymour's letters had urged his arrival specifically "to help him discern between that which was real and that which was false" because "spiritualistic manifestations, hypnotic forces and fleshly contortions as known in the colored Camp Meetings in the south, had broken loose in the meeting."[7] Parham arrived at Azusa determined to restore order and exert his authority; he suffered an almost immediate defeat. As he later recalled the encounter, he entered an environment totally out of control and clearly resentful of his spiritual leadership.

I hurried to Los Angeles, and to my utter surprise and astonishment I found conditions even worse than I had anticipated. Brother Seymour came to me helpless, he said he could not stem the tide that had arisen. I sat on the platform in Azusa Street Mission, and saw the manifestations of the flesh, spiritualistic controls, saw people practicing hypnotism at the altar over candidates seeking the baptism; though many were receiving the real baptism of the Holy Ghost.

After preaching two or three times, I was informed by two of the elders, one who was a hypnotist . . . that I was not wanted in that place.[8]

Parham subsequently accused Seymour of becoming "possessed with a spirit of leadership" and declared that "two-thirds of the people professing Pentecost are either hypnotized or spook-driven."[9]

There was more afoot than the degree of emotion deemed proper in a worship service. Azusa had already been rocked by dissension as rival leaders left the mission to establish other works in the city. Now, eight months into the revival, a new authoritarian figure was entering the fray. Many Azusa worshippers rejected the idea that an "outsider" could suddenly arrive and "correct" their revival pattern.[10] In addition,

Parham's demeanor reduced his chances for a peaceful assumption of power. Turned off by the amount of emotional display, he prefaced his first remarks at Azusa by declaring unequivocally, "God is sick at his stomach!"[11] Little wonder he met with a less than enthusiastic welcome.

There were other problems as well. The publicity from Azusa revealed two things which significantly disturbed Parham. One was the degree of racial equality tolerated by participants; the other concerned the reported lack of palpable evidence for xenoglossa in the revival services. Parham had demonstrated sensitivity to the spiritual needs of blacks; however, he was hardly an advocate of racial equality. Like the large majority of whites at the turn of the century, he assumed white superiority and feared miscegenation. The Anglo-Israel theory convinced him that white Anglo-Saxons enjoyed a unique place in God's historical drama, and miscegenation could only weaken the bloodlines of this chosen race. Parham graphically explained to his audiences that the "sin" of intermarriage in the days of Noah had been the chief cause of the Flood and the root of all inherited disease and abnormalities up to the present time.[12]

When confronted with a lack of racial distinction at Azusa, Parham was personally revolted. He feared such a breakdown in social custom and favored race-mixing only under controlled conditions. There was a place for interracial cooperation, and Parham had demonstrated it in his ministry among blacks in Houston. As recently as August 1906 he had demonstrated his willingness toward this type of cooperative effort by having Lucy Farrow as a guest speaker at the Houston Camp Meeting. Farrow, fresh from her experience at Azusa Street, captivated the audience with her ability to bring on Pentecostal baptism through "the laying on of hands."[13] Parham was certain that cooperation and goodwill did not necessitate a complete blurring of racial roles. Part of Azusa's problem, as he saw it, was Los Angeles itself. Already a bustling metropolis of two million people, the city exhibited the greatest cosmopolitan flavor of any area of Pentecostal penetration.

Unlike the more racially homogeneous centers of the Midwest, high concentrations of ethnically diverse groups created a climate much more open to a flaunting of social norms.[14]

For black participants the brief interracial climate at Azusa symbolized the outbreak of an overdue genuine Christian fellowship. However, Parham, and the overwhelming majority of white participants, concluded that the freedom of God's spirit did not extend quite so far.[15] For Parham, the distinction proved tragic. The paternalistic racism which he had practiced prior to Azusa Street gave way to a harsher, more blatant racism. In the wake of his disappointment and bitterness over the rejection suffered there, he became openly critical of black religious expression and wantonly careless in his remarks about Seymour and the Azusa faithful. The change was sadly clear in Parham's attack on the Azusa "counterfeit" late in 1912.

Men and women, whites and blacks, knelt together or fell across one another; frequently, a white woman, perhaps of wealth and culture, could be seen thrown back in the arms of a big "buck nigger," and held tightly thus as she shivered and shook in freak imitation of Pentecost. Horrible, awful shame![16]

Quite apart from Parham's inability to justify the initial racial openness at Azusa was his concern that verifiable xenoglossa should mark the reception and exercise of Holy Spirit power in the life of every Pentecostal believer. Parham's theological platform of Pentecost contained three vital planks, each of which was adopted by Azusa worshippers. First, tongue-speaking served as the *sine qua non* of Holy Spirit baptism. Tongue speech was not synonymous with the baptism, but its presence at the time of reception was considered sacrosanct by all early pioneers.[17]

The second fundamental underpinning explained the historical significance of Pentecostal recipients themselves. Those who received Pentecostal power had been "sealed" for the impending rapture and would soon form a pivotal role as Christ's "bride" during the eschaton. The most common analogy used was that of the parable of the ten virgins. All were pure (sanctified) but only the five wise virgins with sufficient oil (Pentecostal power) were prepared for the bridegroom's appearing (Second Coming). In this way Pentecostals assured themselves of the importance of their religious movement and took comfort in the knowledge that the powerless in this world would exercise considerable authority in the next.[18]

The third timber in Parham's theological platform emphasized the missionary role behind his movement's justification as an endtime revival. Xenoglossic tongues would make Pentecostal evangelism effective. Its supernatural character would also make the claims of Pentecostals undeniable. The Azusa participants shared this vision of world conquest by xenoglossa. By midsummer 1906, missionaries with the "call" had set out to foreign lands to test their wares.[19]

The theological foundation of the Azusa revival pleased Parham; however, he maintained grave reservations about the authenticity of some of the tongue speech he heard there. Though no linguistic scholar, he castigated Azusa worshippers for their "babbling" and accused some of the seekers of trickery through "the suggestion of certain words and sounds, the working of the chin, or the massage of the throat."[20] Anything failing to resemble real foreign language became suspect since its utilitarian value was lost. Worse, in Parham's mind, was the lack of authenticity which nonxenoglossic tongues seemed to portend.[21] Had Parham succeeded in securing control of Azusa in late October 1906, he would have concentrated on this qualitative distinction which, in conjunction with a recognition of his authority over worship style and a modified racial policy, would have significantly altered the future of the Pentecostal movement.[22]

In the final analysis, Parham was simply unable to pull off such an impressive coup. Rejected after only two or three sermons, he opened a rival mission in the W.C.T.U. (Woman's Christian Temperance Union) building on the corner of Broadway and Temple Streets. There Parham claimed a remnant of two to three hundred former Azusa faithful who followed his teachings and received "real Pentecost." Still, it was a pale imitation of what Parham had hoped to accomplish upon his arrival in late October. In early December he considered his work in the city at a standstill and decided to return to Zion City. He telegraphed Carothers and explained that the two men should switch places. When Carothers arrived in Los Angeles to assume control of the mission there, Parham left for a return engagement with the faithful in Zion.[23]

Parham's return to the city of Dowie in mid-December created a local media blitz. At the height of the controversy in Los Angeles, he had unexpectedly resigned his position as Projector of the Apostolic Faith. Perhaps in an effort to combat Azusa claims that he craved power, Parham gambled that control of the developing movement could be achieved through the role of general evangelist. It was a direct reversal of his organizational efforts from earlier in the year. The move created considerable disarray in Zion City where Voliva and his associates leaked rumors that they had paid Parham off.[24] To quell those rumors and restore order, Parham reestablished himself among Zion Pentecostals and explained his new role in the January issue of the *Apostolic Faith:*

In resigning my position as projector of the Apostolic Faith Movement, I simply followed a well-considered plan of mine, made years ago, never to receive honor of men, or to establish a new church. I was called a pope, a Dowie, etc., and everywhere looked upon as a leader or a would-be leader and proselyter. These designations have always been an abomination to me, and since God has given almost universal light to the world on Pentecost there is no further need of my holding the official leadership of the Apostolic Faith Movement, which was only a cart in which we pushed the gifts along. Now that they are generally accepted, I simply take my place among my brethren to push this gospel of the kingdom as a witness to all nations.

I shall still remain the same to my brethren in assistance, advice and in donating to them my extra cash as when I bore the meaningless title of projector.

Yours sincerely,
C. F. Parham[25]

Parham's decision was less magnanimous than his explanation indicated. He clearly desired leadership and his "resignation" resulted from both his frustration at having lost authority and his desperate hope to gain it back. But he would never enjoy so much authority again. Parham's star was on the wane; the weeks and months ahead would produce even more cracks in his ecclesiastical armor.

Already he faced competition within his own inner circle. Like Parham, W. Faye Carothers possessed experience in holiness churches and was far more educated than the majority of his peers.[26] Carothers' early months in the movement were somewhat restricted by his failure to receive Holy Spirit baptism; however, after his reception early in 1906 he quickly assumed a position of prominence. By March 1906 he carried a great deal of the editorial responsibilities of the *Apostolic Faith* and, by May, felt free to offer theological advice about the Baptism of the Holy Ghost to his readers. Parham honored him by placing him in charge of the important Texas wing of the movement with the official title State Director. Late in 1906 Carothers seems to have served as much more than that, coming first to Zion City and then to Los Angeles to coordinate the revivals Parham had begun. He was, by every indication, the most capable and trusted member of Parham's unofficial board of advisors.[27]

The relationship between Parham and Carothers rapidly deteriorated during the early months of 1907 for reasons which remain shrouded in mystery. Initially Parham's return to Zion had seemed promising. His following in the city approached one thousand and his was clearly the second most powerful religious influence in the city. Ambitious plans were outlined, including a tabernacle with a seating capacity of two thousand. In the short run, however, Parham settled for a large circus tent and began holding unified meetings with all his Zion converts. With continued success it looked as if the Apostolic Faith might actually succeed in toppling Wilbur Voliva from his position of leadership.[28] But in the heat of the battle Parham left town. Around January twenty-first he embarked with a handful of followers on a three-month tour of the Northeast with stops in Cleveland, Toronto, Boston, and New York.[29] At precisely the same time his contact with Carothers was abruptly broken. The Texan returned to his home state and immediately entered into a power struggle with his former boss for the Apostolic Faith churches there. Parham reached Texas early in April in time for the second anniversary of the inaugural Orchard revival. Already the Lone Star State was split evenly in a bitter rivalry.[30]

The key issue of the struggle was Charles Parham himself. Rumors of immorality began circulating as early as January 1907.[31] Local papers suggested that Parham's sudden departure on a northeastern tour had been prompted by the arrival of "mysterious men, said to be detectives, [who] were ready to arrest him on some equally mysterious charge."[32] Parham defectors made vague references to their former leader's "failure" and "awful sin." By early summer his name was anathema, and he had been officially "disfellowshipped" by a large segment of the Texas organization now directed by Carothers and Howard Goss.[33] The nature of the rumors became public knowledge in San Antonio, Texas on Friday, July nineteenth when Parham suffered the humiliation of widespread news coverage. A story in the *San Antonio Light* on that day broke the first genuine scandal in Pentecostal history.

EVANGELIST IS ARRESTED

C. F. PARHAM, WHO HAS BEEN
PROMINENT IN MEETING HERE,
TAKEN INTO CUSTODY

C. F. Parham . . . about 40 years old, and J. J. Jourdan, 22 years old, were arrested about noon today upon an affidavit made before Justice of the Peace Ben S. Fisk, charging the commission of an unnatural offense. . . . In default of $1000 bond each, the men were committed to jail to await the action of the grand jury.[34]

Officially, Parham was charged with committing sodomy— a felony under Texas statute 524.[35] On Tuesday, July twenty-third, he was released from jail with payment of the one thousand dollars bail by two Houston friends, J. Ed Cabaniss and F. Cullen.[36] Parham secured a local lawyer, C. A. Davis, and announced to his following there that he was the victim of an elaborate frame devised by his old rival Wilbur Voliva. The San Antonio mission where he had been speaking was under the direction of Lemuel C. Hall, a former disciple of John Alexander Dowie. Thus Parham alleged that since he had convinced Hall to abandon his connection with the Christian Catholic Apostolic Church and ally with the Apostolic Faith, the Zion kingpin was now fighting back with a vengeance. He pledged to clear his name by fighting the case against him and indignantly rejected suggestions that he leave town to avoid prosecution.[37]

Conspicuously silent in the days after the arrest was J. J. Jourdan, Parham's codefendant. Newspapers covered Parham's release from jail without any word on Jourdan's status. His association with Parham both prior and after this event cannot be substantiated. Ominously, the only known event in Jourdan's life other than this July charge is another alleged criminal offense. Two months earlier he had been indicted by the grand jury on a charge of "theft over $50." Jourdan was accused of stealing sixty dollars from C. J. Sedlmayer of San Antonio's Hotel Arthur. Despite three witnesses, the district attorney's office requested a dismissal— presumably from lack of evidence or as a result of an out-of-court settlement. The Bexar County District Court dismissed the case on June twenty-ninth.[38]

The Parham-Jourdan case met a similar fate. After July twenty-fourth, there was simply no local press coverage of the matter. Parham passed from the San Antonio public page almost as mysteriously as he had suddenly appeared on it five days earlier. No formal indictment was ever filed; Mrs. Parham recalled traveling to Texas to be with her husband at the scheduled indictment, "but the case was never called, the prosecuting attorney declaring that there was absolutely no evidence which merited any legal recognition."[39]

Despite Mrs. Parham's optimistic assessment, publicity of

the scandal through religious newspapers and word-of-mouth was only beginning. The lack of a clear acquittal in San Antonio along with rumors of Parham's impropriety over the past six months combined to create the public impression of guilt. Few allegations were more damaging and publicly reprehensible in 1907 than homosexuality. Parham could never quite free himself from that millstone.[40] The articles printed in the religious press were far more detailed than those in the San Antonio papers. They probably were less reliable and undoubtedly were more guilty of rumor and innuendo. Consequently they were much more damaging to Parham's ministerial career. The most explicit of the accounts offered a mountain of "evidence" aimed at discrediting the Kansas evangelist and putting him out of business.[41]

The first such attack appeared on July twenty-sixth, barely a week after the arrest itself. Not surprisingly it came from the official organ of Wilbur Voliva's church. In a hastily attached supplement, the *Zion Herald* staff constructed a story from a telegram wired on request from the *San Antonio Express*. The brief exchange had included enough information for the subsequent story to forever brand Parham as a social delinquent.

Zion City, Ill., July 23, '07 To Editor San Antonio Express, San Antonio, Texas

Parham reported arrested your city held thousand dollars bond. Wire particulars twenty word reply paid.

ZION HERALD

Received at CH 5A RW Collect.

San Antonio, Texas
July 23rd, 1907

Zion Herald, Zion City, Ills.

San Antonio Texas held on charge Sodomy with Jew boy. Made written confession then decided to fight case. Great indignation. Was holding apostolic meeting.
830 PM

Express[42]

Most damaging was the *Herald*'s unscrupulous practice of attributing the story as written to the San Antonio newspaper—thus crediting the account to an unbiased source. The same combination of fact and allegation was published the following day in the *Waukegan Daily Sun* and, two months later, in the *Burning Bush*, a Wisconsin-based holiness periodical. Both of these sources quoted directly from the *Herald* and gave credit to the *Express* for the content.[43]

Readers were treated to a variety of incriminating "evidence." J. J. Jourdan became a "young man hymn singer" staying in the same quarters with Parham and referred to by the evangelist as "an angel-voiced boy." An abundance of witnesses stood ready to testify against the two men, including the landlady at Parham's boarding house—the lone eyewitness—and former Texas supporters with letters and affidavits accusing him of the same offense on earlier visits to Waco, League City, and Orchard. Most damning were the reports of a written confession originally signed by Parham on the condition that he be allowed to leave town. Even the accused's defense was portrayed as an admission of guilt.

> "This is a plot to drive me from my work," [Parham] exclaimed. "My enemies have pursued me from city to city, and they are aided by the devil." . . . "The confession was wrung from me by force!" exclaimed the preacher. "*I am the victim of a nervous disaster* and my actions have been misunderstood." . . . "*I am a helpless degenerate physically,*" Parham says in explanation. "I will swear, however, that I never committed this crime intentionally. What I might have done in my sleep I can not say, but it was never intended on my part." . . . "I am not guilty of intentional crime," he kept repeating. Jourdan refused to make a statement.[44]

The charges as specified in this *Zion Herald* account are suspect at best. The lack of any corroborating evidence suggests that Voliva was making the most of Parham's dilemma by leaving no rumorous stone unturned. He had much to gain in ensuring his chief competitor's reputational demise.[45] Of course Voliva's involvement does not ensure Parham's innocence either. It is difficult to imagine that such an elaborate scheme could have been totally fabricated by Voliva or any other of Parham's rivals. Nevertheless, that is the defense most often engineered by Parham's apologists. Parham himself later claimed that the charges and rumors were the result of "scandalous lies and slanderous reports" by certain Pentecostals who desired leadership for themselves. Specifically he believed himself the victim of some of his former associates who rejected him as a result of his refusal to organize Pentecostalism into a denomination with all the trappings of wealth and fame. He refused, however, to publish a full defense of his actions or name his accusers and portrayed his "persecution" as a type of Christ's suffering.[46]

Recent defenders of Parham's reputation have focused on W. Faye Carothers as the mastermind behind the calculated frame to remove the Kansas evangelist from his position of prominence. Once again the motive is alleged to be Parham's refusal to organize and Carothers' desire for the glories of leadership.[47] Yet here the conspiracy theory completely breaks down. No substantial evidence exists to implicate Carothers and, if anything, the alleged motive suggests his innocence. Carothers clearly opposed strong organization throughout his career and made no effort to institute any program of central government after Parham's downfall. Rather, it was Parham who had deviated from the ideal by inaugurating the first vestiges of organization in March 1906. Carothers seemed perfectly content to continue that loose structure in the aftermath of the scandal.[48]

In addition the timing of the rumors would appear to clear Carothers. Reports of immorality first circulated shortly after Parham's resignation as Projector in November 1906—a time when Carothers was his strongest supporter. Carothers obviously believed the rumors and organized an independent wing of the Texas Apostolic Faith in response to the dilemma. Carothers was thus effectively free of Parham months before the charges in San Antonio were filed. As an independent Pentecostal leader in Texas still actively promoting the name of the Apostolic Faith, he had absolutely nothing to gain by destroying Parham's reputation. In fact, he too suffered the consequences of the adverse publicity.[49]

In the final analysis the Parham scandal remains a mystery. There is neither enough hard evidence to condemn him nor enough doubt to sufficiently explain the preponderance of rumor which circulated during his lifetime. Unfortunately, Parham neglected—or was unable—to secure San Antonio officials' testimony in clearing his reputation. He naively left the matter to the discretion of his followers, believing that those faithful to the cause of the Apostolic Faith would never believe the rumors, and those opposed to his ministry would never accept a defense.[50]

Several things are clear in hindsight. The charges abruptly ended Parham's chances of maintaining leadership over the growing Pentecostal movement. The impact on his following in the Midwest was devastating. David Lee Floyd, an early Pentecostal from Missouri, remembered that the rumors of Parham's alleged sodomy were "rampant and without mercy."[51] Likewise, the Texas work split into two competing groups, and the Zion campaign deteriorated into a small band of discredited zealots. Elsewhere, the movement spread with followers oblivious to the contribution of the first Pentecostal teacher.[52]

The charges also placed a tremendous burden on Charles Parham. The incident was a source of immense embarassment for him and his wife. Throughout his life, he faced the sting of widespread gossip and continually lamented the fact that his position as Pentecostal father had been impugned.[53]

Finally, the sodomy charge created a more callous Charles Parham than the world had known previously. Though his theological message remained the same, the rhetoric of his sermons became much harsher and less optimistic. Attacks on other Pentecostals now formed an almost relentless theme in his ministry. Gone, or at least subdued, was the radical optimism of a Christianity united by endtime signs of God's power. Somehow the message of world conquest seemed lost in the shadow of a fallen prophet.[54]

The 1907 sodomy charge was the turning point in Charles Parham's life. Yet there was more to Parham's decline than just that event. Carothers' break with Parham included a rejection of the leader's authority quite apart from the question of morality. Upon arriving in Los Angeles in December 1906, Carothers seems to have questioned Parham's judgment about the Azusa revival. He reasoned that the Kansas evangelist had acted hastily in dismissing the revival as a counterfeit under the control of "hypnotists." Carothers later insisted that if Seymour had appealed the matter to the entire Apostolic Faith body, "we would have remained united, because the older part of the movement approved the action which he thought we would condemn."[55] Clearly, Parham's role as authoritarian diminished quickly in the wake of the Azusa debacle. What was essential, Carothers thought, was a higher degree of tolerance than Parham had been willing to exhibit. Parham's frank pulpit mannerisms were effective for attracting needed publicity and urging the unrepentant to make a radical decision for Christ. Yet the "Apostle of Unity" fell far short of the moderating leadership needed to ensure cohesion.[56]

In addition Parham's authority was undermined by the phenomenal growth of the movement. Even before the disappointing debut at Azusa Street, Parham had faced competition. The missionaries from Azusa fanned out into small towns across America. Inherent in their message was religious individualism and power through the presence of God's spirit. There was little room for a single domineering personality like Charles Parham. Rather, there would be a series of dominant personalities as the more "spiritual" members of each community took charge by popular consent. Nowhere was this trend more apparent than in Zion City, where new Pentecostal leaders rose to the fore alongside Parham's rapid decline.[57]

In September 1907 one of the extreme factions of the splintering Pentecostal movement created a nationwide sensation. Harold Mitchell, a Zion convert originally associated with Parham's following there, was tried and convicted of manslaughter in the death of an invalid woman, Letitia Green-halgh. Mitchell, along with Greenhalgh's son and daughter, engaged in a bizarre healing session which included the physical straightening of the elderly woman's severely restricted arms and legs. Mitchell convinced Greenhalgh's children that this radical step of faith was needed to remove the "demon of rheumatism" that had possessed their mother. The unorthodox maneuver resulted in several broken bones and, with the accompanying trauma, in the poor woman's demise. Newspaper accounts made only a token effort to point out that Mitchell was, in fact, independent of any organized Pentecostal mission and was himself obviously mentally disturbed. They painted the event with broad strokes, most often using Charles Parham's name as a synonym for Pentecostal believers worldwide. The result was a series of sensational news accounts and the predictable public outcry that followed.

Murdered in the most brutal manner by being torn limb from limb, while her son and daughter watched and prayed, her cries for help stifled by means of a hand laid over her mouth, the death by violence of Mrs. Letitia Greenhalgh of Zion City, Wednesday noon, may result in the extermination of the most vicious and brutalized religious sect on the face of the earth, the Parhamites.[58]

Though Parham and other Pentecostals separated themselves from this extreme practice and totally disavowed any connection with Mitchell, such press releases undoubtedly hindered their climb toward credibility. For Parham the publicity was the second major disaster of 1907.

In the face of such adversity the Apostolic Faith doctrine continued to spread. By the fall of 1908 there were over sixty different Pentecostal missions scattered throughout the United States.[59] One Canadian Pentecostal publication noted that outside Anglo-America workers had been no less zealous in spreading the new spirit-filled faith. Already missionaries were reporting from "Jerusalem, Syria, Arabia, Persia and Armenia . . . China . . . India . . . Scotland . . . England, Ireland, Wales, Sweden, Norway, Switzerland, Holland, Germany,

Australia, Russia and Thibet, Africa west and south, San Marcial, New Mexico, Jeruca, Cuba, Egypt, Torr-Pellice, province of Torino, Italy, and Japan."[60] Everywhere the message was the same; God was pouring out the Spirit in the last days in the same way that He inaugurated the church age nineteen hundred years earlier. The bookends of church history were laced together with glossolalia. It was an exciting time for the faithful.

Despite his loss of status, Charles Parham had played a leading role in the establishment of Pentecostalism as a national and international movement. His influence on Seymour and the Los Angeles outpouring is undeniable. The apostles flowing from Azusa Street carried with them the central corpus of Parham's message. Outside Los Angeles his impact was even more profound. The Midwestern and Texas centers remained major areas of Pentecostal concentration. Specifically, Zion City loomed large in the successful expansion. Though attempts at a complete Zion takeover by Pentecostals ended with the Mitchell debacle, Parham's work there produced an enduring force in the movement. A missionary training school, a faith healing home, and several independent churches were established in the city and have remained in operation over the decades.[61]

Even more impressive was the large number of evangelists and denominational leaders who traced their roots to Zion. Among them were several figures who subsequently achieved international significance. Fred F. Bosworth established an independent healing ministry which carried the Pentecostal message to crowds as large as twenty thousand. Through his successor, William Branham, the campaigns continued to reach new generations of Americans and Europeans on into the 1960s. John G. Lake of Zion City formed a similar independent ministry which bore particularly fruitful results in South Africa and along the west coast of the United States. Also out of the Zion connection came Elim N. Richey and his son Raymond. The Richeys formed an evangelistic crusade which targeted American army personnel training for service

Located on the corner of Fourth and Jackson Streets in Topeka, Kansas, this building was rented by Parham for his Beth-el Healing Home from fall 1898 to June 1900.
(*Used by permission of Kansas State Historical Society*)

Stone Mansion, Topeka, Kansas, ca. 1901. Known locally as
Stone's Folly, the mansion served as the site of Parham's Bethel
Bible School from October 1900 to July 1901.
(*Used by permission of Kansas State Historical Society*)

The Apostolic Faith.

Lift up a Standard for the People.—Isaiah 62:10

VOL. 1   HOUSTON, TEXAS, DECEMBER 1905   NO. 7

Apostolic Faith, December 1905. Begun in June 1905, this second of four separate editions was published sporadically from Melrose, Kansas; Houston, Texas; and Zion City, Illinois.
(*Used by permission of the Assemblies of God Archives*)

SPECIMEN OF MISS AUSWIN'S HANDWRITING WHICH THE APOSTOLIC BRETHREN CLAIM, IS INSPIRED BY GOD HIMSELF.

From the *Topeka Daily Capital,* January 6, 1901, p. 2. Though rare today, glossographia was a frequent claim among early Pentecostals. This sample, collected by a reporter at the Topeka Revival in January 1901, was attributed to Agnes Ozman whom the reporter erroneously referred to as "Auswin."
(*Used by permission of Kansas State Historical Society*)

Parham (center, seated) and his Houston evangelistic team at Bryan Hall, July-August 1905.
(*Used by permission of the Assemblies of God Archives*)

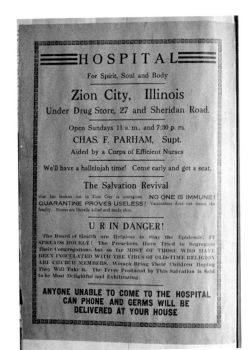

To capture public attention, Parham distributed numerous cleverly designed handbills advertising his messsage.
(*Used by permission of the Assemblies of God Archives*)

Parham and a group of Apostolic Faith followers at Brunner Tabernacle outside Houston, Texas, September 1906. Howard Goss is on the first full row, far right, standing. W. Faye Carothers is on the same row, eighth person to the left of Goss. Parham is the fifth person to the right behind Carothers.
(*Used by permission of the Assemblies of God Archives*)

This poster, printing Parham's alleged confession, was widely distributed by the followers of Wilbur Glenn Voliva in Zion City, Illinois. The poster reads in part "I hereby confess my guilt in the commission of the crime of Sodomy with one J. J. Jourdan in San Antonio, Texas on the 18th day of July, 1907. Witness my hand at San Antonio, Texas this 18th day of July 1907. Signed, Chas. F. Parham." The confession, however, cannot be confirmed by San Antonio court records.
(*Used by permission of the Assemblies of God Archives*)

Charles F. Parham, ca. 1925.
(*Used by permission of the Assemblies of God Archives*)

Upon Parham's death early in 1929, friends began collecting contributions for this pulpit-shaped marker to be placed over his grave in Baxter Springs, Kansas.
(*Used by permission of the Assemblies of God Archives*)

in two world wars. The Richeys also conducted huge city campaigns across America and throughout the Caribbean.[62]

In addition to the international evangelists, a considerable number of denominational leaders and independent churchmen were spawned from Zion. Three of them, J. Roswell Flower, Cyrus B. Fockler, and Daniel C. O. Opperman, served on the first General Council of the Assemblies of God in 1914. Another, Fred Vogler, rose to a position of prominence as Assistant General Superintendent of the denomination. Marie Burgess Brown, also an Assemblies of God affiliate, founded Glad Tidings Hall on Forty-Second Street in New York City in May 1907 and personally pastored the urban work until her death in 1971. Independent Pentecostal William Piper established a strong work at the Stone Church in Chicago and edited the influential *Latter Rain Evangel*. Other Zionites who made similar contributions to the growing movement were F. A. Graves, Lemuel C. Hall, and Mrs. Martha Wing Robinson.[63]

By 1908 Pentecostalism, toughened by adverse publicity, progressed steadily through the evangelistic zeal of thousands of converts. Yet the father of the Apostolic Faith stood increasingly on the outskirts of the movement, rejected by many of his own and ignored by the bulk of the incoming numbers. Parham tried valiantly to hang on to the burgeoning movement. His schedule remained busier than ever as he crisscrossed the nation in an effort to gather support.[64] To ensure his place in the movement, he emphasized his role as the original teacher and founder of Pentecostalism. His faithful responded by affectionately dubbing him "Daddy"—a practice encouraged by Parham himself, continued throughout his life.[65] For most Pentecostals, however, Charles Parham remained an enigma.

One final indignity and embarassment awaited Charles Parham. Early in 1908 he began raising funds for a personal archaeological expedition. A lifelong goal had been to travel to the Holy Land and search for the lost Ark of the Covenant. He explained to intrigued crowds that he would also undertake a search for the remains of Noah's ark. Undoubtedly Parham hoped that the trip would shift the attention of Pentecostals back his way. The slightest measure of success would ensure him favorable publicity and reestablish his position as the best-known Pentecostal in America. At the very least, the trip itself would guarantee him a spot at the top of the list of eligible speakers in a variety of religious circles. After parading the plan before the press and raising sufficient funds, Parham journeyed to New York in December 1908 to board a steamer for Jerusalem.[66]

His ticket for the Middle East was never purchased. Parham returned home to Kansas in January 1909 on money loaned to him by a friend. Dejectedly, he explained to his followers that he had been mugged shortly after arriving in New York and never even had an opportunity to buy his ticket.[67] It was a fitting conclusion to two years of frustration—two years which had taken him from sole Projector of the Apostolic Faith assemblies and chief contender for the religious mantle of John Alexander Dowie to rejected prophet of Pentecost and despondent dreamer of lost artifacts. God would speak again, but His voice would seem a bit softer and a lot less optimistic.

7

Perseverance and Obscurity 1909–1929

During the pivotal years from 1906 to 1908, Charles Parham tried a variety of approaches to solve the problem of his splintering Apostolic Faith movement. At Los Angeles he got tough and attempted to force authority upon a new wing of believers. In Zion he backed down to the charge of personal ambition and resigned his position as Projector of his newly organized church. In Texas and the tri-state region he rode out the storm of controversy over his alleged immorality and clung to the naive belief that no explanation of the charges was necessary for the true possessors of God's spirit. He continued to hold periodic meetings in all three Pentecostal centers almost as if nothing had changed. Yet the defections continued and most new growth experienced by the young movement eluded him. By 1909 he found his ministry badly in need of some sort of reorganization.[1]

As in the past, Parham found solace in the lead-mining region of southeast Kansas. In March 1909 he moved his family to Baxter Springs and coordinated his evangelical ministry from his home there for the remaining twenty years of his life. The move provided a needed sense of security for his children, now approaching puberty, and established a level of continuity his ministry had not enjoyed since the early years in Topeka.

Baxter Springs had been an important community for Parham since his successful campaign in nearby Galena five and a half years earlier. As an overflow from the revival in Galena, a small band of Baxter residents accepted the Apostolic Faith message early in 1904. In the wake of the Nettie Smith crisis later that year Parham had attained celebrity status in the town by forging on with his campaigns despite much local opposition. The Kansas City papers took note of his success:

In Baxter the city hall was rented, after Mr. Parham was refused admittance to the churches, but after three nights' meetings the electric light wires were cut to force a close of the services. Then a billiard hall was tendered for his use. Through it all Mr. Parham has achieved the greatest religious success ever known here.[2]

Also attractive to Parham was the town's role as commercial center of the southeast Kansas mining region. A community of several thousand, Baxter Springs offered the promise of sustained growth. During the half decade after the Civil War, the small crossroads had blossomed into a boom town of over ten thousand as the new cattle industry sparked its emergence as the first "cow town" of the West. A promoter of Kansas in 1871 boasted of the new settlement: "Nature has made the site of this place for a city. No human effort can prevent Baxter from becoming a large place, or from doing a most extensive business."[3] Despite such lofty predictions the cattle business pressed on westward and, by the mid-1870s, Baxter Springs found itself eclipsed by more prominent cow towns like Abilene.

However, a second boom—more modest in its growth patterns and yet more enduring—reached the town almost on the heels of the first. By the late 1870s lead and zinc mining entered the region and, as an established town, Baxter Springs drew its share of the resulting commercial activity. During the early years of the twentieth century this measure of prosperity seemed assured. As a sideline the town hosted an annual Old Soldier's Reunion for veterans of the Civil War. The affair drew thousands of visitors for a week-long celebration until its decline and ultimate cancellation during the second decade of the century.[4]

So it was to a small but bustling Baxter Springs that Parham relocated in 1909. From there he planned and then resumed his travels to literally all regions of the nation. But his impact was not limited to his travels alone. He remained a visible public figure in the town. Each year, beginning in 1910, his birthday on June fourth brought hundreds of his followers throughout the Midwest for an all-day religious celebration.[5] In addition, Parham brought his printing operation to Baxter Springs. In December 1910 he reorganized the *Apostolic Faith*—defunct since the Zion City campaign of early 1907— by issuing a special Christmas edition. The following year he convinced one of his young disciples, Francis Rolland Romack, to set up shop as the permanent editor of the publication. Regular issues began appearing in January 1912.[6]

These accomplishments and the publicity he received from occasional press releases were enough to make Parham one of the town's most noted citizens. Formal acceptance came in 1911 when, after a similar offer from friends in Texas, locals raised money to purchase a building in downtown Baxter Springs to convince the rent-poor Parhams to stay. The large brick structure, originally built as a brewery, became the Parham home and the Apostolic Faith headquarters for the next two decades.[7] Even residents theologically opposed to Pentecost were impressed by their new neighbor. The local paper noted that "while we can not swallow some of the doctrine preached by the eloquent Rev. Parham, we cannot help but say his meetings have been beneficial to the city and the means of saving many souls."[8]

It is difficult to assess the size of Parham's following after the divisions of 1906 and 1907. The oldest surviving subscription list for the *Apostolic Faith* dates to the mid-1930s, several years after Parham's death. The information is enough to make an educated guess of Parham's support during the final two decades of his life. Distributed across thirty-two states, the paper was being mailed to approximately fourteen hundred followers by Mrs. Parham with the help of Evangelist Gail W. Schultz of Selman, Oklahoma.

The bulk of the mailings were directed, as might be expected, to six states with a significant legacy in the Parham ministry—Arkansas, California, Kansas, Missouri, Oklahoma, and Texas.[9] In addition, one copy each was mailed to England and Japan, and two copies went to subscribers in Canada.[10] Considering each paper as an item mailed to all members of a particular household, an estimate of four persons per copy would yield a total Apostolic Faith following of around fifty-six hundred. One thing is clearly evident from the list. Though Parham's following may have been somewhat larger before his death than at the time of the composite listing, the numbers are still significantly lower than the projected estimate of eight to ten thousand for 1906. More than two decades after the debacle in San Antonio he had not matched the numbers he had enjoyed the previous year.[11]

Parham continued to draw occasional crowds of several thousand in small towns and cities where he gave stock sermons and lectures and presented a variety hour of gospel music entertainment.[12] As always, healing provided a focal point for many and could occasionally generate the kind of local enthusiasm he had known in his earlier ministry.[13] One early supporter compared him with Billy Sunday and recalled Parham's use of humor to "get the mouth open to put the 'Gos-pill' in."[14] Another remembered him as "a tremendously annointed preacher" and noted "I never heard anyone with such an annointing until Oral Roberts' time."[15] Partisans have also been quick to recall the judgment of an unnamed New York statistician who calculated in the 1920s that Parham's personal appeals, combined with those of ministers he had influenced through Pentecostal teaching, had produced a full two million converts to Christianity.[16]

Nevertheless, by the 1920s most Pentecostals paid little tribute to the man from Baxter Springs. New and brighter stars had arisen in their midst, some of whom proved particularly adept at drawing crowds and media attention. At the top of the list, Aimee Semple McPherson preached to thousands on a daily basis, raised over a million dollars to build Angelus Temple in Los Angeles, entertained the faithful with a sixty-piece "silver band" which played nightly at her crusades, and supplemented the work with her own gospel radio station. Next to such glitter, Parham's work seemed humble indeed.[17]

Few could match Sister Aimee's flair for drama or her penchant for publicity. Parham clearly lacked the spotlight during his mature years but to his small group of Apostolic Faith supporters he remained the premier prophet of Pentecost. For them he pursued his ministry with the same tireless energy he had always displayed. Up until 1916 Parham met his commitments by railroad fare; in that year he joined the new transportation revolution and bought an automobile. The switch made the small towns of the Midwest and elsewhere even more accessible.[18]

The sheer upkeep for the kind of schedule he kept made a certain income level necessary. In 1913 Parham boasted: "When I first took this way I was getting from $500 to $700 a year in a Methodist pulpit; I now get from $5000 to $7000 a year."[19] A considerable sum for most Americans in the early twentieth century, that income level would have placed him, by 1919, in the top 12.3 percent of all U.S. taxpayers. However, Parham undoubtedly quoted figures for his entire evangelical operation and not his own personal net gain. Monetary contributions were typically given directly to him without benefit of record. In turn, he used the funds for both living and ministerial expenses. For Parham there was little distinction between the two.[20] At any rate, he never amassed a significant estate. He also does not seem to have attained a lifestyle dramatically different from that of the majority of his followers, most of whom were working-class people with at least sufficient means to travel to the annual rallies and voluntarily contribute to Parham's evangelical ministry. A handful were perhaps at an income level which placed them solidly in the middle class.[21]

Parham's contact with other Pentecostal leaders decreased

after 1909 as a result of the irrepressible rumors of sexual misconduct and his conviction that the bulk of the movement carelessly flaunted a counterfeit experience of emotionalism. On occasion, he pointed with pride to the rapid growth of Pentecostal sects and claimed, via seniority, one hundred thousand adherents worldwide.[22] At other times he severely criticized the new Pentecostals and seemed almost pleased at the further splintering of the movement due to rival leadership and theological disputes. With each division Parham sensed a loss of the "pure" doctrine God had given him a decade earlier. Incensed at the Pentecostal evangelist William H. Durham, whose "finished work theory" of sanctification rejected the Wesleyan interpretation that he had personally taught since the movement began, Parham prayed in January 1912 that God would prove the proper doctrine by taking the life of whichever prophet taught in error. When Durham died suddenly six months later, Parham felt assured that God had properly answered his prayer.[23]

Ironically, one major division of the new Pentecostal movement drew support from ideas which began, in part, from Parham's thought. Early in his ministry Parham had struggled with variant interpretations of the water baptism formula. For a time he settled on triune immersion. Then, while at Bethel Bible School in Topeka in 1900, he hit upon a new idea which settled the issue for him.

We were waiting upon God that we might know the Scriptural teaching of water baptism. Finally the Spirit of God said: "We are buried by baptism into His death." We had known that for years; again the Spirit said: "God the Father, and God the Holy Ghost never died."

Then how quickly we recognized the fact that we could not be buried by baptism in the name of the Father, and in the name of the Holy Ghost, because it stood for nothing as they never died or were resurrected. . . . So if you desire to witness a public confession of a clean conscience toward God and man, faith in the divinity of Jesus Christ, you will be baptized by single immersion, signifying the death, burial and resurrection; being baptized in the name of Jesus, into the name of the Father, Son and Holy Ghost; they are one when in Christ you become one with all.[24]

As Parham's explanation makes clear, his preference for a baptism in the name of Jesus in no way lessened his conviction in the orthodox doctrine of a triune Godhead. He never emphasized the formula and does not seem to have considered it a crucial issue. However, by 1915 through a collection of events led primarily by Frank J. Ewart and Glenn A. Cook, the Pentecostal movement was rocked with controversy over not only the single baptismal formula but also the accompanying Unitarian denial of the Trinity. Ultimately the controversy resulted in almost a quarter of all Pentecostals separating into newly formed "Oneness" denominations. Though Parham never acknowledged the position himself, the Oneness organizers no doubt found a receptive audience among Pentecostals previously baptized by the Parhamite model.[25]

On one theological issue Parham had been isolated from mainstream Pentecostalism almost from the beginning. Since his association with David Baker in Tonganoxie, Kansas, he had rejected the idea of eternal punishment in hell on the simple logic that eternal existence was rewarded only to the righteous. Mankind received eternal life through the salvational power of Jesus Christ; those who rejected that salvation were punished in a literal burning hell which ultimately consumed them and ended their existence.[26] Though Parham taught the idea from the earliest years of his ministry, it never took root among Pentecostal pioneers outside his own faithful Apostolic Faith contingency. He argued in vain that "Conditional Immortality" and "Destruction of the Wicked" were original Pentecostal teachings consistent with scripture and a part of the latter-day revival's corrective to traditional theology.[27]

On another issue Parham was out of step because he refused to moderate what had been the hallmark of the Pentecostal revival itself. As late as 1908, many latter rain advocates were still hopeful that tongues would prove the agent

for a worldwide missions conquest. In short, glossolalia had
been confused with xenoglossa and Pentecostals quite naturally assumed that God would preach sermons of salvation to
the heathen in literally every known tongue. But by 1909
many had grown skeptical of this utilitarian function of the
Pentecostal gift. John G. Lake, a missionary to South Africa,
noted that native-born South Africans were generally better
equipped for mission work since they tended to be bilingual
from an early age.[28] Three years later, in October 1912, E. N.
Bell blasted the naive assumption of xenoglossic tongues and
issued an adamant call for more organized mission efforts, including trained missionaries.

Our people are tired, sick, and ashamed of traveling, sight-seeing
experimenting missionaries, who expect to make a trip around the
world and come home. . . . We want men to settle nown [*sic*] to
learn the language, to *establish assemblies* of saved people, to stay
with these, *teaching* them and *using* them to reach their own
people.[29]

Parham, however, clung tenaciously to the vision of world
conquest via mission tongues. He insisted that all authentic
tongue speech was xenoglossic and blamed the counterfeit
experiment of the newer Pentecostals for any failures in the
mission field. Despite Parham's claim that the phenomenon
worked well for missionaries he had sponsored, most Pentecostals abandoned the original interpretation in favor of a
moderate position which defined "heavenly languages" (i.e.,
glossolalia) as the norm and missionary tongues (i.e., xenoglossa) as the extraordinaire.[30]

In 1910, partly out of concern for the theological diversity
developing within Pentecostalism, Parham organized the National Camp Meeting in Baxter Springs. Essentially a forum
for his own followers, he billed the affair as a corrective to
"fanatical spiritualistic counterfeit movements."[31] One of the
highlights of the annual camp meeting was Parham's sermons
on eschatology. Though not substantially different from the
premillennial themes preached by other Pentecostals, his messages were more in-depth and more speculative with regard to

current world events. As early as 1899 he had shown a clear interest in the subject and had predicted an oncoming war between labor and capital. Researching the apocalyptic portions of scripture and available interpretations from within the premillennial camp, Parham dutifully labored in his 1902 publication *Kol Kare Bomidbar* to decipher the eschatological puzzle by placing the appropriate symbol with its corresponding nation.[32] As the years passed, he read with interest newspaper articles about developing tensions in Europe and took upon himself in 1912 the responsibility to write the royal heads of state and warn them of the impending prophetic struggle.[33]

When the European conflict erupted in 1914, Parham increased his eschatological comment. In April 1916 he changed the name of his monthly publication from the *Apostolic Faith* to the *Everlasting Gospel* and geared the articles toward the war and its relationship to biblical prophecy. By 1919 he published his second book, also entitled *The Everlasting Gospel*, and tailored a large portion of the text toward eschatological concerns such as the prophetic significance of Bolshevism and the League of Nations.[34] During the 1920s, Parham restored the original title to his journal and, like all premillennialists, decreased the amount of print given to the imminent eschaton. Nevertheless, the subject remained a lifelong passion; few Pentecostals could match Parham's knowledge and conviction concerning endtime chronology.[35]

On political and social issues Parham mirrored the ambiguity which lay behind the Pentecostal struggle for identity. Like most early Pentecostals he demonstrated a sense of alienation from the American system. At times he sounded closely akin to the Socialist leaders of the Midwest and clearly identified with their hostility toward capitalism.

The past order of civilization was upheld by the power of nationalism, which in turn was upheld by the spirit of patriotism, which divided the peoples of the world by geographical boundaries, over which each fought the other until they turned the world into a shamble. The ruling power of this old order has always been the rich, who exploited the masses for profit or drove them en masse to war, to perpetuate their misrule. The principle teachers of patriotism maintaining nationalism were the churches, who have lost their spiritual power and been forsaken of God.[36]

Revolutionary rhetoric in the pulpit did not always transfer to radical political alliances. Frustrated by the failure of Populist organizers to foment change through government channels, Parham determined that real justice could come only through divine intervention. Thus while the socialist cause was in some respects admirable, it was impractical and unnecessary. What interested Parham most about the social struggle was its role in God's endtime plan. He steered clear of political involvement, frequently advertising his lecture on "Christianity vs. Socialism" with the vague postscript: "He is a Christian, not a Socialist, but graduated from a School of Socialism."[37] Certain that the final answer would be a divine one, he advised his readers that "the cry of socialism . . . is the heart-cry to see Jesus."[38] Taking this apolitical stand served him well before Midwestern audiences who often favored the message of socialism but were equally influenced by the capitalistic message of the American Dream.[39]

Parham's response to World War I was equally enigmatic. His early position on warfare had been strictly pacifistic. He had opposed the Spanish-American War and American involvement in the Philippines. War volunteers, in his words, were "self-appointed murderers" who earn "less even than thirty pieces of silver, and purchance [sic] live to receive the plaudits and honor of more cowardly countrymen and an imbecile nation."[40] When America entered World War I, Parham urged his followers to file exemptions from combat service. Such exemptions, however, were not routinely granted to Pentecostals and several of Parham's closest associates were pressed into duty overseas.[41]

In November 1917, the *Apostolic Faith* temporarily halted publication when Rolland Romack, Parham's editor for the past six years, answered his draft notice and reported ultimately to the Allied front in France. Parham maintained a lively correspondence with his young friend until Romack was killed in action on September 19, 1918. The death had a notable impact on Parham's attitude toward the war. Reacting from grief, he initially considered enlisting to "avenge the death of one we loved so well." When his rage subsided, he purchased a liberty bond instead to show his support for "the great cause" for which Romack had died.[42]

In the 1920s Parham tempered his antiestablishment views even further. Concerned by the anarchy that seemed to pervade America after the war, he became increasingly critical of radical ideology. Already hardened on the race issue by his experience at Azusa in 1906, Parham felt no qualms at offering high praise for the reorganized Ku Klux Klan. The relationship was ironically similar to that which he had held with socialism a decade earlier. Parham admired many Klan leaders but considered their efforts ultimately fruitless since they lacked a purely spiritual agenda. He issued a call in 1927 to all members of the "invisible empire" to coordinate their "high ideals for the betterment of mankind" with the genuine Pentecostal restoration of "Old Time Religion."[43]

On education and higher learning, Parham perfectly demonstrated the paradoxical attitudes of Pentecostal pioneers. Intense anger and frustration at the educational elite who belittled his movement as simplistic and chaotic merged with a sense of awe and respect for the accomplishments of the well educated. In 1905 Parham featured an article in his journal which aptly described one reader's skepticism of college-trained professionals:

Here comes a *college* doctor, a *college* lawyer and a *college* preacher, and the devil, their friend and brother! . . . Now his three friends will get down to business in some city; each one putting up a sign reading something like this: Doctor Curem; Lawyer Knowall, and Preacher Good. . . . Reader, have you a son at home? If you have, keep him there, and away from all high schools and colleges, and raise him in the fear of God, as Abraham brought up his son Isaac.[44]

Parham himself displayed a similar hostility, citing with aplomb the liabilities of those trained in "cemetaries" with "die-plomas" which christened them "G.D.'s—Greedy Dogs

. . . and D.D.'s—Dumb Dogs."[45] He related with pride his response to a Baptist preacher, with "a Ph.D., D.D., and L.L.D. on the hind end of his name," who tried to convince one of the Apostolic Faith followers that people cannot speak true foreign languages without formally learning them.

I challenged that preacher to come to my school for just one week. I promised him a post graduate course that would enable him to put another degree on the end of his name. I would have gotten him so humble before God, and so willing to let God use him, that he would have come out of the post graduate course with A.S.S., on the end of his name. Could I have gotten him to become as humble as was Balaam's mule, God would have talked through him in tongues.[46]

Yet the rhetoric was a mask. Behind it lay the insecurities developed when ambitious youthful plans did not develop quite as expected. Parham actually admired authority and quoted respected authors whenever possible. He read a much wider variety of literature than the average person of his day and was respected by his followers precisely because he held greater knowledge. Like other Pentecostal leaders he established schools—institutions designed to perpetuate certain ideas and to give their graduates a level of respect above that of the average member of the religious community. In short, Parham, and most Pentecostals, imitated those whom they criticized. Desperately, if unconsciously, they needed status and status, by definition, came through certain procedures.[47]

In December 1927 Parham embarked on a long-awaited trip to the Holy Land. Already in declining health, he made the three-month journey alone with funds raised by friends intent on making his lifelong dream come true. His earlier dream of digging for ancient biblical relics abandoned, he spent the three months traveling in a tour group and reveling in the sights of historic Palestine. Along the way he managed to write extensive letters for publication in the *Apostolic Faith,* preach several sermons in American missions, and baptize an old acquaintance from his work in California in the Jordan river.[48]

He returned to the States in April 1928 and arrived home in Baxter Springs in early May. Soon he was on the road again, armed with a selection of slides purchased in the Holy Land and prepared to give audiences a thrilling account of his adventure.[49] Yet Parham's body proved unable to rise to the task at hand. While in Jerusalem he had suffered intense chest pain and had been forced to schedule regular rest periods between his daily tours. Though only fifty-five years old in the summer of 1928, he found himself in increasingly poor health. The lifetime struggle with rheumatic fever, despite long periods of remission, had caused significant heart damage. In January 1929 he was forced to cancel the remainder of his scheduled appointments after suffering periods of unconsciousness during a service at Temple, Texas. He returned to Baxter Springs for bed rest and rapidly his condition worsened.[50]

On the afternoon of January 29, Charles Parham died. True to his convictions, he refused in his final hours to take any medicine for the relief of pain.[51] His death received only minor national attention through an obituary in the *New York Times*. Nonetheless, despite a severe snowstorm, twenty-five hundred people attended his funeral held in the local Baxter Springs theater. Shortly after the funeral, Apostolic Faith followers erected an impressive monument shaped like a pulpit over his gravestone. The tribute reminded the world through its inscription that Parham was the "Founder of the Apostolic Faith Movement."[52]

The memorial meant little for the majority of Pentecostals in 1929; the man who had established their theological identity almost three decades earlier had been lost amidst scandal and doctrinal debate. The mass endtime revival that had promised Christian unity in 1901 had failed to materialize. Instead, a divided movement of Pentecostal sects, peopled largely by the working class and the undereducated, emerged and slowly embarked on the trek toward denominational respectability. The ironic twist would be that the post-World War II success of those denominations would salvage Charles Parham's reputation and establish him as an important religious pioneer of the twentieth century.

Conclusion

Pentecost and the Legacy
of Charles Parham

Parham's death left the small Apostolic Faith affiliation in disarray. The revivals and annual camp meetings depended heavily on his charismatic presence and, particularly, on the friendships he had built through three decades of preaching. The absence of any coherent organization made holding the alliance together a formidable task. Sarah Parham inherited the position of leadership almost by default. She commanded respect throughout the Apostolic Faith fellowship and had, on occasion, taken the pulpit herself. Upon her husband's death she became editor of the *Apostolic Faith* and provided publicity for the traveling evangelists and ministers who served the local congregations.

But Sarah Parham was not alone. Ultimately three of her four sons became ministers. In 1923 Wilfred Parham had begun traveling with his father as an active worker and Apostolic Faith preacher. Two years later he met and married Alice Wilson, pastor of the Foursquare Gospel Church in Pomona, California. The newlyweds formed an evangelistic team and traveled throughout the United States, occasionally teaming with the elder Parham in citywide meetings. Though Wilfred Parham officially joined the Foursquare Gospel denomination, he remained a regular speaker in Apostolic Faith circles.[1]

Parham's youngest son, Robert, accepted the "call" to preach in January 1929 while Charles Parham lay on his deathbed. With his wife, Pauline, Robert picked up the bulk of his father's annual schedule and held revivals and camp meetings in virtually every region of the country.[2] Claude Wallace Parham, the eldest son, made a somewhat belated entry into the ministry in the 1930s when he and his wife, Lula, began supplementing Robert Parham's schedule with evangelistic campaigns of their own.[3]

More than anyone else Robert Parham accepted the mantle of his father's ministry. In addition to the evangelistic work, he aided his mother in coordinating church activities and in publishing the *Apostolic Faith*. In early 1937 the Parham homeplace was converted into a short-term Bible school to train new ministers and provide training for lay workers. Robert directed the Bible school with the help of his mother and the popular Oklahoma evangelist Gail Schultz. With Sarah Parham's death later that same year, the young man assumed full editorial responsibilities and stood as the logical successor to fill his parents' leadership roles.[4]

Despite Robert Parham's efforts, the glorious past of the Apostolic Faith movement was not reborn. Membership remained relatively small despite some growth during the depression years of the 1930s.[5] Charles Parham's distaste for organization contributed to the sect's unspectacular growth. Most Pentecostal churches had been organized into denominations for years. Organizational structure allowed them to coordinate the church growth that came during the depression. Robert Parham considered the same sort of action. He also advocated closer ties with other Pentecostals and did not actively promote the unorthodox ideas of "destruction of the wicked" and "conditional immortality."[6] However, a generation of Pentecostals bred on the philosophy that organization brought "worldliness" and spiritual bankruptcy could hardly be expected to suddenly embrace central control and worship alongside those who had settled for a "counterfeit" experience. Given time, perhaps Robert Parham might have succeeded. Second generation Pentecostals like himself were much more likely to see the need for moderate change. But time proved to be the one thing the youngest Parham would not have. He died of a heart attack in 1944, not yet thirty-eight years old.[7]

In the late 1940s the Apostolic Faith movement suffered divisions over the issues Robert Parham had hoped to handle peacefully. By that time a new generation of healing evangelists were raising the visibility of Pentecostalism across the nation. William Branham, Oral Roberts, and others fashioned an evangelistic message of healing and Holy Ghost power not unlike that which Charles Parham himself had preached decades before. Yet to older members of the Apostolic Faith the new brand of Pentecostalism was emotionalism at its worst. They were convinced that a real difference existed between these sawdust-strewn revivals and the ones they had known years ago. Younger ministers supported the work of the evangelists, however, arguing that God worked through these individuals for the good of all Pentecostal believers. Also at issue was the question of increased organization. Younger ministers argued for a stronger central base complete with elected officers and a structured financial system. The old guard preferred the purity of strict local autonomy without organizational strings of any kind.[8]

In the early 1950s these disagreements led to an open rupture within the Apostolic Faith fellowship. Representatives from affiliated churches met in Spearman, Texas, in 1951 to resolve the issues. An evenly divided caucus resulted in schism. Many of the younger ministers, including Robert Parham's widow Pauline, bolted the fellowship and rescinded their ties with the *Apostolic Faith* journal and the Bible School in Baxter Springs. Subsequently they formed the Full Gospel Evangelistic Association which fostered a tolerant view toward the healing evangelists and allowed for greater organization, including structured offerings during worship services. A total of 136 ministers and eighty-three churches in thirteen states divided with slightly less than half opting for the new organization.[9]

Over thirty years later the two groups remain apart. The Full Gospel Evangelistic Association claims 134 ministers and thirty-one "member churches" and mission stations. There are about an equal number of "cooperating churches"; however, statistics for those groups are unavailable. Estimates of church members affiliated with the association are arbitrary since those figures are also not listed, but forty-five hundred is probably a fair assessment. The membership churches are loosely organized for the purpose of a cooperative foreign missions effort and support of the Midwest Bible Institute in Houston, Texas. Although centered in the South-Central United States, the organization is global in its outreach and maintains a fairly cooperative approach toward other Pentecostal groups. Theologically, the association maintains a faith statement virtually synonymous with the beliefs of the bulk of Wesleyan-Pentecostal denominations.[10]

Parham's namesake association in Baxter Springs is slightly smaller, with 109 ministers and approximately fifty churches. It probably has a total membership of about thirty-five hundred. These churches, also centered in the South-Central United States, have no general officers or yearly business meetings but tend to support the Apostolic Faith Bible College in Baxter Springs and an annual camp meeting held alternately in Baxter Springs and Laverne, Oklahoma.[11] The Apostolic Faith fellowship maintains Parham's firm denunciation of organized offerings and insists that authentic tongue speech is xenoglossic. Also unique among Pentecostals is their perpetuation of the "destruction of the wicked" and "conditional immortality" doctrine.[12]

Charles Parham's direct legacy, then, is scant. Less than ten thousand of the world's estimated fifty-one million Pentecostals have a direct link with the last twenty years of his thirty-six year ministry. Yet Parham's importance cannot be gauged by those figures. More than anyone else, he forged the movement which has mushroomed in the second half of the twentieth century. Parham was one of many ministers influenced by the evangelical "Spirit age" of the late nineteenth century and the accompanying thirst for divine power. Like a host of others he preached a message of radical conversion which promised hope to the dispossessed. Disillusioned by political methods and society's standards of progress, he adopted from his contemporaries a trio of religious doctrines—sanctification of sinful human nature, divine healing of all bodily weaknesses, and millenarian justice through a soon-coming Christ. But it was Parham alone who formulated the distinguishing ideological formula of tongues as initial evidence for Holy Spirit baptism. That discovery, in effect, created the Pentecostal movement. It set Pentecostals apart from the overall pneumatic revival by tying them to a stricter theological creed and, more than any other feature, served as their identifying badge within an often hostile community of Christian denominations.

Parham also infused the movement with a zeal for missions. Xenoglossic tongues provided the key to an endtime missions thrust which would close the last of God's historical dispensations—the church age. Pentecostal preaching via tongues would draw unbelievers to gospel truth in a glorious eleventh-hour revival, after which God's eschaton would shower the faithful with eternal joy. Later Pentecostals altered the definition slightly to include glossolalic tongues, but the essential features of initial evidence and endtime missions remained intact. As a result, Pentecostalism, born at the turn of the twentieth century, became the sleeping religious giant of the twentieth century.

Convinced that time was short and that the mission fields of the world were now ripened for an endtime harvest of souls, Pentecostal evangelists and missionaries forged on in spite of limited funds and rough-hewn talents. Their message, buoyed by demonstrable displays of spiritual power, found converts. By midcentury, they had created sizable denominations and institutions worldwide. A byproduct of the growth after 1960 was the Charismatic movement, a related but fundamentally different movement. Charismatics accepted some of the principles of Pentecostalism but, by and large, rejected the theological rigor inherent in the initial tongues doctrine.

Though spawned by interest in the fast-growing Pentecostals, these mainline churchmen were theologically more akin to Parham's predecessors—the evangelical disciples of the Spirit age. Nevertheless, their acceptance of the validity of charismata in twentieth century church life brought increased respectability to Pentecostals and encouraged their goal of global conquest.

Charles Parham is also significant because he mirrors the complex origins of Pentecostal growth. Fused with the intellectual roots of biblicism, holiness theology, divine healing, and millenarianism were a parallel series of social forces. Biblicism reflected alienation from modernist thought. Holiness theology presupposed, at least in part, dislocation from contemporary lifestyles. The attractiveness of divine healing in American society revealed the presence of both physical and psychological pain. Millenarianism prospered on the heels of political discontent as campaigns and candidates gave way to a spiritual rendition of social justice.

Parham and his Pentecostal successors were thus the products of both ideological and social forces. They consciously sought a theology rooted in the traditional authority of scriptural exegesis and early church practice. Their interpretation of those sources merged with their devotional experience to confirm the hardened theological definition of Holy Spirit baptism evidenced by glossolalia. All the while, they preached a message which met the needs of people in social flux. The social thesis waxes strong in Pentecostal origins. All Americans were affected, to varying degrees, by disappointments and the rapid forces of change in the nineteenth century. Yet when combined with conviction of religious truth, those forces provided an increased incentive to touch the divine. Collectively, they help to explain how a phenomenon like Pentecostalism attracted and comforted so many.

Finally, Charles Parham symbolizes the determination of the individual religious spirit. Weak from birth, he overcame innumerable physical obstacles and became an example of the human capacity to conquer adversity. Disenchanted with the religious status quo, he left the security of a firm denominational structure to launch an independent healing ministry and to begin a search for the consummate spiritual experience. Despite embarrassing rumors of immorality, he maintained a visible profile among a sizable segment of America's Midwestern population. And long after most Pentecostals had moderated their vision of xenoglossic tongues for end-time missions, Parham clung steadfastly to the optimism of global conquest by divinely inspired messengers. Courageous, innovative, implacable, and pugnacious, he stands as an example of the admirable, if disconcerting, qualities of generations of American evangelists.

Convinced that he personally stood at the center of the Creator's plan for eschatological salvation, Charles Parham dared to proclaim a radical new experience of Holy Spirit baptism as normative for twentieth-century Christians. He drew from the expectations of endtime power promised by late nineteenth century evangelicals and harnessed his new experience with the theological firmness of the initial tongues doctrine. Ultimately, the success of the new movement over its first three generations made him an important historical figure.

Equally intriguing, however, is the religious motivation that convinced Parham of his message. Although the most difficult factor to define, this impulse is fundamental to any religious prophet. The religious impulse allows the prophet to defy logic and endure despite frequent failure. Called into service by God, his life assumes purpose and meaning far beyond that of ordinary human beings. Atop this lofty perch any difficulty seems manageable and all success looms large. Charles Parham tasted success only amidst a lifetime of difficulties, discouragements, and disappointments. But like others before and after him, he acknowledged only the success. When one talks to God, success can come in strange and inexplicable ways.

Appendices, Notes, Sources, and Index

Appendix A

Estimate of Apostolic Faith
Followers in mid-1906

Estimates of Parham's following in the Midwest during the initial five years of the Pentecostal movement are extremely contradictory due to the rapid rate of growth and the lack of any consistent organizational framework. Figures range from one thousand to twenty-five thousand. The lower estimate seems totally unjustified since Howard Goss noted as early as 1916 that over one thousand people in Texas alone had received Holy Spirit baptism before the Azusa revival broke in April 1906 [Lawrence, p. 66]. The higher estimate is equally unreliable. Parham first claimed the twenty-five thousand figure two decades after the fact in an article in which he erroneously stated that Seymour had attended his Houston school "daily for three months" [*Apostolic Faith* (Baxter) 2 (July 1926):5].

Nevertheless, historians have generally based their accounts on one of these two dubious estimates. Stanley Frodsham cited Goss but interpreted his one thousand spirit-filled saints as a national figure rather than an estimate of the work in Texas, though Goss clearly referred only to Texas [Frodsham, p. 29]. The error was later repeated by Michael Harper [Harper, p. 25]. The more optimistic estimate of Parham's was accepted uncritically by Vinson Synan, Howard Kenyon, Morris Golder, and Richard Quebedeaux [Synan, *Latter Days*, p. 48; Kenyon, p. 20; Golder, p. 22; and Quebedeaux, p. 29].

A careful analysis of other primary sources indicates that a more accurate estimate of Parham's movement in 1906 should fall somewhere between those figures. In September, a Waukegan, Illinois, newspaper listed Parham's following as five thousand and noted that they were mainly in Kansas and California [*Waukegan Daily Sun,* 26 September 1906, 7]. Earlier, in March, Parham's own *Apostolic Faith* had claimed a somewhat higher number of twelve thousand—though the figure is less than half that he remembered twenty years later [*Apostolic Faith* (Melrose-Houston) 1 (March 1906):6]. Seymour quoted a similar figure of thirteen thousand in the inaugural issue of the Los Angeles journal [*Apostolic Faith* (Los Angeles) 1 (September 1906):1]. It is likely that both Parham's and Seymour's figures are inflated; however, the newspaper account is equally suspect since it doesn't acknowledge Parham's extensive work in Texas.

A reasonable estimate of eight to ten thousand may be reached by taking a combination of factors into consideration. In the first place, only a percentage of Parham's followers would have actually received the Baptism of the Holy Spirit. If modern day Pentecostals are a correct gauge, only one-half of all active Apostolic Faith followers would have received that experience (see introduction, p. 4). In addition, a large number of regular attenders would have stopped short of the commitment of active membership. Thus a guess at the number of people who regularly attended Parham's campaigns and loosely affiliated with his ministry could have easily been as high as four times the number of spirit-filled believers. This assessment is supported by the experience at Azusa Street where, in September 1906, 150 had received Holy Spirit baptism but crowd attendance had swelled to over one thousand (see chapter 5, p. 194). Applying this rule of thumb to Goss' estimate, the Texas following would increase to four thousand. Allowing for at least an equal number of followers in the Kansas-Missouri area (supported by Parham's decision to create two separate state organizations there), Parham's Midwestern following is judged to be around eight thousand.

Added to that number would be the followers loosely affiliated with Azusa Street. The same formula would suggest six hundred active Azusa participants by August 1906. That figure would not conflict with occasional crowd sizes of over one thousand. Seymour's assessment of thirteen thousand in September 1906 was probably an optimistic estimate of one thousand for his own mission added to Parham's recent estimate of twelve thousand. At any rate, eighty-six hundred would be a conservative estimate of "active" followers; both Parham and Seymour had certainly attracted an additional number of curious onlookers.

Appendix B

Parham's Break with Azusa Street as Recorded in the Apostolic Faith Los Angeles

Parham's break with the Azusa Street revival is evident in the pages of the *Apostolic Faith* (Los Angeles). The Azusa-based journal credited Parham in its inaugural issue as "God's leader in the Apostolic Faith Movement" [1 (September 1906):1]. The October issue gave a glowing biographical sketch of the Kansas evangelist and detailed his importance in developing Pentecostal doctrine [1 (October 1906):1]. The November issue, however, conspicuously omitted any reference to Parham. Significantly, the publishing name was changed without explanation from "The Apostolic Faith Movement of Los Angeles" to "The Pacific Apostolic Faith Movement, Headquarters, Los Angeles" [1 (November 1906):2]. The December issue then opened with a clear-cut statement of independence: "Many are asking how the work in Azusa Mission started and who was the founder. The Lord was the founder and He is the Projector of this movement." [1 (December 1906):1]. With no mention of the Midwestern roots, a brief history of the Azusa Street revival followed. The scenario now centered only on the local saints who had sparked Seymour's success. The article subsequently added:

Some are asking if Dr. Chas. F. Parham is the leader of this movement. We can answer, no he is not the leader of this movement of Azusa Mission. We thought of having him to be our leader and so stated in our paper, before waiting on the Lord. We can be rather hasty when we are very young in the power of the Holy Spirit. We are just like a baby—full of love—and were willing to accept anyone that had the baptism with the Holy Spirit as our leader. But the Lord commenced settling us down, and we saw that the Lord should be our leader. So we honor Jesus as the great Shepherd of the sheep. He is our model." [1 (December 1906):1, quoted in Nelson, p. 212].

[Note: The most available reprint of the Azusa papers—Fred T. Corum, comp., *Like as of Fire* (Wilmington, Massachusetts: By the Compiler, 1981)—contains only the top half of page one and thus omits this final quote.]

Appendix C

Shifts in Pentecostal Theology after Charles Parham

Charles Parham fused three theological planks into the first Pentecostal doctrine: 1) Tongue speech as the initial evidence of Holy Spirit baptism, 2) Spirit-filled believers as the "sealed" Bride of Christ, and 3) Xenoglossic tongues as the tool for a dramatic end-time revival. Parham retained all three beliefs throughout his lifetime but Pentecostals after 1910 have gradually rejected the last two. Only tongues as initial evidence survived in its original form.

Occasional claims of xenoglossa date to after 1910 but increasingly those occurrences were interpreted as infrequent miracles while the more "normal" tongue speech involved "divine languages" (i.e. unknown tongues or, technically, glossolalia). Thus the missionary context of tongue speech was lost. Coincidentally, many Pentecostals softened their stance on requirements for bridal membership though this plank was not totally abandoned by all. More often than not, Pentecostals simply avoided making such a blanket statement out of fear of creating an elitist attitude among spirit-filled believers. Nevertheless, the assumption that Holy Spirit baptism is at least a prerequisite for bridal membership is a widely-held belief among Pentecostals today. [Note: For a fuller discussion of these changes, see Goff, "Pentecostal Millenarianism," pp. 14–24. In this early research article, I erroneously noted that Parham later changed his position that Holy Spirit baptism must be evidenced by tongues (p. 22). Further research revealed that Parham did not change his position, but was merely distinguishing between "Holy Spirit annointing" and Holy Spirit baptism. Parham, and most later

Pentecostals, taught that believers receive an annointing of the Holy Spirit at conversion with subsequent annointings available to them thereafter. The Baptism of the Holy Spirit, however, was taught as a distinct experience which included tongues as the initial evidence of reception. See Parham, *Everlasting Gospel,* pp. 16–18, 63–69.]

Notes

Introduction

[1] David B. Barrett, ed., *World Christian Encyclopedia* (Oxford: Oxford University Press, 1982), p. 838 and Richard N. Ostling, "Counting Every Soul On Earth" *Time* (May 3, 1982): 67.

[2] Henry P. Van Dusen, "The Third Force in Christendom" *Life* (June 9, 1958): 124. Sydney Ahlstrom's celebrated religious survey obviously underestimated Pentecostals, noting their worldwide numbers for 1970 at eight million with one and a half million in the United States. *A Religious History of the American People* (New Haven and London: Yale University Press, 1972), pp. 819–22. Barrett's estimate for 1970 is 36,794,000 (Barrett, p. 838).

[3] These figures come from a *Christianity Today*-Gallup Poll survey reported in Kenneth S. Kantzer, "The Charismatics Among Us" *Christianity Today* 24 (February 22, 1980): 25–29.

[4] Barrett, p. 838. Barrett's definition is tailored toward the loose theological construction of the Charismatic movement.

[5] For a discussion of the issues involved in Pentecostal-Charismatic dialogue, see Ray H. Hughes, "A Traditional Pentecostal looks at the New Pentecostals" *Christianity Today* 18 (June 7, 1974): 6–10.

[6] Kantzer, p. 26.

[7] This is the presentation of Pentecostalist Vinson Synan in *In the Latter Days: The Outpouring of the Holy Spirit in the Twentieth Century* (Ann Arbor, Michigan: Servant Books, 1984).

[8] The census figure is from Barrett, p. 818. On Korea, see Colin Whittaker, "The Korean Pentecost" *Dedication* 9: 20–22. On Latin America, see Emilio Willems, "Religious Mass Movements and Social Change in Brazil" in E. N. Baklanoff, ed. *New Perspectives of Brazil* (Nashville: Vanderbilt University Press, 1966), pp. 205–32 and *Followers of the New Faith* (Nashville: Vanderbilt University Press, 1967), pp. 118–53. Also Christian Lalive D'Epinay, "The Pentecostal 'Conquista' in Chile" *Ecumenical Review* (1968): 16–32. On the worldwide growth in general, see Peter Wagner,

"The Greatest Church Growth is Beyond Our Shores" *Christianity Today* 28 (May 18, 1984): 25–31.

⁹On the Wesleyan holiness movement, see Melvin Easterday Dieter, *The Holiness Revival of the Nineteenth Century* (Metuchen, New Jersey and London: Scarecrow Press, 1980); Charles Edwin Jones, *Perfectionist Persuasion: The Holiness Movement and American Methodism, 1867–1936* (Metuchen, New Jersey: Scarecrow Press, 1974); and Vinson Synan, *The Holiness-Pentecostal Movement in the United States* (Grand Rapids, Michigan: William B. Eerdman's Publishing Co., 1971), pp. 13–54.

¹⁰On the Reformed-Pentecostals and their roots, see Edith Lydia Waldvogel, "The 'Overcoming Life': A Study in the Reformed Evangelical Origins of Pentecostalism" (Ph.D. dissertation, Harvard University, 1977), pp. 14–148 and William W. Menzies, "The Non-Wesleyan Origins of the Pentecostal Movement" in Vinson Synan, ed., *Aspects of Pentecostal-Charismatic Origins* (Plainfield, New Jersey: Logos International, 1975), pp. 81–98.

¹¹On the oneness-Pentecostals, see Frank J. Ewart, *The Phenomenon of Pentecost* rev. ed. (Hazelwood, Missouri: Word Aflame Press, 1975), pp. 108–34; Arthur L. Clanton, *United We Stand* (Hazelwood, Missouri: Pentecostal Publishing House, 1970), pp. 13–34; and David Reed, "Aspects of the Origins of Oneness Pentecostalism" in Synan, *Aspects,* pp. 145–68.

¹²William Warren Sweet, *The Story of Religion in America* rev. ed. (New York: Harper and Bros., 1950), p. 422.

¹³Winthrop S. Hudson, *Religion in America* 2nd ed. (New York: Charles Scribner's Sons, 1973), p. 346.

¹⁴Synan, *Latter Days,* p. 20. The 1986 figure comes from denominational records for "active adherence." Stricter formal membership in 1986 totaled a still impressive 1,258,724. Telephone interview with Wayne Warner, Archivist, Assemblies of God Headquarters, Springfield Missouri, 18 March 1988.

¹⁵Major treatments of Pentecostalism have agreed with the central thesis of a Parham-Seymour connection and have credited Parham with the theological roots and Seymour with the evangelistic outreach. See John Thomas Nichol, *Pentecostalism* (New York, et al.: Harper and Row, 1966), pp. 26–39; Nils Bloch-Hoell, *The Pentecostal Movement* (Oslo: Universitetsforlaget; London: Allen and Unwin; New York: Humanities Press, 1964), pp. 18–52; and Walter J. Hollenweger, *The Pentecostals* (Minneapolis: Augsburg

Publishing House, 1972), pp. 22–24. Hollenweger's work remains the most in-depth global treatment of Pentecostalism.

¹⁶ Anderson's is the most sophisticated treatment of social dislocation as a key to unlocking Pentecostal origins. His work presupposes that of sociologists who study the intergroup dynamics of similar religious sects; for example, see Luther P. Gerlach and Virginia H. Hine, *People, Power, Change: Movements of Social Transformation* (Indianapolis: Bobbs-Merril Educational Publishing Co., 1970). Anderson's work is compatible with Waldvogel's in that he emphasizes the Reformed roots of Pentecostalism. Synan's Wesleyan argument has received support in a recent dissertation by Donald R. Wheelock, "Spirit Baptism In American Pentecostal Thought" (Ph.D. dissertation, Emory University, 1983).

¹⁷ Douglas J. Nelson, "For Such A Time as This: The Story of Bishop William J. Seymour and the Azusa Street Revival" (Ph.D. dissertation, University of Birmingham, England, 1981). Nelson's treatment suffers from the romanticism involved in a historically defamed Seymour, victim of white prejudice, now under rescue by the author to rewrite the book on American Pentecostalism. Under close scrutiny, Nelson aborts his own thesis in admitting that early white Pentecostals were unwilling to obliterate the color line and that non-Pentecostal blacks, such as W. E. B. DuBois, were already championing integration. Cf. pp. 71, 81, 88–89, 94, and 102. Other writers who have stressed Seymour's prominence as founder and the importance of interracial worship are Leonard Lovett, "Black Holiness-Pentecostalism: Implications For Ethics and Social Transformation" (Ph.D. dissertation, Emory University, 1978); James Maynard Shopshire, "A Socio-Historical Characterization of the Black Pentecostal Movement in America" (Ph.D. dissertation, Northwestern University, 1975); and James S. Tinney in Randall K. Burkett and Richard Newman, eds. *Black Apostles: Afro-American Clergy Confront the Twentieth Century* (Boston: G. K. Hall and Co., 1978), pp. 213–25. Tinney goes so far as to suggest that Seymour, not Parham, introduced the link between Holy Spirit baptism and tongues (p. 214), though there is no evidence given for the claim and no other Pentecostal writer has offered any support.

¹⁸ Grant Wacker has best demonstrated the religious significance of healing within the Pentecostal tradition. Recognizing the existence of purely religious motivations in the rise of the movement, he

notes that "the true significance of divine healing and other miracle experiences is that they have functioned as sacraments, palpable symbols, of those rare but unforgettable moments of grace in the life of the believer." "Into Canaan's Fair Land: Brokenness and Healing in the Pentecostal Tradition," in Ronald Numbers and Darryl Amundsen, *To Care and To Cure: Health and Healing in the Faith Tradition* (New York: Macmillan Co., forthcoming).

[19] My analysis differs markedly with that of Bloch-Hoell who noted that eschatology was important but not of "unusual importance" among Pentecostals (Bloch-Hoell, pp. 87–88). The millenarian emphasis, at least for first generation Pentecostals, was crucial. Cf. James R. Goff, Jr., "Pentecostal Millenarianism: The Development of Premillennial Orthodoxy, 1909–43" *Ozark Historical Review* 12 (Spring 1983): 14–24. On the rise of millenarian doctrine in the United States, see J. F. C. Harrison, *The Second Coming: Popular Millenarianism, 1780–1850* (New Brunswick, New Jersey: Rutgers University Press, 1979). The best treatment of millenarian thought in the late nineteenth and early twentieth centuries is Timothy P. Weber, *Living in the Shadow of the Second Coming* (New York and Oxford: Oxford University Press, 1979).

[20] Prior to Parham's theological formulation, "Pentecostal" had been used quite frequently by holiness groups as a synonym for sanctification. In 1919, the Church of the Nazarene (a holiness body) dropped the word from their name to clearly separate their organization from the tongue-speaking Pentecostals. Timothy L. Smith, *Called Unto Holiness* (Kansas City, Missouri: Nazarene Publishing House, 1962), pp. 319–20.

[21] Nichol, p. 81. Also cited in Howard Nelson Kenyon, "An Analysis of Racial Separation Within the Early Pentecostal Movement" (M.A. thesis, Baylor University, 1978), p. 22. Actually Parham's editorial work in Topeka should be classified as holiness; he was not yet Pentecostal. The first Pentecostal edition of the journal dates to 1905 when Parham reorganized the publication and issued it from Melrose, Kansas. See chapter 4, p. 99–100.

[22] Frank J. Ewart, *The Phenomenon of Pentecost* (St. Louis: Pentecostal Publishing House, 1947), pp. 30–35 and Klaude Kendrick, *The Promise Fulfilled: A History of the Modern Pentecostal Movement* (Springfield, Missouri: Gospel Publishing House, 1961), pp. 37–64. A short analysis emphasizing Parham's role is James R. Goff, Jr., "Charles F. Parham and His Role in the Development of the Pentecostal Movement: A Reevaluation" *Kansas History* 7 (Au-

tumn 1984):226–37. One of the earliest histories credits Parham
but tends to downplay his contribution in favor of his successors.
See Bennet F. Lawrence, *The Apostolic Faith Restored* (St. Louis:
Gospel Publishing House, 1916), pp. 52–68. For examples of Pen-
tecostal historians who refer to Parham's work without mentioning
his name, see Stanley H. Frodsham, *With Signs Following* 3rd ed.
(Springfield, Missouri: Gospel Publishing House, 1946), pp. 19–29;
Donald Gee, *The Pentecostal Movement* (London: Elim Publishing
Co., 1949), pp. 11–17; and G. H. Montgomery, "The Origin and
Development of the Pentecostal Movement" *Pentecostal Holiness
Advocate* (March 14, 1946):3–5, 10.

[23] Charles William Shumway, "A Study of 'The Gift of Tongues'"
(A.B. thesis, University of Southern California, 1914), pp. 164–71;
Nichol, pp. 26–32; and Anderson, pp. 47–61.

[24] For this type of presentation, see Donald Gee, "Movement
Without a Man" *Christian Life* 28 (July 1966):27–29; Carl Brumback, *A Sound From Heaven* (Springfield, Missouri: Gospel Publishing House, 1977), pp. 55–61; and Kenyon, p. 8. Pentecostals
have often tried to create a historical link to apostolic Christianity
by noting the periodic appearance of glossolalia in church history
since the Acts 2 phenomenon. In 1946, G. H. Montgomery traced
the movement specifically to A.D. 30 "at about 9 A.M., May 28"
(Montgomery, p. 3).

[25] For the spontaneous theories, see John L. Sherrill, *They Speak
With Other Tongues* (New York: Pillar Books, 1964), pp. 44–46;
W. H. Turner, *Pentecost and Tongues* 2nd ed. (Franklin Springs,
Georgia: Advocate Press, 1968), pp. 97–115; and *Historical Ac-
count of the Apostolic Faith* (Portland, Oregon: Apostolic Faith
Publishing House, 1965), p. 19.

[26] See William S. Merricks, *Edward Irving: The Forgotten
Giant* (East Peoria, Illinois: Scribe's Chamber Publications, 1983),
pp. 179–262; J. Edwin Orr, *The Flaming Tongue* (Chicago: Moody
Press, 1975), pp. 178–85; Larry Christianson, "Pentecostalism's
Forgotten Forerunner" in Synan, *Aspects*, pp. 15–37; and Charles
W. Conn, *Like a Mighty Army* (Cleveland, Tennessee: Church of
God Publishing House, 1955), pp. 3–55. On the implausibility of
this approach, see Waldvogel, pp. 9–10; William W. Menzies, *An-
nointed to Serve: The Story of the Assemblies of God* (Springfield,
Missouri: Gospel Publishing House, 1971), pp. 39–40; and Harold
Hunter, "Spirit-Baptism and the 1896 Revival in Cherokee County,
North Carolina" *Pneuma* 5 (Fall 1983):3.

²⁷This is the essential position contained in Synan, *Holiness-Pentecostal Movement,* pp. 95–116.

²⁸Glossolalia—glossa (tongues) + lalia (to speak)—is used specifically to mean unintelligible syllables uttered by Pentecostals as a phenomenon associated with an intense religious experience. It is often expressed within Pentecostal circles as "heavenly language" or "unknown tongues." Xenoglossa is used to indicate an actual existing language which the speaker is privileged to utter without any apparent previous knowledge of the mechanics of that language. The word is derived from xeno (foreign) + glossa (tongues). Here I follow the practice of Anderson (pp. 16–19) who uses xenoglossy and William J. Samarin [*Tongues of Men and Angels* (New York: MacMillan Co., 1972), pp. 109–15] who uses xenoglossia. Harold Hunter, on the other hand, uses xenolalia for the same term (p. 13). The correct derivative, of course, would be xenoglossolalia but the term is too laborious.

²⁹Anderson, pp. 90–92. Pentecostal writers have failed to note the extent of the mission tongues concept, often attributing it to a few eccentrics—most notably, Parham. See Synan, *Holiness-Pentecostal Movement,* p. 103, n. 19 and Morris E. Golder, *History of the Pentecostal Assemblies of the World* (Indianapolis: By the author, 1973).

1

¹Here I am not offering a revamping of the much-maligned "Turner thesis." Rather, I am simply submitting that the late-nineteenth-century frontier was a region of instability. New arrivals were forced to cope with changes in environment and, often, in lifestyle. Most importantly, their sense of security was threatened by the break with their cultural roots. Religion then became, for some at least, an important factor in coping with the changes and adjustments brought on by their frontier experience.

²On Parham genealogy, I am indebted to Byron A. Parham of the National Archives and Records Service for information on the origins of the Parham name. "The name is English and geographical in its origin (as opposed to occupational, viz., Miller, Smith, etc.). It first appeared in written form in the Doomsday Book of William I,

in an entry for Suffolk County, and it means a hamlet where pears grow (pear + ham). . . . Its present-day English pronunciation is still "Pear-rhum"; here in the U.S., it is more likely to be pronounced "Parr-rhum." Parham also notes the relatively small number of Parhams in the United States. In 1960, the Social Security Administration listed 23,000; the current number is still estimated at less than 100,000. Letter from Byron A. Parham, Supervisory Archivist, General Services Administration, National Archives and Records Service, Washington, D.C., 23 August 1984.

[3] The most comprehensive work on Parham is the biography written by his wife, Sarah E. Parham, *The Life of Charles F. Parham* (Joplin, Missouri: Tri-State Printing Co., 1930; reprint ed., Birmingham, Alabama: Commercial Printing Co., 1977). Though hagiographical, the work remains valuable as a source of varied contributions by Parham's followers and as a detailed chronology of his life and ministry. There is an interesting entry on William Parham in Alfred T. Andreas, *History of the State of Kansas* (Chicago: A. T. Andreas, 1883), p. 1,415. It confirms the move to Iowa, the marriage to Ann Eckel, and the birth of the first four sons. Andreas listed the date of William Parham's marriage as 1878 though the birth dates of the children are all prior to that. There is a lack of any corroborating evidence on the date and since 1878 occurs in the previous sentence as well, the best explanation is typographical error.

[4] On Muscatine, see Alfred T. Andreas, *Illustrated Historical Atlas of the State of Iowa* (Chicago: Andreas Atlas Co., 1875), pp. 448–50. The population figure is from *The Tribune Almanac for 1871* (New York: New York Tribune, 1876), p. 30. The Parham childhood photograph is in the Parham Showcase, Apostolic Faith Church, Baxter Springs, Kansas. It appears to have been taken when Parham was between the ages of one and three.

[5] On Sedgwick county, see Lawrence D. Burch, *Kansas as It Is* (Chicago: C. S. Burch and Co., 1878), p. 139 and L. T. Bodine, *Kansas Illustrated* (Kansas City, Missouri: Ramsey, Millet, and Hudson, 1879), pp. 6–8. Burch and Bodine are typical of a host of works praising the opportunities of Kansas. Bodine subtitled his work "An accurate and reliable description of this marvelous state for the information of persons seeking homes in the great West."

[6] Andreas, *History of Kansas,* p. 1415. I am indebted to Joanne Black of the Conference Archives, Kansas West Conference, United

Methodist Church for location of the now defunct town of Anness, Kansas. Anness maintained a separate post office until the 1950s.

[7] William Frank Zornow, *Kansas: A History of the Jayhawk State* (Norman: University of Oklahoma Press, 1957), pp. 159–62, 171–72. The Preemption Act of 1841 provided for squatters who already inhabited land prior to government surveys to buy that land at the minimum price of $1.25 per acre. The Homestead Act allowed settlers to claim 160 acres without payment provided they lived on that land for five years and made a significant improvement in its market value.

[8] Zornow, pp. 163–65. *The World Almanac and Encyclopedia: 1908* (New York: Press Publishing Co., 1907), p. 623 lists Kansas' population for the latter half of the nineteenth century as follows: 1860—107,206; 1870—364,399; 1880—996,096; 1890—1,427,096; 1900—1,470,495.

[9] Zornow, pp. 167–73.

[10] John D. Hicks, *The Populist Revolt* (Minneapolis: University of Minnesota Press, 1931), p. 60. Lease was from Wichita, Kansas, thus, like Parham, a native of Sedgwick County. Parham's family had previously been exposed to agrarian discontent in Iowa where the proto-Populist Greenback Party had been strong in the 1870s. See Leland L. Sage, *A History of Iowa* (Ames: Iowa State University Press, 1974), pp. 186–99. In adulthood, Parham claimed Jeremiah D. Botkin as an old family friend. Botkin, an early gubernatorial candidate for Kansas' Prohibition Party, was elected to the United States Congress in 1896 on a "fusionist" ticket of Democrats and Populists. See Kirke Mechem, ed., *The Annals of Kansas: 1886–1925* 2 vols. (Topeka: Kansas State Historical Society, 1954–56) 1:62, 205 and *Apostolic Faith* (Topeka, Kansas) 2 (January 1, 1900):7.

[11] Ibid., p. 162.

[12] Zornow, pp. 198–208.

[13] Ibid.

[14] This is the general thesis of Wiebe in *The Search for Order: 1887–1920* (New York: Hill and Wang, 1967).

[15] In 1878 Lawrence Burch had written of Kansas: "There is less cant, less loud profession, less expression of objectionable self-consciousness . . . here than further east. . . . " Burch, p. 89. This appraisal would shift dramatically in the hands of other writers as the century came to a close. By the 1920s Kansas was generally acknowledged as a breeding ground for religious prophets. See

Charles B. Driscoll, "Major Prophets of Holy Kansas" *American Mercury* 8 (May 1926):18–26.

[16] Patricia R. Spillman, "The Kansan Ethos in the Last Three Decades of the Nineteenth Century" *Emporia State Research Studies* 29 (Summer 1980):13.

[17] Zornow, pp. 190–92 and Anderson, pp. 47–48. For a highly critical view of Kansas schools during the period, see Driscoll, pp. 24–25.

[18] Parham, *Life,* p. 2.

[19] This is from Parham's earliest recorded testimony in *Apostolic Faith* (Topeka) 1 (March 30, 1899):6.

[20] The childhood picture of Parham taken in Muscatine, Iowa, does indeed display a rather prominent forehead. Descriptions of Parham later in life often made exaggerated references to his "remarkably-shaped head." See "Wonderful Cures in Kansas" *Joplin News-Herald* and *Cincinnati Examiner* (27 January 1904) in the Parham Scrapbook, Private possession of Mrs. Pauline Parham, Dallas, Texas (hereafter referred to as *PSD*. See Sources Consulted, Collections). The articles are quoted in *Apostolic Faith* (Baxter Springs, Kansas) 1 (July 1912):2.

[21] For the analysis of Parham's physical deficiencies, I am indebted to interviews with two physicians personally interested in nineteenth-century medical terminology: Charles Chalfant, M.D., Fayetteville, Arkansas, 2 May 1983 and Wade W. Burnside, M.D., Fayetteville, Arkansas, 31 January 1986. Dr. Burnside noted that although there are no medical records from Parham's death in January 1929 at age fifty-five, the description by relatives indicates death by heart failure directly related to the damage sustained from rheumatic fever.

[22] Burnside interview.

[23] Charles F. Parham, *Kol Kare Bomidbar: A Voice Crying in the Wilderness* (Kansas City, Missouri: By the author 1902; reprinted ed., Joplin, Missouri: Joplin Printing Company, 1944), p. 12. Also Parham, *Life,* p. 2.

[24] Ibid., p. 13.

[25] David McCullough, *Mornings on Horseback* (New York: Simon and Schuster, 1981), p. 107. For a complete look at McCullough's analysis of similar effects on the personality of Theodore Roosevelt, see pp. 90–108.

[26] Parham began his own life sketch with "The call to preach:— Preachers are born, not manufactured; this fact is proven by the

record of nearly all Bible characters." Parham, *Voice,* p. 11.

²⁷ Ibid., p. 12.

²⁸ Parham, *Life,* pp. 1–2. After his mother's death, Charles Parham assumed the major responsibility for care of the new baby. The following year his father remarried.

²⁹ Parham, *Voice,* p. 14.

³⁰ Ibid., p. 15. Parham's experience with a flashing light was strikingly similar to that of major Christian figures such as the Apostle Paul (Acts 9:3) and Martin Luther.

³¹ Parham's school records indicate that he was technically a part of the Normal School. He had taught in the local village school prior to entering college and may have entertained thoughts of teaching as a career. Still his "call" to the ministry and activity in evangelism suggest that he was interested in furthering his religious training as well. Parham erroneously gives his age as sixteen at the time of his matriculation. College records show that he attended three full years at Southwest Kansas (1890–91, 1891–92, and 1892–93) but did not graduate. Letter from Ralph W. Decker, Jr., Registrar, Southwestern College, Winfield, Kansas, 25 November 1985. Parham's educational background has generally been underestimated. Lyle P. Murphy referred to his college experience as "a short time": "Beginning at Topeka" *Calvary Review* 13 (Spring 1974):2. Anderson reported Parham "had the equivalent of less than a year." Anderson, p. 102. Mario G. Hoover, on the other hand, overestimated Parham's education, reporting that he "completed his studies." "Origin and Structural Development of the Assemblies of God" (M.A. thesis, Southwest Missouri State College, 1968), pp. 4–5.

³² Elmer Dean Farnsworth, ed., *The Story of Southwestern* (Winfield, Kansas: Anderson Press, 1925), pp. 9–11. Southwest Kansas College subsequently changed its name to Southwestern.

³³ Ibid. Though Parham doesn't mention it, there is little doubt that the economic downturn played at least a small part in ending his education. What is striking here is that Parham's family had been able thus far to afford the one hundred dollar per year (in advance) tuition despite the agricultural depression that had begun in Kansas as early as 1887. William Parham apparently enjoyed quite a bit of prosperity during the boom years prior to that date. Cf. Zornow, pp. 167–68.

³⁴ Parham, *Voice,* pp. 15–16.

³⁵ Ibid., p. 16.

³⁶Ibid. Parham's course record is still on file at Southwestern College and could possibly confirm the extent of his career goals as well as his aptitude for certain subjects. However, the Buckley Family Rights and Privacy Act prevents the release of that record to anyone outside the direct family descendants. Repeated efforts to secure a release from Parham's descendants have proven unsuccessful.

³⁷Parham, *Life,* pp. 8–9 and Parham, *Voice,* pp. 16–17. None of the Parham accounts adequately date the experiences of his college years. I have reconstructed them as accurately as possible by taking into account all available data. The sickness and healing both occur between Parham's matriculation in the fall of 1890 (Decker letter) and the "Christmas time" experience when his ankles were finally made well (*Life,* p. 9). Parham clearly preached after the healing at Tonganoxie in May of 1892 (*Life,* p. 15). Allowing for the months involved in the illness (*Voice,* p. 16) and the handicapped period (*Voice,* p. 18), it seems apparent that the "oak tree" healing came in December 1891 rather than 1890.

³⁸Parham, *Voice,* pp. 18–19. Dramatic healings have served as a springboard for many Pentecostal leaders including Florence Crawford, a contemporary of Parham's, and Oral Roberts. On Crawford, see *Historical Account of the Apostolic Faith,* pp. 59–61. On Roberts, see David E. Harrell, Jr., *All Things Are Possible* (Bloomington and London: Indiana University Press, 1975), p. 42.

³⁹Parham, *Life,* p. 11.

⁴⁰Ibid., p. 12.

⁴¹Farnsworth, p. 6.

⁴²Ibid., p. 16.

⁴³Ibid., pp. 17–18.

⁴⁴Ibid.

⁴⁵Letter from Joanne Black, Commission on Archives and History, Kansas West Conference, United Methodist Church, Winfield, Kansas, 26 November 1985 and Letter from Harold Kolling, Curator of the Baker University United Methodist Collection, Baldwin City, Kansas, 10 December 1985.

2

¹Kolling letter. *Official Minutes of the Thirty-Ninth Session,* (Kansas Annual Conference, Methodist Episcopal Church, Abilene,

Kansas, March 7–12, 1894), p. 25 lists Parham as a supply appointment for a second term. This confirms Parham, *Life,* p. 20 with respect to Dr. Davis' death but not Parham's age. He would have been twenty, not nineteen, at the time of the appointment.

[2] Florence Quinlan, "History of the United Methodist Church in Linwood, Kansas" (Manuscript, Baker University United Methodist Collection, Baldwin City, Kansas, August 13, 1970), p. 1 and Parham, *Life,* pp. 20–21.

[3] On the extreme tenets of some holiness evangelists, see Synan, *Holiness-Pentecostal Movement,* pp. 45–54 and Anderson, pp. 36–37.

[4] Entire sanctification" was a term used to distinguish between the definite act of grace described here and the ongoing process of seeking a life of holiness. It was used only by those who saw sanctification as a "second work of grace." The Keswickian and higher life advocates did not accept this theology of a totally eliminated sin nature. For John Wesley's rather vague explanation of sanctification, see his *A Plain Account of Christian Perfection* (Kansas City, Missouri: Beacon Hill Press, 1966). There were a number of theological treatments of entire sanctification by prominent Methodist writers in the late nineteenth century. See B. Carradine, *The Old Man* (Kentucky Methodist Publishing Co., 1896) and George D. Watson, *Coals of Fire* (Boston: McDonald and Gill, 1886).

[5] Parham, *Voice,* p. 18. Parham's complete view of sanctification is detailed in Charles F. Parham and Sarah E. Parham, *Selected Sermons of the Late Charles F. Parham and Sarah E. Parham.* Compiled by Robert L. Parham (Baxter Springs, Kansas: By the compiler, 1941), pp. 51–63.

[6] Mrs. Parham affirms that Charles Parham was teaching the doctrine of entire sanctification by the time of his pastorate in 1893. Parham, *Life,* pp. 20–21.

[7] That Parham's penchant for emotional worship was not yet completely outdated in the Methodist Church is evidenced by a Methodist leader's enthusiastic support as late as 1901 of a young minister who had created a stir at a recent service when he stood and shouted aloud "Hurrah for Jesus!" See E. F. Walker, "Pentecostal Praise" *Way of Faith and Neglected Themes* (Columbia, South Carolina) 12 (August 22, 1901):1.

[8] The terms "Baptism of the Holy Spirit" and "Baptism of the Holy Ghost" were often used interchangeably with "sanctification."

Toward the end of the nineteenth century, a growing number of holiness advocates began to distinguish between the two experiences. Anderson suggests this was true only of the Keswickian and higher life movements, but there is evidence of a distinction among Wesleyan advocates as well. The most obvious proponents of a split in terminology within the Wesleyan camp were the Fire-Baptized Holiness Associations which Anderson dismisses due to their "heretical" doctrine of a "third blessing." Nevertheless, the Fire-Baptized movement remained staunchly Wesleyan with regard to entire sanctification and it is difficult to exclude them so easily. Cf. Synan, *Holiness-Pentecostal Movement,* pp. 62–63 and Anderson, pp. 41–43. At any rate, it is inaccurate to describe Parham in 1900, as Anderson does, as "a typical Holiness preacher of the Keswick variety" (p. 50). Parham seems to have been equally affected by both the Wesleyan and Reformed aspects of holiness theology.

[9] Parham actually went through a progression of positions on water baptism. After his initial indifference, he became convinced by scripture that single immersion was commanded. By 1898 he changed to advocate triune immersion in the name of Father, Son, and Holy Spirit. Finally around 1900, he settled on single immersion with the dual application of "in the name of Jesus, into the name of the Father, Son, and Holy Ghost." Parham, *Voice,* pp. 21–24.

[10] Parham, *Life,* p. 24.

[11] Ibid., p. 14. Parham published a complete account of his views on total annihilation first in "Questions on Immortality" *Apostolic Faith* (Topeka) 2 (January 1, 1900): 4–5 and then later in Charles Parham, *The Everlasting Gospel* (n.p., [1919–20]), pp. 92–95, 111–17. The timing of his friendship with Baker suggests, as Anderson noted, that the innovative Quaker gentleman may have influenced Parham's ideas on water baptism, church membership, and sanctification as well.

[12] Cf. Parham, *Life,* pp. 24–25 and Quinlan, p. 1.

[13] This is Parham's account as relayed in Shumway, p. 164. The timing is confirmed by *Official Minutes of the Fortieth Session* (Kansas Annual Conference, Methodist Episcopal Church, Abilene, Kansas, March 1895), p. 27 which lists D. L. McCreary as having been appointed to the Eudora church at that time. Kolling letter.

[14] Parham, *Voice,* p. 19. An example of Parham's rebel attitude toward authority is his description of "most sectarian schools" as

188   *Notes*

"dominated by back-slidden, superannuated preachers . . . out-classed by younger men of more progressive, and in many cases, deeper spiritual truths" (p. 15). Parham was twenty-nine years old when he wrote the book.

[15] Parham, *Life*, p. 25. In 1913, Parham elaborated on his experience in Methodism with: "I had the confines of a pastorate, with a lot of theater-going, card-playing, wine-drinking, fashionable, unconverted Methodists; now I have a world-wide parish, with multitudes to preach the gospel message to. . . . " Parham, *Everlasting Gospel*, p. 7.

[16] This comes from an anonymous news source quoted in William E. Connelley, *History of Kansas State and People* 5 vols. (Chicago and New York: American Historical Society, 1928), 2:1,342–43.

[17] Such was the case described for Parham's father and stepmother who remained loyal Methodists after their son's defection. With Parham's direction, they achieved an assurance of salvation in the early 1920s. See Parham, *Life*, pp. 282–83, 287–88.

[18] Ibid., pp. 25–26.

[19] Parham, *Voice*, p. 19.

[20] Parham, *Life*, p. 11. Sarah Parham indicates that her mother and brothers and sisters also lived with her grandfather. She never mentions her father and it is probable that he either died or abandoned the family sometime prior to her thirteenth birthday. Cf. pp. 15 and 28–29.

[21] Ibid., pp. 28–31. Sarah Parham's grave marker lists her as "Co-founder of the Original Apostolic Faith Movement." William Connelley cited Mrs. Parham's alma mater as "Friends Academy." He erroneously gave December 29, 1895 as their marriage date. Connelley, pp. 1,342–43.

[22] Ibid., pp. 31–33.

[23] Ibid., p. 32. The scripture is from Luke 4:23.

[24] Parham, *Voice*, p. 19.

[25] Parham, *Life*, p. 32. There is no evidence that Parham ever personally consulted a physician or used medicines after this event.

[26] Ibid., pp. 14, 32–33.

[27] Ibid. pp. 33–35.

[28] Ibid., p. 34. The exact nature of Mrs. Cook's condition cannot be determined. *Black's Medical Dictionary* defines "dropsy," or hydrops, as "an abnormal accumulation of fluid beneath the skin, or in one or more of the cavities of the body. . . . Dropsy is not a

disease, although this is a popular idea, supported by the fact that at one time many deaths were recorded as due to 'dropsy' without a further statement of the cause." The condition is often associated with either heart disease or Bright's disease but may also be caused by a series of other ailments. William A. R. Thomson, M.D., *Black's Medical Dictionary* 31st ed. (London: Adam and Charles Black, 1976), pp. 266–67.

[29] Ibid., pp. 36–39.

[30] Spillman, pp. 42–44.

[31] John Duffy, *The Healers: A History of American Medicine* (Urbana: University of Illinois Press, 1979), p. 232.

[32] On Parham's distinction between divine healing and "divine healers," see Parham, *Voice,* pp. 46–47.

[33] Parham's home visits are recorded in testimonies in *Apostolic Faith* (Topeka) in almost every issue printed during its run from March 1899 to April 1900. The descriptions of Parham's larger healing services indicate that he generally prayed for the sick after a preaching service, often with other workers joining in the ceremonial "laying on of hands." In this way he tailored a communitarian healing ministry based on James 5:14–15 rather than the individual "gift of healing" model described in I Corinthians 12:9. Parham never claimed the "gift" though others, including his wife, suspected that he had it. See Parham, *Life,* p. 33.

[34] *Apostolic Faith* (Topeka) 1 (October 18, 1899):7. On the rise in medical sophistication and social status, see Gerald N. Grob, *Edward Jarvis and the Medical World of Nineteenth-Century America* (Knoxville: University of Tennessee Press, 1978), pp. 1–8.

[35] Parham, *Voice,* p. 41.

[36] *Apostolic Faith* (Topeka) 1 (September 13, 1899):7. The verses are from Jeremiah 30:13 and 46:11. Both refer to the uselessness of medicine when applied to the allegorical "wound" of the wrath of God. Thus they are somewhat out of context as used here. Parham also overlooks examples which seem to sanction the use of medicine, for example, Proverbs 17:22 and Ezekiel 47:12.

[37] Charles F. Parham, "Divine Health" (Pamphlet by S. B. Echols and Elbert Pool, August 1959) in Marjorie Haire Collection, personal possession of Mrs. Geralean Harshfield, Oklahoma City, Oklahoma. For a synopsis of Parham's healing theology while at Beth-el, see *Apostolic Faith* (Topeka) 1 (May 24, 1899):5–6.

[38] Parham, *Selected Sermons,* p. 43.

[39] Ibid., pp. 43–44. Parham seems a bit inconsistent in his logic here since he generally based healing on James 5:14–15 and refused to acknowledge a special gift of healing on his part. He would no doubt have distinguished between the gift of healing and this authority required to cast out demons. A "gift" was something given directly from God; "authority" came through the depth of one's own spiritual commitment. Parham's opposition to Mary Baker Eddy and Christian Science centered on his conviction that their power-of-the-mind techniques failed to acknowledge the reality of real disease and, thus, of God's supernatural power to heal. See "They Believe in a Personal God," *Kansas City World* (22 January 1901): 8. On Christian Science, see Stephen Gottschalk, *The Emergence of Christian Science in American Religious Life* (Berkeley: University of California Press, 1973).

[40] Ibid., p. 44.

[41] Murphy, p. 3. Charles M. Sheldon, *In His Steps* (Old Tappan, New Jersey: Fleming H. Revell Co., 1972). By the time of this 1972 printing, Sheldon's book had sold over eight million copies and enjoyed an estimated circulation in excess of twenty million. See Hudson, p. 312.

[42] *Topeka Capital,* 12 November 1951, Kansas Historical Society (Topeka, Kansas) "Newsclippings File," pp. 25–26. Parham criticized Sheldon for failing to include an example of faith healing in *In His Steps* since that would have been Jesus' response to disease. See John W. Ripley, "Erastus Stone's Dream Castle—Birthplace of Pentecostalism" *Shawnee County Historical Bulletin* (Topeka, Kansas) 52 (June 1975): 48.

[43] *Apostolic Faith* (Topeka) 1 (March 22, 1899): 8.

[44] Ibid.

[45] Sarah Parham seemed to date the journal to the fall of 1898. See Parham, *Life,* p. 39. The cover of Parham's later journals proclaimed "first published 1897." See *Apostolic Faith* (Baxter) 1 (August 1925): 1. However, the earliest extant copy is Volume 1, Number 2 which is dated March 22, 1899. Page four of that issue refers to "last week's paper" thus effectively dating the inaugural issue to March 15, 1899. This was the first of four *Apostolic Faith* journals published by Parham, each beginning as Volume 1. The Topeka paper ran from March 1899 to April 1900. A second paper was begun in Melrose, Kansas, around June 1905 and was published sporadically in Melrose and Houston, Texas, until March 1906. The

third paper began in Baxter Springs, Kansas, in December 1910 and continued through October 1917. A final *Apostolic Faith* was reorganized at Baxter Springs in January 1925 and continues today under the title *Apostolic Faith Report*. For consistency, I have noted each journal by city; the two Baxter Springs editions may be distinguished by the date. The name was also used by Parham's successors in at least four separate places: 1) William J. Seymour's paper in Los Angeles, California (1906–08); 2) Florence Crawford's paper in Portland, Oregon (1909–present); 3) W. Faye Carothers and Eudorus N. Bell's paper in Houston, Texas (1908–11); and 4) J. G. Campbell's paper in Goose Creek, Texas (1921).

[46] *Apostolic Faith* (Topeka) 1 (March 22, 1899):4.

[47] Ibid., (March 30, 1899):4.

[48] Ibid., (May 3, 1899):7.

[49] Ibid., (June 7, 1899):8 and (August 9, 1899):5.

[50] Ibid., (November 1, 1899):7 and (June 28, 1899):8. In the November 1 issue, Parham indicated that his goal for January 1 was five hundred subscribers. Along with the number of complimentary copies, that would seem to indicate a regular rate of several hundred.

[51] Ibid., (March 30, 1899):4.

[52] Ibid., (July 19, 1899):8.

[53] Ibid., (June 14, 1899):5–8. Most issues ran at least a page of such testimonies. For a physician's analysis of the Beth-el home, see David E. Gray, M.D., "Lean Not Thou On the Arm of Flesh" *Shawnee County Historical Bulletin* 57 (November 1980):143–50.

[54] Ibid., p. 4 and (June 28, 1899):8. This estimate calculates from January 1, 1899, thus eliminating the last few months of 1898 when there were presumably few clients for the new work.

[55] Ibid., 2 (February 15, 1900):6. Also Parham, *Life*, p. 39.

[56] Ibid., 1 (July 19, 1899):8. See also (July 12, 1899):8.

[57] Ripley, p. 48. Ripley calls these "Parham's branch missions"; however, that indicates stronger ties than there actually were. It is true that these missions are occasionally referred to in *Apostolic Faith*, but there is no evidence that Parham actually exercised any control over them. It is probable that he was influential in their establishment, although other healing homes existed in the Midwest as well.

[58] *Apostolic Faith* (Topeka) 1 (March 22, 1899):8 and (July 26, 1899):7.

[59] Pentecostals—and evangelicals in general—are often portrayed

as "otherworldly" since they emphasize the spiritual, rather than social, salvation of mankind. Timothy L. Smith, however, has pointed out that social reform was a cardinal plank within the nineteenth-century evangelical tradition. See *Revivalism and Social Reform: American Protestantism on the Eve of the Civil War* (Gloucester, Massachusetts: Peter Smith, 1976), pp. 148–237. Smith's critics have noted that evangelical reform took the form of individual social welfare and thus was philosophically foreign to the larger aims of the Social Gospel. Cf. Anderson, pp. 195–202. Parham's own views toward social reform were quite enigmatic. At times he made radical calls for governmental responsibility in relief efforts and unemployment programs. Yet he was inherently skeptical of such programs and clearly favored relief efforts through local churches. Cf. Parham, *Voice*, p. 119; "He Has A New Way" *Topeka Daily State Journal* (26 July 1906): 10; and "Demand Prisoners Be Given Liberty," Miscellaneous newsclipping in *PSD*.

[60] *Apostolic Faith* (Topeka) 1 (April 21, 1899): 7.

[61] Ibid., (July 5, 1899): 8; (July 19, 1899): 8; (July 26, 1899): 4; (August 9, 1899): 7 and "Beth-el Rest," Handbill in *PSD*.

[62] Ibid., (November 15, 1899): 7; 2 (January 1, 1900): 7; 2 (April 15, 1900): 4–5 and Parham, *Life*, pp. 37 and 48.

[63] *Apostolic Faith* (Topeka) 1 (August 30, 1899): 7 and (November 1, 1899): 7. In September 1899 the paper was on the verge of failing despite Parham's shift to bimonthly issues one month earlier. See (September 13, 1899): 7.

[64] Ibid., (November 1, 1899): 7. Parham and his family moved out of the Beth-el home during this period and rented a separate apartment at 226 Van Buren Street. They did not return to Beth-el until February 1900. See 2 (February 15, 1900): 6.

[65] Ibid., (July 5, 1899): 3–4.

[66] Grant Wacker, "Marching to Zion: Religion in a Modern Utopian Community" *Church History* 54 (December 1985): 496–502. Wacker notes that at the Chicago fair Dowie also criticized journalists, politicians, Masons, Roman Catholics, and denominational clergy, making—in one reporter's estimation—"Billy Sunday's preaching seem 'prim in comparison'" (p. 499).

[67] On Dowie's social concerns, see Philip Lee Cook, "Zion City, Illinois: Twentieth Century Utopia" (Ph.D. dissertation, University of Colorado, 1965), pp. 43–44. An example of Dowie's use of spectacular healings is a front page story which proclaimed that a gun-

shot wound had been healed through prayer without any medical attention. See *Leaves of Healing* 9 (June 15, 1901):1–4.

[68] For a complete discussion of the postmillennial tie to American progress, see Robert T. Handy, *A Christian America* (New York: Oxford University Press, 1971); Nathan O. Hatch, *The Sacred Cause of Liberty* (New Haven and London: Yale University Press, 1977); and James H. Moorhead, *American Apocalypse: Yankee Protestants and the Civil War, (1860–1869)* (New Haven and London: Yale University Press, 1978).

[69] On Darby's importance, see Weber, pp. 17–24. On American millenarianism, see Edwin S. Gaustad, ed., *The Rise of Adventism* (New York: Harper and Row, 1974). On millenarian movements in general, see Norman Cohn, *The Pursuit of the Millennium* 2nd ed. (New York: Oxford University Press, 1970) and E. J. Hobsbawm, *Primitive Rebels: Studies in Archaic Forms of Social Movement in the Nineteenth and Twentieth Centuries* (New York: Frederick A. Praeger, 1963). An apologetic account which links Darby's ideas to that found in the early apostolic church is Charles C. Ryrie's *Dispensationalism Today* (Chicago: Moody Press, 1965), pp. 65–85. For an example of American premillennial literature at the turn of the century, see the widely read W. E. Blackstone, *Jesus Is Coming* (Chicago: Fleming H. Revell, Co., 1898; rev. ed., 1908). A European example is Charles J. T. Bohm's *The Second Coming of Christ and His Kingdom in Visible Glory* (Glasgow: D. Hobbs and Co., 1902).

[70] Grant Wacker, "The Holy Spirit and the Spirit of the Age in American Protestantism, 1880–1910" *Journal of American History* 72 (June 1985):45–62. On Moody's influential career, as well as that of other urban evangelists, see William G. McLoughlin, Jr., *Modern Revivalism: Charles Grandison Finney to Billy Graham* (New York: Ronald Press Co., 1959). The standard biography of Moody is James F. Findlay, Jr.'s *Dwight L. Moody: American Evangelist, 1837–1899* (Chicago and London: University of Chicago Press, 1969). On the premillennial roots of Fundamentalism; see Ernest R. Sandeen, *The Roots of Fundamentalism: British and American Millenarianism, 1800–1930* (Chicago: University of Chicago Press, 1970) and the more recent analysis by George M. Marsden, *Fundamentalism and American Culture: The Shaping of Twentieth Century Evangelicalism, 1870–1925* (New York and Oxford: Oxford University Press, 1980).

[71] Waldvogel, pp. 77–121, 149–52. Parham refers to Keswick in *Apostolic Faith* (Topeka) 1 (November 15, 1899):7.

[72] Ibid., pp. 122–48. For a thorough study of the origins of the divine healing movement in America, see Paul G. Chappell, "The Divine Healing Movement in America" (Ph.D. dissertation, Drew University, 1983).

[73] On Irwin, see Synan, *Holiness-Pentecostal Movement*, pp. 61–67 and Joseph Hillery King, "History of the Fire-Baptized Holiness Church" (Manuscript, Pentecostal Holiness Church Archives, Oklahoma City, Oklahoma). This manuscript was published as a serial in *Pentecostal Holiness Advocate*, March 24–April 21, 1921.

[74] *Apostolic Faith* (Topeka) 1 (March 22, 1899):8.

[75] Ibid., (June 7, 1899):5–6.

[76] King, pp. 10–11. Both King (p. 9) and George Harold Paul, "The Religious Frontier in Oklahoma: Dan T. Muse and the Pentecostal Holiness Church" (Ph.D. dissertation, University of Oklahoma, 1965), p. 23 credits Irwin's *Live Coals of Fire*, which began in October 1899, as "the first journal in the United States to teach that the experience of baptism was separate from and subsequent to the experience of sanctification." However, Parham's *Apostolic Faith* had openly professed the doctrine since March 1899. Later in life Parham accused the Fire-Baptized of having been overly emotional and listed them under the general category of "Counterfeit." See *Apostolic Faith* (Baxter) 1 (April 1925):9–15.

[77] Dillard L. Wood and William H. Preskitt, Jr., *Baptized With Fire: A History of the Pentecostal Fire-Baptized Holiness Church* (Franklin Springs, Georgia: Advocate Press, 1982), p. 16 which quotes from the 1905 *Constitution and General Rules of the Fire-Baptized Holiness Church*. Also George Floyd Taylor, "Our Church History" (Manuscript, Pentecostal Holiness Church Archives, Oklahoma City, Oklahoma). This manuscript was published in the *Pentecostal Holiness Advocate* as a twelve-part serial beginning January 20, 1921.

[78] Synan, *Holiness-Pentecostal Movement*, p. 66. References to a "dynamite" experience began in 1899 and continued in the Fire-Baptized movement as late as 1906. See Irwin's editorial in *Live Coals of Fire* (Lincoln, Nebraska) 1 (October 6, 1899):1 and various testimonial accounts in *Live Coals* (Royston, Georgia) 1 (January 11, 1905):2; 2 (May 9, 1906):4; and 2 (July 25, 1906):4.

[79] See "Letter from Mrs. J. A. Haskins" in *Apostolic Faith* (Topeka) 1 (March 30, 1899):6–7.

[80] The authoritative work on Sandford is William Charles Hiss, "Shiloh: Frank W. Sandford and the Kingdom, 1893–1948" (Ph.D. dissertation, Tufts University, 1978). On his association with Parham, see p. 247. The visit by Sandford's students seems to be the same as that of the "evangelists from the East" mentioned in Parham, *Life,* p. 48.

[81] Ibid., pp. 59–336. On Sandford's search for Holy Spirit baptism, see especially pp. 101–4. In 1900 Parham estimated Shiloh's partially completed complex at a value of $150,000. See *Topeka State Journal* (20 October 1900): 14.

[82] Ibid., pp. 223–24. Also *Kansas City Times* (2 January 1900): 8.

[83] The model is based on Luke 10: 1–12.

[84] *Apostolic Faith* (Topeka) 2 (February 15, 1900): 7 and (April 1, 1900): 6.

[85] Ibid., (April 1, 1900): 5. The quotation (and all subsequent scriptural references) is from the Authorized, or King James, Version.

[86] Ibid., p. 7.

[87] *Apostolic Faith* (Baxter) 2 (July 1926): 1. Also Parham, *Life,* p. 48. Sarah Parham's account lists "Malone's work" as based in Cleveland but the older account by Parham himself locates it in Cincinnati. Parham seems to have visited these other holiness works in the company of Sandford and the band of students. They stopped not only to visit but also to wait for God to supply enough money to buy a ticket to the next destination. It was Parham's first encounter with the drama of faith travel. See *Topeka State Journal* (20 October 1900): 14.

[88] *Topeka State Journal* (20 October 1900): 14 and Hiss, p. 247. Others who note Sandford's extensive influence on Parham are Shumway, p. 158; Anderson, p. 50; and Edith Waldvogel Blumhofer, *The Assemblies of God: A Popular History* (Springfield, Missouri: Gospel Publishing House, 1985), pp. 24–25.

[89] Ibid. and Parham, *Life,* pp. 48–49.

3

[1] The statement follows a series of "signs" Jesus gives in answer to the disciples' question, "What shall be the sign of thy coming,

and of the end of the world?" (Matthew 24:3). The parallel to Matthew 24:14 is Mark 13:10 which reads: "And the gospel must first be published among all nations." Parham's use of the verses is referred to in *Houston Post* (20 August 1906):10.

²Anderson, pp. 42 and 81. The best description of the concept by an early Pentecostal is in George Floyd Taylor, *The Spirit and the Bride* (Dunn, North Carolina: By the author, 1907), pp. 90–96. See also *Latter Rain Evangel* (Chicago) (January 1929):2. The biblical reference is to Joel 2:23.

³Parham, *Voice*, pp. 30–31. Cf. the optimistic appraisal of Shiloh in *Topeka State Journal* (20 October 1900):14.

⁴Throughout I have used Bethel for the Bible school and Beth-el for the healing home. Both terms mean "the house of God." Not only is this a convenient distinction, but the early literature clearly uses the hyphenated form for the healing home. Since Parham ceased publication of *Apostolic Faith* in May 1900, the earliest references to the Bible school are in the local press which consistently used "Bethel."

⁵*Topeka Capital* (12 November 1951) Kansas Historical Society "Newsclippings File," pp. 25–26. The site of Parham's Bible school is now near Seventeenth and Stone Streets in downtown Topeka and is the current property of Most Pure Heart of Mary Catholic Church. The original building burned in 1901. See Ripley, p. 42. Photos indicate that the Stone mansion was quite an impressive structure. The earliest descriptions estimated from fourteen to eighteen large rooms. Later news accounts erroneously reported that the building had thirty rooms.

⁶Ibid., (November 18, 1951), p. 27. Also Ripley, pp. 42–45 and Shumway, p. 165. For dating purposes, I have generally favored Shumway who personally interviewed Erastus Stone sometime around 1913.

⁷*Topeka State Journal* (20 October 1900):14.

⁸Ibid.

⁹*Topeka Daily Capital* (7 December 1901) Kansas Historical Society "Newsclippings File," p. 161.

¹⁰*Topeka State Journal* (20 October 1900):14 and Shumway, pp. 165–66.

¹¹*Apostolic Faith* (Baxter) 2 (July 1926):2. Also Parham, *Life*, pp. 51–53. Watch-night services were commonplace among Parham's holiness peers including Moody, Dowie, and Sandford. See

Cook, pp. 46–47 and Hiss, p. 191. According to this account, Bethel's student body had increased from its opening enrollment of thirty-four to forty.

[12] Parham, *Life*, pp. 53–54. Also *Apostolic Faith* (Baxter) 2 (July 1926):2–3.

[13] Ibid., pp. 53, 61. Also *Topeka Mail and Breeze* (22 February 1901) Kansas Historical Society "Newsclippings File," p. 276.

[14] *Apostolic Faith* (Baxter) 2 (July 1926):3. Also Parham, *Life*, pp. 54–55.

[15] The most dramatic account is that related in Ethel E. Goss, *The Winds of God: The Story of the Early Pentecostal Days (1901–1914) in the Life of Howard A. Goss* (New York: Comet Press Books, 1958), pp. 23–26. The midnight, New Year's Eve version was also recounted in some early newspaper coverage. See "Are From Kansas" *Kansas City Journal* (February 1901) in *PSD*. Other accounts place Ozman's reception earlier in the evening of December 31. See Michael Harper, *As at the Beginning: The Twentieth Century Pentecostal Revival* (Plainfield, New Jersey: Logos International, 1965), p. 25; Richard Quebedeaux, *The New Charismatics: The Origins, Development, and Significance of Neo-Pentecostalism* (Garden City, New York: Doubleday and Co., 1976), pp. 28–30; and Sherrill, p. 38. The dating problem has often simply been overlooked. Sarah Parham's account includes both traditions without explanation. Cf. Parham, *Life*, pp. 52–53, 59, and 66.

[16] Parham, *Life*, p. 63. Sarah Parham's account includes the chapter by Thistlethwaite entitled "The Wonderful History of the Latter Rain" (pp. 57–65). The denominations listed are exactly what one would expect. Parham had been a Methodist, the Thistlethwaites Quaker, and all were now loosely identified as holiness workers. Anderson speculates that the twelve ministers are subconsciously modeled after the twelve disciples and that the 115 present at the watch-night service (i.e., forty students and seventy-five visitors) correspond to the "about an hundred and twenty" present at the first Pentecostal outpouring (Acts 1:15 and 2:1). See Anderson, pp. 56–57.

[17] Parham's earliest recounting of Topeka dates to 1902 and contains a couple of significant differences from the later, more elaborate, account. He places Ozman's experience on "New Year's night" and fails to mention that the students had independently concluded that tongues were the indisputable evidence of Holy Spirit baptism.

See Parham, *Voice,* pp. 33–34. Parham first related the student consensus idea in his interview with Charles Shumway around 1913. Shumway included the information in his narrative but then concluded that Parham had consciously "determined to turn the attention of the School to the gift of tongues" and that he "urged them all, including himself, to seek the baptism of the Holy Spirit with the accompanying sign." See Shumway, pp. 166–67.

[18] Agnes N. O. LaBerge, *What God Hath Wrought* (Chicago: Herald Publishing Co., 1921), pp. 7–28 and "History of the Pentecostal Movement from January 1, 1901" (Manuscript, Editorial files of the *Pentecostal Evangel,* Springfield, Missouri). The manuscript accompanies a letter from LaBerge to E. N. Bell dated 23 February 1922. Also see Murphy, p. 3.

[19] *Apostolic Faith* (Houston, Texas) 2 (October 1908):2. Also *Apostolic Faith* (Baxter) 1 (December-January 1912–13):4. Ozman's story is substantiated by Lilian Thistlethwaite in Parham, *Life,* p. 59.

[20] LaBerge, "History," p. 3.

[21] *Apostolic Faith* (Houston) 2 (October 1908):2 and LaBerge, *What God Hath Wrought,* p. 29.

[22] See J. Roswell Flower, "Birth of the Pentecostal Movement" *Pentecostal Evangel* no. 1907 (November 26, 1950):3. Flower focused on the conclusion by Parham's students as a "most momentous decision . . . which has made the Pentecostal Movement of the Twentieth Century." While he was correct in noting the theological significance of the initial evidence position, Flower failed to recognize the problems the student search theory posed when compared to Agnes Ozman's testimony. Incredibly enough, he included Ozman's account in the article but overlooked the incongruity. Cf. pp. 3 and 12.

[23] LaBerge, "History," p. 3.

[24] In 1914, Parham confided to Charles Shumway that, without exception, everyone at Bethel had verbally acknowledged that the Second Coming would occur before 1925. See Shumway, p. 166. This intense millenarian emphasis is also noted by Gee, p. 2 and Anderson, pp. 90–92.

[25] *Apostolic Faith* (Topeka) 1 (June 21, 1899):4.

[26] Ibid., (May 3, 1899):5. Also on Glassey, see Hiss, p. 163 and Parham, *Voice,* p. 29.

[27] See Parham, *Voice,* pp. 27–28.

28 *Apostolic Faith* (Topeka) 2 (April 1, 1900):7.

29 Shumway, p. 165. Also *Kansas City Times* (27 January 1901): 15 and "New Kind of Missionaries" *Kansas City Times* (17 May 1901) in *PSD*. Parham's missionary tongues concept was occasionally alluded to by other holiness leaders, though he was the first to emphasize and actively seek the phenomenon. Arthur T. Pierson interpreted Acts 2 as a case of xenoglossic tongues; A. B. Simpson was quoted by later Pentecostals as having predicted the return of mission tongues during the last generation; and Mary Woodworth-Etter remembered the reception of such a gift as early as 1890. On Pierson, see *Holiness Advocate* (Clinton, North Carolina) 7 (May 15, 1907):1; on Simpson, Frank Bartleman, *Azusa Street* (Plainfield, New Jersey: Logos International, 1980), pp. 65–66; and on Woodworth-Etter, George R. Stotts, "Mary Woodworth-Etter: A Forgotten Feminine Figure in the Late Nineteenth and Early Twentieth Century Charismatic Revival" (Paper presented to the American Academy of Religion, Washington, D.C., October 26, 1974), p. 17.

30 The emphasis on missionary training was made the month the school opened. See *Topeka State Journal* (20 October 1900):14.

31 LaBerge, *What God Hath Wrought*, p. 28 and "History," p. 2.

32 The search for evidence is included in Parham's earliest account. Parham, *Voice*, pp. 33–34. See also Thistlethwaite's account in Parham, *Life*, pp. 58–59 and *Apostolic Faith* (Baxter) 2 (July 1926):2. That Parham centered his studies on Acts is confirmed in *Topeka State Journal* (9 January 1901):6. The biblical account of xenoglossa is in Acts 2:5–12, 41.

33 *Apostolic Faith* (Baxter) 2 (July 1926):2. Though Ozman never engaged in foreign missions, she did frequently refer to her Christian efforts as "missionary work." It is quite likely that during this period, she considered going abroad. Ozman's sister, Mary Ella Ozman, decided to go to South America as a missionary at approximately the same time, though there is no hard evidence that she had any direct contact with Parham. See LaBerge, *What God Hath Wrought*, pp. 25–27.

34 Ibid. Also Parham, *Life*, pp. 51–52. The allusion is to Balaam's talking donkey of Numbers 22:30.

35 LaBerge, "History," pp. 3–4.

36 Shumway, p. 168. Leading experts on glossolalia comprise two schools of thought. Most studies have preferred to link glossolalia

with some aspect of an altered state of consciousness. See Felicitas D. Goodman, "Phonetic Analysis of Glossolalia in Four Cultural Settings" and Virginia H. Hine, "Non-pathological Pentecostal Glossolalia: A Summary of Relevant Psychological Literature" *Journal for the Scientific Study of Religion* 8 (1969):211–239. William J. Samarin has championed an alternate thesis that glossolalia is learned, albeit subconscious, behavior. *Tongues of Men and Angels: The Religious Language of Pentecostalism* (New York and London: Macmillan Co., 1972). All agree that glossolalia is technically not language since it is not a systematic collection of syllables designed for human communication. Thus glossolalia serves strictly a religious function. Xenoglossa, of course, would serve as communication for the listener if not for the speaker. On the problems of verifying xenoglossa as authentic, see Samarin, pp. 109–15.

[37] *Topeka Daily Capital* (6 January 1901):2. "Auswin" here is undoubtedly a misprint for Ozman since the article identifies her as the initial recipient of the experience. The reference to "laundry talk" is in "Converts in Zion City Get 'Gift of Tongues'," Miscellaneous newsclipping in *PSD*. On glossographia (glossa—tongues + graphia—to write), see Samarin, pp. 185–87; Nickels J. Holmes and Lucy Simpson Holmes, *Life Sketches and Sermons* (Royston, Georgia: Press of the Pentecostal Holiness Church, 1920), p. 181; and *Topeka Mail and Breeze* (22 February 1901) Kansas Historical Society "Newsclippings File," p. 276. As with xenoglossa, the claims for glossographia declined after the initial years of development. Cf. *Apostolic Faith* (Los Angeles) 1 (September 1907):2. A fourth type phenomenon is sometimes mentioned in Pentecostal literature though with less frequency than glossolalia, xenoglossa, and glossographia. Akolalia (Akouw—to hear + lalia—to speak) describes the incredible claim that a speaker's known language would be heard by someone else in their own different language. See Shumway, pp. 50–58 and Hunter. p. 13. Akolalia is fundamentally different from glossolalia and xenoglossa since it would be essentially a miracle of hearing rather than speech. Parham makes no reference to the phenomenon.

[38] On cryptomnesia, see Samarin, pp. 115–18. Shumway explains the same phenomenon but uses hypermnesia in Shumway, "Gift of Tongues," pp. 19–29 and "A Critical History of Glossolalia" (Ph.D. dissertation, Boston University, 1919), outline b–4.

[39] Zornow, pp. 174–83. The figures come from *The Tribune Al-*

manac for 1893 5 vols. (New York: Tribune Association, 1893), 5:123 and *The World Almanac and Encyclopedia: 1915* (New York: Press Publishing Co., 1914), pp. 711–12.

[40] The testimony of foreigners, or persons familiar with some foreign language, who confirmed xenoglossa is quite common in early Pentecostal literature. For a wide range of examples, see Ralph W. Harris, *Spoken by the Spirit* (Springfield, Missouri: Gospel Publishing House, 1973). In Parham's circle, there was even an official affidavit sworn verifying such a claim. See *Apostolic Faith* (Melrose, Kansas and Houston, Texas) 1 (May 1906): 13–15. It is significant that, as the century progressed, reports of xenoglossa became less frequent. Along with a shift away from the foreign missions concept of tongues, which decreased the importance of xenoglossa, most Pentecostals—like most Americans—were less affected by immigration as tighter controls created a more homogeneous American landscape.

[41] Parham, *Voice*, p. 31.

[42] Parham, *Everlasting Gospel*, p. 68. Though the "Foreword" in the most recent reprinting of the book claims it was written in 1911, internal evidence strongly suggests that the original edition was published ca. 1919–20 (see p. 31).

[43] Ibid., pp. 68–69. Howard Goss, later a prominent Pentecostal leader himself, was converted under Parham's ministry after being convinced by the unique feature of glossolalia (or, as he supposed, xenoglossa). See Gordon Lindsay, *They Saw It Happen!* (Dallas: Christ For the Nations, 1972), pp. 11–12.

[44] For the concept of a bride within the holiness ranks, see George D. Watson, *The Bridehood Saints* (Cincinnati, Ohio: Office God's Revivalist, Ringgold, Young, and Channing St., n.d.). Pentecostal baptism as evidence of bridal membership was an important theme among the early participants of the movement. The idea brought an often deserved criticism that the movement claimed spiritual superiority since, for many theorists, it followed that only spirit-filled Christians would be taken in the rapture. Recent Pentecostals have rejected the notion and assigned its belief to only a fringe of the movement. See Harris, p. 121. However, first-generation Pentecostals generally supported the concept. Cf. Taylor, *Spirit and Bride*, p. 115 and *The Rainbow* (Franklin Springs, Georgia: Publishing House of the Pentecostal Holiness Church, 1924), p. 213; *Holiness Advocate* (May 15, 1907):5; and *Latter Rain Evangel*

(January 1918): 6–9. See also Goff, "Pentecostal Millenarianism," pp. 20–21.

⁴⁵ Parham, *Voice,* p. 32. See also Parham, *Everlasting Gospel,* pp. 74–76.

⁴⁶ Ibid., p. 35. Glossolalia had been an occasional phenomenon in holiness meetings but Parham was the first to link the occurrence as evidence of one's reception of the Baptism of the Holy Ghost. His stand thus created a new, definable theological position which forged the Pentecostal movement. For examples of glossolalia among pre-Pentecostal holiness groups, see Maria Beulah Woodworth, *Life and Experiences of Maria B. Woodworth* (Dayton, Ohio: United Brethern Publishing House, 1885), p. 28 and *The Life, Work, and Experience of Maria B. Woodworth* (St. Louis: By the author, 1894), p. 202. Also Paul, pp. 44–45 and Synan, *Holiness-Pentecostal Movement,* p. 65.

⁴⁷ *Topeka Daily Capital* (6 January 1901): 2. In this earliest press coverage of events at Bethel, the general outpouring is dated to the previous Friday night (January 4) and thus conflicts with the later accounts which identify January 3. However, the article misprints "Auswin" for Ozman and is, by itself, insufficient evidence to refute the more traditional timetable. Years later, Parham explained Riggins' departure by noting that he was upset at having failed to receive the new experience himself. See Shumway, "Gift of Tongues," p. 168.

⁴⁸ *Topeka State Journal* (7 January 1901): 4. This quote is noticeably "edited out" of the news article contained in *PSD.*

⁴⁹ Ibid., (9 January 1901): 6. See also (6 January 1901): 2 and (21 January 1901): 7.

⁵⁰ Ibid. (9 January 1901): 6 and (15 January 1901): 3. Later reports confused Riggins with a spirit-filled student named Samuel Higgins. Cf. *Kansas City World* (15 January 1901): 7.

⁵¹ Ibid. (21 January 1901): 7.

⁵² See "At Academy of Music," "Throws Away Crutches As Effect of Prayer," and "Six Hours of Prayer," Newsclippings dated as "Kansas City, 1901" in *PSD.*

⁵³ "Are From Kansas" *Kansas City Journal* (February 1901) in *PSD.* Parham did grow a beard during this period as is evidenced by photos and sketches in *PSD.* It seems to have been the only time during his life that he did so.

⁵⁴ "Gift of Tongues," Newsclipping dated "Kansas City, 1901" in *PSD.*

⁵⁵ Ibid. Carry Nation's prohibition crusade had arrived in Topeka at about the same time Parham had left for Kansas City. See Mechem, pp. 332–34 and Robert Smith Bader, "Mrs. Nation" *Kansas History* 7 (Winter 1984–85): 246–62.

⁵⁶ "Preacher Issues A Defi" *Kansas City Times* (1901) in *PSD*. The smallpox epidemic in Kansas City was actually quite small when compared to other major cities at the same time. See *Kansas City World* (2 February 1901): 1.

⁵⁷ *Kansas City Times* (27 January 1901): 15. Also *Kansas City Journal* (22 January 1901): 1.

⁵⁸ "The Pathological Conditions of the Bethel Bible School at Topeka" (Senior Graduate paper, Kansas State University, 1901) as quoted in *Apostolic Faith* (Goose Creek, Texas) no. 20 (May 1921): 2–4. A similar analysis is contained in *Kansas City World* (15 January 1901): 7.

⁵⁹ *Kansas City World* (4 February 1901): 1.

⁶⁰ For an example of this type of skepticism, see *Gospel Trumpet* (Moundsville, West Virginia) 22 (September 18, 1902): 3.

⁶¹ "Parham Home" *Topeka Capital* (1901) in *PSD*. Parham told the Topeka reporters that his efforts in Kansas City had drawn "large and enthusiastic meetings." However, Kansas City newspapers estimated nightly attendance between seventy–five and one hundred. See *Kansas City World* (22 January 1901): 8 and "Six Hours of Prayer" (Kansas City, 1901) in *PSD*.

⁶² Ibid.

⁶³ "Prayer Is His Cure" *Kansas City Times* (11 March 1901) and "Says They Are Persecuted" (Kansas City, 1901), both in *PSD*.

⁶⁴ Parham, *Life,* pp. 76–79.

⁶⁵ "New Kinds of Missionaries." A more realistic estimate of Parham's following by mid-1901 would be a combined total of five hundred. That would allow for a student body and local Topeka following of around two hundred and congregations in Kansas City and Lawrence of one hundred and fifty each.

⁶⁶ *Apostolic Faith* (Houston) 2 (October 1908): 2.

⁶⁷ *Topeka Daily Capital* (7 December 1901): 3.

⁶⁸ Parham, *Life,* p. 80. Anderson and Nelson indicated that the Bethel students repudiated their belief in Pentecost, noting that Ozman returned to work in a non-Pentecostal holiness mission. The implication is that Parham's early converts were then subsequently "reminded" of their Pentecost after the Los Angeles revival of 1906. See Anderson, p. 58 and Nelson, p. 69. However, Ozman

asserted that her experience remained valid and that she occasionally preached Pentecostal doctrine during this period. See LaBerge, *What God Hath Wrought,* pp. 26–27, 33–34 and "History," p. 5. While it is apparent that many of the students were disillusioned with the meager results of the movement, there is no reason to suspect that they personally rejected either Parham or the Pentecostal message. It would be natural for them to return to holiness missions since Parham remained an avid supporter of holiness doctrine and continued to make his appeal in those circles.

[69] The biblical reference is to Mark 1:3 et al. Parham had used the analogy with John the Baptist as early as January 1901. See *Kansas City Journal* (22 January 1901):1. That he secured enough funds to publish the book indicates that he continued to maintain a small following in the Kansas City area. Shumway noted that after moving to Kansas City in 1901, Parham broke up several churches and made "much trouble . . . for the evangelical ministry." "Gift of Tongues," p. 169.

[70] *Topeka Daily Capital* (7 December 1901):3 and Parham, *Life,* pp. 80–81.

4

[1] Parham collected almost any news reference to his work, including those poignantly critical of him, and kept them in a scrapbook. In later years, he reprinted such articles in his journal, editing out the more unfavorable comments. See *Apostolic Faith* (Baxter) 1 (July 1912):1–12.

[2] Parham, *Life,* pp. 81–86.

[3] Ibid., p. 87. See also Chappell, p. 345. Parham had not abandoned his teaching on divine healing, but his efforts at world evangelism via mission tongues had overshadowed that part of his ministry during the previous two years.

[4] Floyd C. Shoemaker, "Cedar County" *Missouri Historical Review* 53 (July 1959):333–34 and Walter Williams, ed., *The State of Missouri* (Columbia, Missouri: E. W. Stephens, 1904), pp. 354–55.

[5] Parham, *Life,* pp. 87–88.

[6] Ibid., p. 88. Also Mary A. Arthur, "Beginning History of Galena Church," (Manuscript, Assemblies of God Archives, Springfield, Missouri, n.d.), p. 1.

[7] Arthur, pp. 3–4. It is interesting that Arthur mentioned return-

ing to the healing springs for a drink of water. Apparently Parham didn't condemn the practice, since mineral springs would not qualify as man-made medicine. Sarah Parham quoted Arthur but failed to include the brief episode at the spring. Cf. Parham, *Life*, pp. 88–90. It is possible that Mrs. Parham quoted Arthur from a different source since there are several other irregularities—including additions—in her account.

[8] Ibid., pp. 4–5. Years later, a news account reported that Parham had originally preached in the Galena Methodist Church in the absence of the pastor, Rev. Frank Otto. Upon Otto's return, Parham was denied use of the church building and separate quarters were secured. There is, however, no further substantiation for this variant account. See "As Galena Knew Parham," Miscellaneous newsclipping in *PSD*.

[9] Arrell M. Gibson, "Lead Mining in Southwest Missouri After 1865" *Missouri Historical Review* 53 (July 1959): 315. Also Anderson, pp. 58–59.

[10] Goss, p. 9.

[11] Gibson, p. 325.

[12] Paul C. Nagel, *Missouri: A Bicentennial History* (New York: W. W. Norton and Co., 1977), pp. 56–57. Population figures are from *The World Almanac and Encyclopedia: 1922* (New York: Press Publishing Co., 1921), p. 700.

[13] Goss, pp. 12–14. Also "Wonderful Cures in Kansas" *Joplin News-Herald* and *Cincinnati Examiner* (27 January 1904) and "'Divine Healer' Next Week" (Nevada, Missouri, 1904), both in *PSD*.

[14] Murphy, p. 9 and Parham, *Life*, p. 98.

[15] Goss, p. 13. Lyle Murphy noted that other religious leaders in Galena offered support for Parham's doctrine of tongues and healing, most notably Rev. Sara Scovell of the First Spiritualist Church and Miss Clara Crawford, a local faith healer (See Murphy, pp. 8–9). There is no evidence, however, that Parham returned their endorsement.

[16] Following the initial success of Parham's revival, the local Methodist Episcopal Church began nightly renewal services of its own. See "A Divine Healer Cured Them?" *Kansas City Times* (2 January 1904) in *PSD*.

[17] An Aged Minister Baptized" *Kansas City Times* (7 March 1904) in *PSD*.

[18] Parham, *Life*, pp. 99–100.

[19] An example of the growing attention brought by the success at

Galena is a letter from a minister in Cincinnati inquiring about the various news accounts. Parham claimed to have received many such letters during his career; this is the only one I have been able to locate. See C. C. Bruner to Rev. C. F. Parham, 7 February 1904, in *PSD.*

[20] See "Parhamism Charged With Death of Innocent" (Baxter Springs, Kansas, October 24, n.d.) in *PSD.* The article appears to come from a regional newspaper as a special story written by a roving reporter in Baxter Springs. A search of the local Baxter Springs newspaper failed to produce a similar story. Since the article doesn't note the year, I was forced to use other means in dating the incident to 1904. There is no record of Nettie Smith's death in the Cherokee County Courthouse. However, her mother died February 28, 1901 at which time Nettie was listed as "child, age 5." Jeanna Zahm, Elinor Makings, and Clione Bieber, comps., *Record of Affidavit of Death: Book A. Cherokee County* (Columbus, Kansas: Cherokee County Genealogy Society, n.d.), p. 85. That would mean her death at age nine could have been in October of either 1904 or 1905. Since the article notes that Parham had recently gone out of town but seems to place him in the same general vicinity, I have chosen 1904. The timing corresponds to a meeting Parham held at nearby Joplin, Missouri. In October 1905, Parham had moved to Texas.

[21] Parham, *Life,* pp. 102–4.

[22] *Apostolic Faith* (Goose Creek) no. 20 (May 1921), p. 5.

[23] *Apostolic Faith* (Baxter) 2 (July 1926):4. Aylor is described as a "wealthy ranchman" in *Houston Chronicle* (13 August 1905):6. See also Parham, *Life,* p. 107 and Frodsham, p. 27. The 1980 census listed Orchard with a population of 403.

[24] Parham, *Life,* pp. 108–9.

[25] Ibid., pp. 109–12.

[26] Anderson, p. 59. In 1910, Houston numbered 78,800 and Galveston reported 36,981. Michael T. Kingston, ed., *The Texas Almanac: 1984–85* (Dallas: A. H. Belo Corp., 1983), p. 349.

[27] Parham, *Life,* pp. 112–13. Mrs. Parham noted that Aylor sold a mule to help cover the costs of starting the Houston campaign.

[28] Frodsham, pp. 27–28 and Menzies, pp. 46–47.

[29] *Houston Chronicle* (13 August 1905):6.

[30] Goss, p. 30; Parham, *Life,* pp. 113–15; and *Apostolic Faith* (Melrose-Houston) 1 (August 1905):8.

³¹[Houston Heights, Texas] *Suburbanite* (12 August 1905) in *PSD*.

³²Parham, *Life*, pp. 104–5.

³³*Apostolic Faith* (Houston-Melrose) 1 (September 1905):7 and "One Clad Triumphant Day" (Joplin, Missouri, 1905), in *PSD*.

³⁴*Houston Chronicle* (13 August 1905):6.

³⁵Parham, *Life*, p. 116.

³⁶Shumway, "A Critical History," p. 114. Shumway's attack on the *Chronicle* was not totally justified. The article in question ("Houstonians Witness the Performance of Miracles," 13 August 1905, 6) actually included the "documentation" of xenoglossa under the special heading "Apostolic Claims" and encased the entire section in asterisks. The bulk of the article was objective in its analysis. Cf. Shumway, "Gift of Tongues," p. 170.

³⁷*Houston Chronicle* (13 August 1905):6 and *Apostolic Faith* (Melrose-Houston) 1 (September 1905):8. Carothers claimed to have studied German earlier in his life.

³⁸It is unclear whether the German sailor received Holy Spirit baptism. The article simply states that when he sailed for Germany, he "took the full gospel with him." That he heard German in his initial visit to the Pentecostal meeting is implied from the context. See *Apostolic Faith* (Melrose-Houston) 1 (October 1905):7.

³⁹Shumway, "Gift of Tongues," p. 164.

⁴⁰Franz Muenzner, "Apostolic Faith! Erste Deutsche gedruckte Predigt von Franz Muenzner" (Orchard, Texas: By the author, [1905]), in *PSD*. Parham had also affiliated with a German evangelist, C. T. Potma, in Topeka in 1899. See *Apostolic Faith* (Topeka) 1 (March 22, 1899):8.

⁴¹Parham, *Life*, pp. 123–24 and *Apostolic Faith* (Melrose-Houston) 1 (October–November 1905):5–6.

⁴²*Apostolic Faith* (Melrose-Houston) 1 (August 1905):16.

⁴³Ibid. Also Dolph Shaner, "John Baxter of Baxter Springs" (Souvenir ed., Eightieth Anniversary of The Baxter State Bank, Baxter Springs, Kansas, 1985), pp. 7–8. Shaner says the "reunion week" pushed the Baxter population past 20,000. The residential population peaked at 10,000 immediately after the Civil War, when it became "the first cow town of the West," then rapidly declined. By 1900, the town had less than 5,000 residents. *World Almanac: 1908*, pp. 635–37. Due to dwindling numbers of veterans, the reunion also declined late in the nineteenth century and was discon-

tinued after 1917. It still seems to have been a fairly well attended meeting in 1905.

⁴⁴ *Apostolic Faith* (Melrose-Houston) 1 (September 1905): 3 and Parham, *Life,* pp. 125–26.

⁴⁵ Goss, p. 17.

⁴⁶ See Theodor Herzl, *The Jewish State,* trans. by Sylvie D'Avigdor, 4th ed. (London: Rita Searl, 1946). For an interpretation of Herzl's significant contribution, see David Vital, *The Origins of Zionism* (Oxford: Clarendon Press, 1975), pp. 234–370 and *Zionism: The Formative Years* (Oxford: Clarendon Press, 1982). Also Walter Laqueur, *A History of Zionism* (New York: Holt, Rinehart, and Winston, 1972), pp. 84–135.

⁴⁷ David A. Rausch, *Zionism Within Early American Fundamentalism: 1878–1918* (New York and Toronto: Edwin Mellen Press, 1979), pp. 83–132. Long after the establishment of the state of Israel in 1948, Pentecostals continued to view the restoration of the Jewish homeland as an eschatological sign linked to the outpouring of Holy Spirit baptism. See W. H. Turner, *Pentecost and Tongues* 2nd ed. (Franklin Springs, Georgia: Advocate Press, 1968), p. 31.

⁴⁸ Parham's remarks were strongly pro-Jewish and, in urban areas, he often drew a sizable representation from the Jewish community. See *Apostolic Faith* (Melrose-Houston) 1 (October–November 1905): 8–9 and (December 1905): 5–6. Also "Restoration of Palestine" *Joplin Globe* (n.d.) and "The Zion Movement" (Houston, n.d.), both in *PSD.*

⁴⁹ *Apostolic Faith* (Topeka) 1 (April 14, 1899): 4. In a letter written after Parham's death, a holiness minister, Bishop J. H. Allen, claimed to have introduced Parham to the Anglo-Israel scheme while Parham was pastor of the Methodist church at Eudora, Kansas. Parham clearly espoused the theory by early 1899. See (March 22, 1899): 2–3. Parham erroneously attributed the derivation of the word Saxon from "Isaac's Sons." See Parham, *Voice,* p. 106.

⁵⁰ *Apostolic Faith* (Melrose-Houston) 1 (October–November 1905): 11–12; "Jews to Found Own Home" (Houston, n.d.), in *PSD;* and Parham, *Voice,* pp. 103–4. Parham's thought on both Anglo-Israel and the discovery of the Ark were reinforced by his association with Frank Sandford. Sandford had been heavily influenced by the extensive writings on the subject by C. A. L. Totten, a professor of Military Science at Yale University. See Hiss, pp. 166–71.

⁵¹ "Creation and Formation" *Houston Daily Post* (13 August

1905) in *PSD*. The same address is repeated in Parham, *Voice*, pp. 81–85 and *Everlasting Gospel*, pp. 1–5. The "1,000 years = 1 day" model was a popular solution for those seeking to rationalize scripture with science. See Hector MacPherson, Jr., "The Creation Story in the Light of Modern Astronomy" *Popular Astronomy* 19 (August 1911): 426–30.

[52] Ibid. A similar solution to the "evolution problem" was proposed in the late 1960s by an Oklahoma State University faculty member. See Bradley O. Brauser, *Yestermorrows* (Ponca City, Oklahoma: By the author, 1969), pp. 38–54.

[53] Ibid. The paradox here is obvious, but it is one which Parham failed to address. He portrayed the sixth-day creation as inferior to the later creation, yet it was the eighth-day creation—not the sixth— which disobeyed its Maker in the Garden of Eden. A second point of incongruity is that while Parham downgraded intermarriage, he noted that the offspring of these first two races "became giants, mighty men of renown." The reference here is to Genesis 6:4.

[54] In later sermons, Parham revealed that, while he accepted some of the concepts of evolutionary creation, he strictly opposed the concept of human evolution from lower animals. See *Apostolic Faith* (Baxter) 3 (February 1927): 1–5. On one occasion, he suggested "an exiling of these professional monkeyfied preachers to the jungles of Africa where they can educate their ancestors. . . ." See Parham, *Selected Sermons*, p. 48.

[55] Parham, *Life*, pp. 126–28 and *Apostolic Faith* (Melrose-Houston) 1 (September 1905): 4.

[56] *Apostolic Faith* (Melrose-Houston) 1 (October–November 1905): 6. The biblical example for such a practice is Acts 19:11–12.

[57] Howard Goss remembered 134 baptized with the Spirit in the Houston suburb of Alvin during one religious campaign in the fall of 1905. He estimated that by the time of the Azusa Street outbreak in April 1906, over one thousand Texans had received the experience and sixty Apostolic Faith workers were actively ministering across the state. Lawrence, pp. 63–66.

[58] *Apostolic Faith* (Melrose-Houston) 1 (December 1905): 15.

5

[1] Parham first used the title under his portrait on the cover of *Apostolic Faith* (Melrose-Houston) 1 (December 1905).

²Parham, *Life,* pp. 136–41 and *Apostolic Faith* (Goose Creek) no. 20 (May 1921):5.

³Goss, p. 34. Goss noted that the school "convened in Caledonia Hall on Texas Avenue near Main Street," but later stated that the "residence and school building was at Rusk Avenue." Apparently Parham opened the school in the larger building on Texas Avenue and, when the turnout for the school failed to require the extra space, he moved the operation to the headquarters building. See *Apostolic Faith* (Melrose-Houston) 1 (December 1905):15.

⁴Nelson, pp. 35, 166–67.

⁵Ibid. A local ordinance had legally segregated Houston's street-car service on October 28, 1903. See B. H. Carroll, Jr., ed., *Standard History of Houston, Texas* (Knoxville, Tennessee: H. W. Crew and Co., 1912), p. 253. See also Parham, *Life,* p. 137.

⁶Marie Deacon, "Kansas as the 'Promised Land:' The View of the Black Press, 1890–1900" (M.A. Thesis, University of Arkansas, 1973), pp. 108–21.

⁷Parham, *Life,* p. 63 and "Prayer Is His Cure."

⁸Lawrence, p. 64. For reference to other blacks associated with the Houston meeting, see *Houston Chronicle* (13 August 1905):6 and Parham, *Life,* pp. 118–20.

⁹*Apostolic Faith* (Melrose-Houston) 1 (March 1906):12.

¹⁰Ibid., (May 1906):10.

¹¹Ibid., (March 1906):12.

¹²Ibid.:12–13.

¹³For further evidence of paternalistic attitudes and continued segregation among Southern Pentecostals after 1906, see Mack M. Pinson, "Sketch of the Life and Ministry of Mack M. Pinson" (Manuscript, Assemblies of God Archives, September 6, 1949), pp. 8–9.

¹⁴On Dowie's racial views, see *Leaves of Healing* 15 (September 24, 1904):801–6, 811; and Wacker, "Marching to Zion," pp. 504–5.

¹⁵For Nelson's analysis of Parham as a racist, see Nelson, pp. 97–98, 208–11. Nelson correctly gauges that Parham's efforts were paternalistic but he fails to distinguish the evangelist's blatant racial remarks in the post-Azusa period from his more benign racial policy during the early years of Pentecostal development. Parham's occasional racial barbs all date to the post-1910 period and are best viewed as a reaction to his disappointing loss of stature after the

Azusa Street breach late in 1906. His laudatory comments of the Ku Klux Klan during the 1920s are as much a reaction to the perceived dangers of modernism as any expression of Parham's racial ideology. See Parham, *Life,* pp. 162–64, 246 and *Apostolic Faith* (Baxter) 1 (December 1912):4–5; 3 (March 1927):5; 3 (January 1927):7. Charles Driscoll's article points out that religious support of the Ku Klux Klan in Kansas was a result, by and large, of a fear of Catholics. See Driscoll, p. 22.

[16]Parham, *Life,* p. 142 and Nelson, p. 66.

[17]The length of time that Seymour spent in the Houston school, and thus under Parham's influence, has been a source of considerable debate. Nelson suggests a very minimal influence, "something between a few days and a few weeks" (p. 67). He concludes from a variety of conflicting primary sources that Seymour's arrival occurred sometime in January. Parham, on the other hand, greatly exaggerated the stay noting that "Seymore [*sic*] . . . had spent six months in getting all the teachings in the Bible school in Houston, Texas." *Apostolic Faith* (Baxter) 2 (August 1926):2. All sources indicate that Seymour left before the temporary school was concluded in early March. Late January would be the earliest possible arrival time and early February, as I have suggested, is a more moderate assessment of the evidence. That would place Seymour in the Houston school for a total of five to six weeks—roughly half of the scheduled ten-week program. On the length of the school session and Seymour's departure, see Nelson, pp. 55–56, 66–67; Parham, *Life,* pp. 140–42; and *Apostolic Faith* (Goose Creek) no. 20 (May 1921):4–6. It is certain that Seymour stayed long enough to grasp the essentials of Parham's doctrine, particularly the concepts of spirit baptism evidenced by tongues and missionary conquest. At any rate, it is inaccurate to infer from the relationship that Seymour "did not accept a large amount of Parham's thought" (Nelson, p. 67).

[18]Parham, *Life,* pp. 143–45.

[19]Ibid., p. 147.

[20]Ibid., p. 148. Hall contributed to the first two issues of *Apostolic Faith* (Los Angeles) but, after Seymour's break with Parham in late October, was conspicuously absent from the periodical. The four additional workers, "Bro. and Sister [Walter] Oyler and Bro. and Sister Quinton," were acknowledged in the November issue as having "arrived in Los Angeles lately" with the note that "God has been using them in Whittier." They also failed to receive any

additional coverage in the periodical. See *Apostolic Faith* (Los Angeles) 1 (September 1906):4, (October 1906):3–4, and (November 1906):1. For Mrs. Oyler's perceptions of Azusa Street, see Parham, *Life*, pp. 161–62.

[21] *Apostolic Faith* (Los Angeles) 1 (September 1906):1 and Nelson, p. 56. Farrow's connection with Parham is certain since she worked in his home in Kansas and received Holy Spirit baptism under his ministry in the fall of 1905. Warren's initial exposure to the Pentecostal movement seems to have been a divine healing experience in Houston associated with one of Parham's 1905 campaigns as well. See *Apostolic Faith* (Los Angeles) 1 (September 1906):4.

[22] Nelson, pp. 55–59, 182–201; Anderson, pp. 62–69; Synan, *Holiness-Pentecostal Movement* pp. 104–10; and *Los Angeles Daily Times* (18 April 1906):Part II, 1.

[23] W. J. Seymour to Bro. Parham, 27 August 1906, printed in Parham, *Life*, pp. 154–5 and W. J. Seymour to Bro. Carothers, 12 July 1906, in *PSD*.

[24] To avoid confusion, this journal is always identified in the text; without such identification, the name refers to Parham's publication. The Azusa-based journal was clearly not edited by Seymour. He was a regular contributor and his articles were always carefully initialed. The editor remained officially anonymous but it was most likely Clara Lum, a white woman who served the Azusa group as Mission Secretary. Morris Golder, quoting from Glenn Cook's account, identifies Lum as the editor. Synan suggests Florence Crawford was the unnamed editor. See *Apostolic Faith* (Los Angeles) 1 (September 1906):4, (October 1906):4, (January 1908):2; Golder, p. 29; and Vinson Synan, Introduction to *Azusa Street,* by Frank Bartleman (Plainfield, New Jersey: Logos International, 1980), p. xix. Nelson notes that Lum alone controlled the mailing lists and, thereby, succeeded in "stealing" the paper away from Seymour. More precisely, Lum kept the Azusa mailing lists and continued to use them after her break with Seymour in May 1908 since she, as editor, considered them a product of her own labor. Seymour did publish at least one separate issue after Lum's departure. See Nelson, pp. 216–18.

[25] *Apostolic Faith* (Los Angeles) 1 (September 1906):1. By September 1906, Azusa had reached approximately one-half the size that the Houston wing of the movement had enjoyed roughly one year earlier when several hundred had received the Pentecostal experience. By Goss' estimate, Texas by the spring of 1906 boasted over one thousand spirit-filled believers and sixty full-time workers

(Lawrence, p. 66). In comparison, Azusa was still a relatively small group. The figures help to explain Parham's delay in going to Los Angeles. Obviously, he felt that his presence was required at the Midwestern pulse of the movement. He could not have known then the tremendous rate of growth that Azusa would experience in the months ahead. The article noted that an additional uncalculated number "have been saved and sanctified." Still the figures were apparently modest as evidenced by reference to 106 baptized at a summer baptismal service and only thirty-eight full-time field workers as late as October 1906. See (October 1906):1 and (September 1906):4.

[26] Anderson, p. 66. My assessment of Azusa's growth differs markedly from that of Nelson who, drawing on the memory of Arthur G. Osterberg, speculates that crowd sizes reached twelve hundred as early as May. Cf. Nelson, pp. 59, 232.

[27] Bartleman, pp. 49–66. *Azusa Street* is an unabridged reprint of Bartleman's 1925 history of the Azusa revival *How Pentecost Came to Los Angeles—How It Was in the Beginning* (Los Angeles: By the author).

[28] Ibid., pp. 67–85. Also Anderson, p. 70.

[29] See appendix A.

[30] *Apostolic Faith* (Houston-Melrose) 1 (December 1905):9–10.

[31] Ibid., p. 10.

[32] Parham, *Everlasting Gospel*, p. 7.

[33] *Apostolic Faith* (Melrose-Houston) 1 (March 1906):9. The notice explained: "It requires about $50 dollars [*sic*] to edit and mail the paper each month, and as we make no charges for it, we feel you dear readers are forgetting your part in contributing any or even all for each month's issue."

[34] Ibid.:9–11. Parham noted that the New Testament uses the words bishop and elder synonymously and listed 1 Timothy 3:1–7 and Titus 1:8–9 as the "spiritual qualifications of an Elder."

[35] Ibid.:9. Howard Goss recognized this move toward organization and acknowledged that Parham "with the advice of others" personally selected the officials. See Lawrence, p. 66.

[36] Ibid., (May 1906):4–6. Lilian Thistlethwaite noted that the name "Assembly Meeting" came from the scriptural injunction to "neglect not the Assembling of yourselves together." The reference is to Hebrews 10:25. Though Parham ceased to use the name after his movement split in 1907, the Pentecostal missions of the Midwest that formed the Assemblies of God in 1914 adopted it as both

a local church name and, collectively, as their denominational designation. Many of those present were quite familiar with the term from their prior association with Parham. On the actual selection of the name, see Carl Brumback, *Like A River: The Early Years of The Assemblies of God* (Springfield, Missouri: Gospel Publishing House, 1977), pp. 31–35.

[37] Seymour to Carothers, 12 July 1906.

[38] Ominously, Parham didn't consider appointing Seymour as a separate state director in California. It is unlikely that he would have appointed any black man to such a prestigious position but he certainly would not have done so without first visiting and determining the need for a new state organization.

[39] On Seymour's Board of Twelve, see Nelson, p. 60 and Anderson, p. 70. Both, following the account of Azusa participant Glenn Cook, suggest that Seymour began ordaining ministers and issuing ministerial credentials at this time. However, given Seymour's letter for credentials and "buttons" in July 1906, it is likely that Cook confused the chronology and Seymour did not assume those roles until after his break with Parham in late October. The Board of Twelve then was initially a body to coordinate the local work of the mission and the paper, presumably until Parham arrived to assume greater control. Seymour knew of Parham's assembly plan; he had in his possession a copy of the March 1906 journal which had outlined the new program. Cf. *Apostolic Faith* (Los Angeles) 1 (September 1906):4 and *Apostolic Faith* (Melrose-Houston) 1 (March 1906):4–5. Seymour used the term "assembly" for the local church in a separate discussion of church government printed almost a year after his formal break with Parham. See *Apostolic Faith* (Los Angeles) 1 (September 1907):3.

[40] Seymour to Parham, 27 August 1906. This source is problematical since it only appears in Mrs. Parham's account and the original can no longer be found in *PSD*. Yet Mrs. Parham notes specifically that she is quoting from the letter now "yellow with age." There is no reason to suspect her transcription, since the letter agrees in spirit with Parham's return letter to Seymour which appeared in *Apostolic Faith* (Los Angeles) 1 (September 1906):1. Significantly, Seymour's reference to "little revivals" seems to parallel the rise of the two other Pentecostal missions led by Fisher and Bartleman. Seymour's reference to "Satan is working" was most likely recognition of an unhealthy competition between the three and he requested Parham's visit to bring unity in a city-wide effort.

[41] *Apostolic Faith* (Los Angeles) 1 (September 1906):1. Parham's reference to "the outside fields I desire" further supports the contention that he exercised firm control over his religious allies. Despite his statements to the contrary, it was a role he would find impossible to relinquish.

[42] Parham, *Life*, pp. 155–56.

[43] Parham clearly knew of Dowie's troubles. In July 1906 he visited Topeka and was interviewed by local reporters. During that six-day visit, the local papers ran almost daily articles on the Zion struggle. See *Topeka Daily State Journal* (25 July 1906):6. On Dowie, see especially "Zion Not Dowie's" (27 July 1906):10.

[44] On the decline of Dowie's Zion, see Cook, pp. 355–401. Cook is generally sympathetic to Dowie, noting that most of Zion's problems can be traced to economic forces beyond the aging leader's control. See also Wacker, "Marching to Zion," pp. 507–8. Dowie's predicament was widely reported by both local and national press. For examples of intense coverage in nearby Waukegan, Illinois, see *Waukegan Daily Sun* (27 July 1906):1; (28 July 1906):1–2; and (12 September 1906):1–2. For examples of national coverage, see *New York Times* (2 April 1906):1; (3 April 1906):4; and (5 April 1906):1.

[45] Brumback, *Sound From Heaven*, p. 70 and Menzies, p. 65. The sequence of events is based on a personal letter from Louise Albach, a Zion school principal, to J. R. Flower, 30 August 1950. It is conceivable that Mrs. Hall is Mrs. Anna Hall of both Orchard and Azusa Street fame but there is no evidence to support such a conjecture. In 1904, Dowie had changed the name of his church by adding "Apostolic."

[46] To stress the divine origins of Parham's call to Zion, Mrs. Parham noted the turmoil in the city and concluded, "From a natural standpoint, it looked like a very unfavorable time to go to Zion City with any hopes of having a meeting." Parham, *Life*, p. 156. Yet the opposite was true. Prior to the religious turmoil of 1906, Dowie's powerful influence would have prevented any competition in the city. Parham, despite an obvious admiration for Dowie's faith healing practice, criticized the prophet as "narrow" and "self-advancing." Most of this criticism came after Dowie's claim in 1901 that he was personally the endtime manifestation of the prophet Elijah. See Parham, *Voice*, pp. 55–56 and *Apostolic Faith* (Topeka) 2 (January 1, 1900):7. On Dowie's claim, see Wacker, "Marching to Zion," pp. 502–3. Wacker cites Dowie's worldwide following as between

25,000 and 50,000.

[47] *Apostolic Faith* (Melrose-Houston) 1 (May 1906): 6, 12.

[48] Cook, pp. 395–96. Cook notes that out of 1,918 total votes, Voliva received an astounding 1,900. Since Dowie's supporters boycotted the election and his name didn't appear on the ballot, his true strength remained unknown.

[49] *Waukegan Daily Sun* (21 September 1906): 1. Newspaper accounts effectively date Parham's arrival to either September 19 or 20. The first reports erroneously referred to him as "Farnum." Parham later told reporters that, upon his arrival, he had visited Voliva to suggest that they work together for the good of Zion. Voliva, however, refused to see him. When Voliva subsequently became alarmed at the size of the Apostolic Faith meetings and wished a conference, Parham returned the insult. See (27 September 1906): 4.

[50] Ibid. (22 September 1906): 1–2. The article included a "partial list" of six Zion "invaders." Another article noted that there were as many as "two-score," though nowhere near that number received individual press coverage. See (27 September 1906): 4. Prior to Parham's success in Zion, reporters considered Crosby—with some sixty converts—Voliva's major opponent. She was accused by her detractors of advocating "free love" since she opposed legal marriage vows. Crosby's following remained small but she invoked continued news coverage with announcements of the expected birth of "holy ghost children." These children, "miraculously conceived and born," would be sinless since they came from unions devoid of any "carnal desire." In May 1907, Crosby and her companion, Arthur Bales, were jailed for three weeks on a charge of "illegal cohabitation." To secure their release, the two finally consented to a shortened form of the traditional marriage ceremony and were legally married by the local justice of the peace. By that time, Crosby's influence in Zion had dropped to only thirty followers. See (20 September, 1906): 1, (23 October 1906): 4, (15 January 1907): 1, and (21 May 1907): 1, 4.

[51] Ibid. (26 September 1906): 7.

[52] *New York Times* (27 September 1906): 7.

[53] *Waukegan Daily Sun* (29 September 1906): 1.

[54] Ibid. Other accounts were only slightly less complimentary. One noted "Tarham [*sic*] is a short man with glossy black hair and black eyes. He has a weak voice and is a poor speaker, but his evi-

dent emotion and seeming sincerity carry conviction and he is rapidly making converts." "New Prophet Invades Zion," Miscellaneous newsclipping from *PSD*.

⁵⁵ Ibid. (28 September 1906):1. Parham, had he won enough local support, could have called for an election between Voliva and himself. A victory in such an election would have ousted Voliva and installed Parham as the general overseer of the Christian Catholic Apostolic Church. See "Former Galena Preacher May Oust Overseer Voliva," Miscellaneous newsclipping in *PSD*.

⁵⁶ Ibid. (26 September 1906):7 and (27 September 1906):2, 4.

⁵⁷ Ibid. Also *Waukegan Daily Gazette,* 28 September 1906 in *PSD* and Chappell, p. 350.

⁵⁸ Ibid. (28 September 1906):1 and (8 October 1906):5. Early accounts accused Parham of the same tactic. See "Under Voliva's Nose Rented Tabernacle," *Waukegan Daily Sun,* in *PSD*.

⁵⁹ Voliva was fighting an internal battle for leadership as well. His succession of Dowie was not yet assured in Zion, much less among the 25,000 church members worldwide. See *Waukegan Daily Sun* (4 October 1906):1, 4. This internal battle would continue for over a year. Philip Cook's study of Zion noted that it was not until April 1908 that Voliva could claim to be the sole Overseer of the Christian Catholic Apostolic Church. Cook, p. 407.

⁶⁰ It is inconceivable that Parham emphasized the experience in his early meetings since no leak of the teaching appeared in the press during that period. Still there can be little doubt that he slowly prepared his followers for the onslaught of Pentecostal power.

⁶¹ *Waukegan Daily Sun* (18 October 1906):2.

⁶² Ibid. (19 October 1906):1. For other articles which denote the dramatic change in press coverage, see (22 October 1906): 4; (22 October 1906):5; and (29 October 1906):6. Also *Atchison* (Kansas) *Globe* (18 October 1906), Kansas Historical Society "Newsclippings File," p. 38. The importance of glossolalia in this turn of events is significant. "Tongues" were perceived as the "badge" of the Pentecostal movement. Since Pentecostals were often ridiculed on this account, it became the single most important identifying phenomenon.

⁶³ "Dowie Has His Say," Miscellaneous newsclippings in *PSD*.

⁶⁴ *Waukegan Daily Sun* (15 November 1906):8.

⁶⁵ Ibid. (23 October 1906):8. On Carothers' leadership in Zion, see (16 November 1906):1. Parham's departure was first recorded

in the October 23 afternoon edition. Ten days earlier, reports had circulated that Parham was raising money to build a tabernacle in Zion. It is reasonable then to speculate that his sudden decision to leave Zion was, in part, a West Coast fund raising effort since he left strong organizational leaders in the city and clearly intended to soon return. Cf. (12 October 1906):1. Nevertheless, his timing was probably conditioned most by the successful outpouring of Pentecost in Zion several days earlier and his concern over the long delay already encountered in the Los Angeles trip. See Parham, *Life,* p. 160.

6

[1] Seymour to Carothers, 12 July 1906. Carothers forwarded the letter on to Parham with the handwritten note: "Bro. Parham, I sent him credentials and wrote Bro. Aylor to send him the buttons." Also *Waukegan Daily Sun* (27 September 1906):7 and (27 September 1906):4.

[2] *Topeka Daily State Journal* (25 July 1906):6. See also *St. Louis Post-Dispatch* (2 August 1906):Part II, 11. The increased publicity from Azusa Street during the final weeks of the summer indicates that the movement there was gaining momentum. It also corresponds to Parham's dispatch of Mrs. Hall to help restore order in the revival effort.

[3] Ibid. (26 July 1906):10. See also (30 July 1906):10 and *St. Louis Post-Dispatch* (5 August 1906):7–b. Parham's political statements revealed a lingering Populist mentality. There was much in the Progressive platform of the first two decades of this century to attract the disgruntled Populists of the 1890s. Yet Populists harbored a profound distrust of government which prevented them from jumping on the Progressive bandwagon. Many, like Parham, found comfort in the dependability of religious faith. Parham then was personally opposed to alcohol but highly skeptical of government programs to solve the problem. His answer lay solely in personal religious conversion. The suspicion of Progressive programs was no doubt heightened by the movement's association with "social Christianity" and the mainline Protestant churches. See Hudson, pp. 315–17.

[4] Ibid. Balancing the favorable newspaper coverage were articles and editorials criticizing Parham for his brash public style and his frequent denunciation of "modern churches." See "Did Not Want to Hear Parham Finish" and "On Second Thought" in *PSD*.

[5] The distinction is one still made by Pentecostals. Ultimately the "discernment" process is highly subjective. An unspoken concensus develops over time within a given community to define "spiritual worship" and "flesh." Those who repeatedly go beyond the accepted bounds of emotional display are then counseled and discouraged from such activity. If they continue, they are ultimately ostracized. Within every Pentecostal community, discernment is intended to create a balance between two extremes all groups hope to avoid. In the lingo of Pentecostals, these are "wildfire" (uncontrolled manifestations in the flesh) and "quenching the spirit" (refusing to yield to valid spiritual manifestations).

[6] Prior to Azusa Street, Parham faced two such major encounters within his movement. The issue of emotion (and ultimately Parham's authority as judge) had resulted in a minor split among his Galena followers sometime early in 1904. The split was probably a major factor in the decline of the revival there. Parham was more successful in "correcting" a similar problem in Galveston during the winter of 1905–06. Cf. Murphy, p. 9 and Lawrence, p. 63.

[7] Parham, *Life*, pp. 155–56. Except Parham's recollection, there is no evidence that Seymour ever wrote such a letter. Seymour clearly desired his teacher's visit; however, Parham's perception of the predicament in Los Angeles was colored by the negative publicity he had encountered during the summer. His harsh recollection was also influenced by his rejection at Azusa. It is probable that others (most notably Anna Hall or the Oylers) had written Parham with negative reports. See Parham, *Life*, p. 168. On this problem, also see Nelson, pp. 95–98.

[8] Ibid., p. 163. Parham later identified the Azusa participant Glenn Cook as one of these "hypnotists" who led the work astray. *Apostolic Faith* (Baxter) 2 (September 1913):9. See also Ewart, pp. 198–99.

[9] Ibid., p. 164 and *Apostolic Faith* (Baxter) 3 (February 1914):9. Though Nelson discounts Parham's assessment of Azusa as a coverup for racial prejudice, Shumway seems to confirm the impression that the atmosphere was fundamentally different from that to which Parham was accustomed. Cf. Nelson, pp. 208–11

and Shumway, "Gift of Tongues," p. 69; "A Critical History," pp. 115–16.

[10] See Bartleman, pp. 68–69 and appendix B.

[11] Shumway, "Gift of Tongues," pp. 178–79.

[12] Parham, *Voice,* pp. 83–84 and 106–7. It doesn't seem to have occurred to Parham that, following this logic, it would have been a most "Christian" act to endorse miscegenation as a way of eventually spreading the benefits of the chosen white race.

[13] Goss, new rev. ed. by Ruth Goss Nortje (Hazelwood, Missouri: Word Aflame Press, 1977), pp. 96–97. Farrow's unique ability was also recorded by Azusa participants. See Mother Cotton, "Inside Story of the Outpouring of the Holy Spirit" *Message of the Apostolic Faith* 1 (April 1939):1–3.

[14] *World Almanac: 1908,* pp. 642–43. The diversity of nationalities and languages in Los Angeles in 1906 is well attested. See Lawrence, pp. 78–79 and Nelson, p. 183. Nelson, however, greatly exaggerated the character of the Azusa Street participants when he noted that "multitudes converged on Azusa including virtually every race, nationality, and social class on earth" (p. 196). Azusa participants, and all early Pentecostals, were predominantly working class. The degree of race mixing allowed in Los Angeles is evidenced by news stories of interracial marriages—one of which appeared alongside the original coverage of the Azusa Street revival. See *Los Angeles Daily Times* (18 April 1906): Part II, 1.

[15] Parham's racial attitudes clearly stiffened after the Azusa Street incident. An early pro-Parham source indicated that race became a factor when the evangelist refused to acknowledge that black believers could be in the elite "bride of Christ" at the time of the Second Coming. See K. Brower letter, Los Angeles, 1909 quoted in *Apostolic Faith* (Goose Creek) no. 20 (May 1921):6–7.

[16] *Apostolic Faith* (Baxter) 1 (December 1912):4–5. For other examples of Parham's growing racist attitude, see *Everlasting Gospel,* pp. 72–73 and 118–19. Despite Parham's shift toward a harsher racism, he still elicited a paternalistic impulse and occasionally ministered to interracial crowds at camp meetings. See Parham, *Life,* pp. 246 and 302.

[17] Nelson errs in contending that "Parham saw [glossolalia] as the only evidence, while Seymour did not" (Nelson, p. 130). Both men denied that tongue speech formed the only evidence; both men also affirmed that it provided the initial evidence. The distinction, of course, was somewhat semantical. Since tongues served un-

equivocally as the initial evidence, it was, in effect, the "only" evidence that mattered. On Parham's views, see *Everlasting Gospel,* pp. 63–69. For Seymour's, see *Apostolic Faith* (Los Angeles) 1 (February–March 1907): 7, (June–September 1907): 3, and 2 (May 1908): 3. Independent articles in the Los Angeles journal affirmed the significance of tongues as "the Bible evidence." See 1 (September 1906): 2–3, (November 1906): 1, and (October–January 1908): 2.

[18] See Parham, *Everlasting Gospel,* pp. 74–76; *Apostolic Faith* (Los Angeles) 1 (November 1906): 4, (January 1907): 2, and Taylor, *Spirit and Bride,* pp. 112–26.

[19] The strength of this belief has been underestimated by previous historians of Pentecostalism because it faded out after the early years of development. Synan suggested that "very few Pentecostal leaders accepted this premise" (*Holiness-Pentecostal Movement,* p. 103, n. 19) and Nelson denied that Seymour taught it (p. 180, n. 109). However, Pentecostal literature prior to 1909 indicates that this was a common assumption throughout the movement. Cf. *Apostolic Faith* (Los Angeles) 1 (September 1906): 1–4, (October 1906): 1, (November 1906): 2–3, (February–March 1907): 1; *Apostolic Faith* (Portland, Oregon) 2 (July–August 1908): 1; *Bridegroom's Messenger* (Atlanta) 1 (December 1907): 1; *Upper Room* 1 (June 1909): 6–7; *Holiness Advocate* (May 15, 1907): 7, (October 1908): 4; and Taylor, *Spirit and Bride,* pp. 17, 35, 51–52, 62–63, 93–94, 102–5. On the same issue, see Shumway, "Gift of Tongues," pp. 42–46, 181; Wayne E. Warner, ed., *Touched by the Fire* (Plainfield, New Jersey: Logos International, 1978), pp. 23–24; and Anderson, pp. 90–91.

[20] Parham, *Life,* p. 169. See also Shumway, "Gift of Tongues," p. 169.

[21] Interestingly enough, anti-Pentecostal writers sometimes accepted the validity of xenoglossa as mission tongues. However, they doubted that Pentecostals had the genuine article and rejected their message precisely on those grounds. See Alma White, *Demons and Tongues,* 4th ed. (Zeraphath, New Jersey: Pillar of Fire, 1949), pp. 119–23.

[22] See appendix C.

[23] Parham, *Life,* pp. 163–64, 171; *Apostolic Faith* (Baxter) 2 (July 1926): 6; and *Waukegan Daily Sun* (5 December 1906): 3.

[24] *Waukegan Daily Sun* (30 November 1906): 1, (1 December 1906): 1, and (3 December 1906): 6.

[25] Ibid. (5 February 1907): 3. The Waukegan paper quotes from

Apostolic Faith (January 1907). An even longer explanation is quoted in Parham, *Life,* pp. 176–77. This issue of Parham's journal, and presumably others, was published in Zion City. I have been unable, however, to locate any surviving copies.

[26] Carothers had been a lawyer prior to entering the ministry and continued to practice at intervals during his life. See *Apostolic Faith* (Melrose-Houston) 1 (September 1905):8 and *Herald of the Church* (Houston) 1 (June 1925):8.

[27] Cf. *Apostolic Faith* (Melrose-Houston) 1 (December 1905):12; (March 1906):11–12; and (May 1906):9–10.

[28] *Waukegan Daily Sun* (5 December 1906):3; (18 December 1906):3; (5 January 1907):4; and (25 January 1907):1.

[29] Parham, *Life,* pp. 191–97. See also *Waukegan Daily Sun* (11 February 1907):1, 5. The newspaper article reported that Parham planned to visit Frank Sandford's community in Shiloh, Maine. Sandford had only recently left Shiloh for a three-year excursion around the world during which he and his band of missionaries anchored off the coast of each continent and fervently prayed for revival. Parham may have figured to exploit the advantage of Sandford's absence by introducing his own theological ideas there. If so, he seems to have made no significant impact and failed even to note Shiloh as a stop on the tour. However, he did recall a visit to nearby Lisbon Falls where he enjoyed the company of "old friends." Cf. Hiss, pp. 416–17 and Parham, *Life,* p. 193.

[30] Lawrence, pp. 67–68 and Goss, rev. ed., pp. 98–102. An incident at the short-lived Waco Bible School in Waco, Texas, in February 1907 illustrates Parham's loss of stature. There, members of the Texas Apostolic Faith questioned the theological doctrine of tongues as the initial evidence. With Carothers leading the way, however, the orthodox position prevailed. The controversy—and particularly Parham's absence in the matter—is indicative of the former Projecter's ouster from an important segment of the Texas wing. On the controversy, see Menzies, pp. 124–26.

[31] Howard Goss' earliest memoirs in the Lawrence account clearly dated the issue of Parham's immorality prior to the Waco school incident in February 1907. Mrs. Parham's account, however, suggested that Parham's arrival in Texas in April 1907 was received in a spirit of unity and affection and postdated the issue of morals until the formal charges in July. She noted that problems began for Parham in Zion City during the period of the Northeast tour but

attributed the conflict to Parham's refusal to organize. Cf. Parham, *Life,* pp. 158, 172–73, 183, and 197.

[32] *Waukegan Daily Sun* (28 January 1907):1. The paper acknowledged that its report was based on widespread rumor and that the Zion police department knew nothing of the report. Mrs. Parham remembered "false accusations" as early as 1902. Parham, *Life,* p. 84.

[33] Lawrence, pp. 67–68 and Goss, rev. ed., pp. 132–33. The issue of Parham's guilt or innocence was such an explosive issue that both Carothers and Goss resigned their official positions to quell rumors that they were attacking Parham for their own personal gain. A more neutral candidate, A. G. Canada was elected in July 1907 as the official leader of the Texas Apostolic Faith work. Nevertheless, Carothers and Goss remained prominent figures among Texas Pentecostals throughout their lives. After July 1907, both this new organization and Parham's loyal churches continued to use the Apostolic Faith name. By 1912, however, the Canada-Carothers-Goss group, now joined by E. N. Bell of Fort Worth, had switched to the more neutral term Pentecostal to distinguish themselves from Parham's work. This element of the Texas Pentecostal movement played an important role in the establishment of the Assemblies of God in 1914. See *Apostolic Faith* (Houston) 2 (October 1908):4; Goss, rev. ed., pp. 262–86; and Brumback, *Like A River,* pp. 1–40.

[34] *San Antonio Light* (19 July 1907):1. Parham's "failure" always contained sexual overtones. The most common charge was homosexuality though both adultery and masturbation were occasionally inferred. The discrepancies were apparently the result of "vague" gossip. On the charges, see Anderson, pp. 140, 272–73; Goff, "Charles F. Parham," p. 233; Bloch–Hoell, pp. 19–20; and Synan, *Holiness-Pentecostal Movement,* pp. 112–13. The insinuation of masturbation was peculiar to Irvine John Harrison who noted that the accusations against Parham were "based upon the statement of one individual, charging that he observed him [i.e., Parham] while peeking through the keyhole of his door, misconducting himself while alone in his room." See Harrison, pp. 97–98. On early-twentieth-century fears and misconceptions of masturbation, see Regina Lois Wolkoff, "The Ethics of Sex: Individuality and the Social Order in Early Twentieth Century Sexual Advice Literature" (Ph.D. dissertation, University of Michigan, 1974), pp. 18–23 and 72–77.

[35] *San Antonio Daily Express* (20 July 1907):12. See William Parker, *Homosexuality: A Selective Bibliography of Over 3000 Items* (Metuchen, New Jersey: Scarecrow Press, 1971), pp. 274–82 on state laws prohibiting homosexuality.

[36] Ibid. (24 July 1907):12. Also *San Antonio Light* (23 July 1907):7. One of the bondsmen, J. Ed Cabaniss of Katy, Texas, had known Parham only since early 1906. He remained a staunch follower throughout the evangelist's career. See Parham, *Life,* pp. 137–40 and 269–70.

[37] *San Antonio Light* (24 July 1907):2. On L. C. Hall, see *Leaves of Healing* 15 (September 24, 1904):819.

[38] File No. 18668, "State of Texas vs. J. J. Jourdan" *Criminal Minutes: District Court, Bexar County, Texas,* May 1907.

[39] Parham, *Life,* p. 198. Interestingly enough, Mrs. Parham fails to mention San Antonio by name anywhere in her book. Lack of any record of indictment in the Bexar County Courthouse is proof enough of Mrs. Parham's contention that the case was dropped, particularly in light of the accurate files for the Jourdan theft case two months earlier. Thus the only official record of the event would have been the arrest affidavit. The San Antonio Police Department routinely disposed of such forms once a case had been dismissed and no such records from 1907 exist. Interview with David J. Garcia, District Clerk, Bexar County, San Antonio, Texas, 14 August 1985.

[40] Several studies have shown that public awareness of homosexual activity increased toward the end of the nineteenth century. The 1895 trial and conviction of the English writer Oscar Wilde jolted the sensibilities of Victorian society. Government response to the increased publicity was an inclusion of sodomy laws throughout much of Europe and the United States. See John Rutledge Martin, "Sexuality and Science: Victorian and Post-Victorian Scientific Ideas on Sexuality" (Ph.D. dissertation, Duke University, 1978), pp. 64–80; Jeffrey Meyers, *Homosexuality and Literature, 1890–1930* (Montreal: McGill-Queen's University Press, 1977), pp. 1–10; and Vern L. Bullough, *Homosexuality: A History* (New York and London: Garland STPM Press, 1979), pp. 39–45. Bullough pays special attention to the development and interpretation of sodomy laws in Texas (pp. 43–45).

[41] The credibility of the religious accounts is a crucial issue. At least two non-Pentecostal papers seem to have taken some liberty with the story. The *Zion Herald* (Zion, Illinois) and the *Burning*

Bush (Waukesha, Wisconsin) reprinted a damaging account of Parham's case supposedly quoted from the *San Antonio Express*. However, quite unlike the matter-of-fact stories which appeared in the San Antonio press, these detailed accounts included references to an eyewitness and a written confession. See *Supplement to the Zion Herald* (26 July 1907) and *Burning Bush* 6 (September 19, 1907):6–7. In addition to my own search, I paid for a thorough check of all daily and weekly editions of the *Express* for the period surrounding Parham's arrest. The *San Antonio Express and News* staff confirmed my own suspicions. The articles "quoted" in the *Herald* and *Bush* never appeared in the San Antonio news releases. Letter from Judy Zipp, Librarian, *San Antonio Express and News*, 29 April 1986.

⁴² *Supplement to the Zion Herald* (26 July 1907). If the *Express* staff informed the *Herald* of a written confession, they neglected to use the information in their own dispatches. There is also no other evidence of a San Antonio paper labeling Jourdan as "Jew boy."

⁴³ Ibid. Cf. *Burning Bush* 6 (September 19, 1907):6–7 and *Waukegan Daily Sun* (27 July 1907):1, 5. As these sources indicate, Parham's problems made headlines in only selective areas and was not a part of a nationwide media blitz. All the sources I have located with this account can be traced to the *Zion Herald*. Presumably, much of the news traveled in Pentecostal circles by way of the grapevine.

⁴⁴ Ibid. The emphasis is contained in the original source. In addition to Parham, Voliva launched a direct attack on "Parham's associates" in Zion. Among them were: "Bingley, a self-confessed dirty old kisser;" "Fockler, a self-confessed adulterer;" and "Brudder Tom, . . . an immoral man . . . caught . . . hugging and kissing Sister Hall." The *Waukegan Daily Sun* reported that the Parham sect in Zion attempted legal redress by presenting the article to United States postal authorities and claiming unlawful defamation of character. The authorities refused to act on the matter. See *Waukegan Daily Sun* (27 July 1907):5.

⁴⁵ Ibid. Portions of the article contradict accepted facts. Parham is made to say "I will not fight this case—even if they kill me I will not resist." Yet the San Antonio papers clearly reported Parham's intention to fight the charges. Also, Jourdan at age 22 could hardly be described as an "angel-voiced boy." Finally, the article erroneously reports that Parham had previously preached in India, though on

this point the San Antonio reporters also erred. Cf. *San Antonio Light* (24 July 1907):2. Although no conclusive evidence points to Voliva as having actually created the scandal, he frequently pedaled rumors of immorality concerning his chief opponents. See *Waukegan Daily Sun* (18 February 1907):1 which includes the accusation of sodomy against one of Dowie's overseers. See also "Voliva To Lay Bare Dual Life of Dowie," Miscellaneous newsclipping in *PSD*.

⁴⁶ For allusions to the charges in Parham's writings and the account by his wife, see *Apostolic Faith* (Baxter) 1 (December–January 1912–13):8–9; 2 (August 1926):1–4; and Parham, *Life*, pp. 178–79, 184–88, 210–13, 260–61, 349.

⁴⁷ Though to date nothing has appeared in print, this is the opinion of Parham's daughter-in-law, Pauline Parham. Mrs. Parham is still a well-known speaker in Apostolic Faith circles. Interview with Pauline Parham, Dallas, Texas, 12 August 1985. The implication of Carothers seems to be based on Charles Parham's recollection that Carothers was "the first man who sought leadership." See *Apostolic Faith* (Baxter) 2 (September 1913):9–10. Significantly Carothers' name was edited out of news articles reprinted by Parham, Cf. *Houston Daily Post* (20 August 1906):10 and (27 August 1906):7 with *Apostolic Faith* (Baxter) 3 (December 1927):5–7. The August 20 article is erroneously attributed to the *Houston Chronicle* (2 September 1906). The intentional editing is clear in *PSD*. Other Parham apologists have attributed the rumors to enemies in New York and Los Angeles. On Los Angeles, see *Apostolic Faith* (Goose Creek) no. 20 (May 1921):6–7. The references to New York were gleaned from an interview with Naomi Busch, former editor of the *Apostolic Faith* (Baxter), Baxter Springs, Kansas, 31 March 1983.

⁴⁸ For Carothers' views on weak organization, see *Apostolic Faith* (Houston) 2 (October 1908):4, 7. This periodical, begun in September 1907 after the break with Parham, was edited by Carothers. He envisioned unity throughout the Pentecostal ranks but via a very loose organizational structure entirely consistent with that begun by Parham in March 1906. See also *Apostolic Faith* (Melrose-Houston) 1 (March 1906):15–16; *Herald of the Church* 1 (June 1925):2–5; "The Church Question," Miscellaneous newsclipping in *PSD;* and Ewart, rev. ed., pp. 66–68.

⁴⁹ Goss, rev. ed., p. 269.

⁵⁰ Though most of Parham's original followers certainly knew

about the rumors, those who joined him later in his ministry often did not. Pauline Parham remembers being shocked when she first learned about the ordeal in the early 1970s while reading Vinson Synan's history of Pentecostalism. She claims that the Parham children were unaware of the charges against their father. Parham Interview. Marjorie Haire, who traveled with Parham during the 1920s, remembered rumors of immorality but had no knowledge of the exact charge. Her reaction to the gossip was simple—"That was a lie." Interview with Marjorie Haire, Rogers, Arkansas, 12 June 1985. Rev. Algernon Benoni Stanberry, Jr., another traveling companion, first heard the rumors in 1931 after Parham's death. His reaction was equally supportive of Parham. "I slept with him, eat [*sic*] with him and . . . I could swear on a stack of Bibles that there was never one immoral approach in our ministry together. I wouldn't no [*sic*] more believe it than . . . [pause] and I wouldn't President Reagan, either." Interview with A. B. Stanberry, Jr., Alvin, Texas, 16 August 1985.

[51] Floyd also recalled that Howard Goss was "one of the main instigators of the prosecution." David Lee Floyd Interview by Wayne Warner, 10 April 1981, Tape no. 3, Assemblies of God Archives, Springfield, Missouri. Curiously, Shumway didn't mention the charges in his 1914 work though he alluded to similar claims against other Pentecostal leaders. See Shumway, "Gift of Tongues," p. 46.

[52] See E. N. Bell's disclaimer of Parham in *Word and Witness* (Malvern, Arkansas) 8 (October 20, 1912): 3 and *Pentecostal Evangel* (January 7, 1922): 8; J. R. Flowers' opinion in Hoover, p. 16; and Howard Goss' recollections in Goss, rev. ed., pp. 132–33. On the denunciation of Pentecostalism in general on account of the charges, see H. J. Stolee, *Pentecostalism: The Problem of the Modern Tongues Movement* (Minneapolis: Augsburg Publishing House, 1936, reprint ed. as *Speaking in Tongues,* 1963), p. 63 and Synan, *Holiness-Pentecostal Movement,* p. 144.

[53] Technically, the accusation against Parham would have been bisexuality, not homosexuality, since there is every indication that he fathered six children. On this note, there is some indication that the charges created a rift between Parham and his wife. A. B. Stanberry recalled that when he first met the Parhams in 1925, he sensed that they were somewhat aloof from one another and noted with curiosity that they always slept in separate bedrooms. Parham later

confided in him that they had had no "mutual relations" since their last child was born in the summer of 1906. Stanberry Interview. The change in their relationship could have been a simple matter of birth control but the timing of the event with the beginning of the sodomy rumors is striking. On abstinence as a common method of birth control during the Victorian era, see Wolkoff, p. 6.

[54] The shift is perhaps best demonstrated by Parham's emphasis after 1909 on eschatology, the dominant theme in *The Everlasting Gospel*.

[55] *Herald of the Church* 1 (June 1925): 10–11. The selection indicates that the problem between Seymour and Parham was a "governmental test" (i.e., Parham's authority) though the question of Parham's alleged immorality may have been an issue. Writing in 1908, Carothers called the Azusa revival "one of the greatest revivals of modern times." He recorded that "in the winter of 1906 the work in Los Angeles separated from us, under circumstances which the present writer believes justified them, but about which it would be painful to write." *Apostolic Faith* (Houston) 2 (October 1908): 1. Agnes Ozman noted that, some years later, Seymour was a guest speaker at Carothers' Brunner Pentecostal Tabernacle in Houston. She seems to have had similar reservations about Parham's quick denunciation of "fanaticism." See LaBerge, "History," p. 6 and *What God Hath Wrought*, p. 51.

[56] Parham's frankness in the pulpit was questioned even by some of his followers. An example of questionable behavior was his practice of asking all females in the audience to cross and then uncross their legs. Following the exercise, he admonished his listeners on the dangers of immorality by exclaiming to the women, "Now you've just opened the gates of hell." Interview with Geralean Harshfield, Oklahoma City, Oklahoma, 14 May 1985.

[57] *Waukegan Daily Sun* (30 November 1906): 6, (18 June 1907): 1, 4, and (2 July 1907): 7. Reporters generally categorized all these groups as "Parhamites."

[58] Ibid. (20 September 1907): 1–2. See also (21 September 1907): 1, 4, (25 September 1907): 1, and (15 November 1907): 1, 6. On the specific linking of Parham's name with the affair and his subsequent disavowal of Mitchell, see (21 September 1907): 5 and (23 September 1907): 1, 5. Shumway uncritically linked Parham with the manslaughter case in his 1914 study. Shumway, "Gift of Tongues," pp. 158–59. The initial reports reached as far South as

San Antonio. See *San Antonio Light* (20 September 1907) : 1.

⁵⁹ The estimate is conservative. Sixty, not including Parham's missions, were listed with addresses in Carothers' *Apostolic Faith* (Houston) 2 (October 1908) : 5.

⁶⁰ *Apostolic Messenger* (Winnipeg, Canada), November 1908 as printed in Zelma E. Argue, *What Meaneth This? The Story of Our Personal Experiences and Evangelistic Campaigns* (Alton, Illinois: By the author, 1924), p. 13. Shumway independently confirmed the tremendous growth in his 1914 account. See Shumway, "Gift of Tongues," p. 191.

⁶¹ Chappell, p. 351.

⁶² Ibid., pp. 351–57. Also see Herbert V. Knight, *Ministry Aflame* (Amherst, Wisconsin: Palmer Publications, 1972), pp. 16–24 and Harrison, pp. 72–73. On Bosworth and Branham, see Parham, *Life,* p. 190 and Harrell, pp. 27–42, 159–65. On Richey, see Lindsay, pp. 29–34. Parham claimed that the Zion experience produced no less than five hundred Pentecostal ministers and workers. *Apostolic Faith* (Baxter) 2 (July 1926) : 5. The evidence for his claim is at least strong enough to forever dismiss Lyle Murphy's suggestion that Parham's work in Zion City resulted in "little gained for the effort." Murphy, p. 10.

⁶³ Ibid. On Brown, see *In Loving Memory: Marie Estelle Brown* (New York: Glad Tidings Tabernacle, 1971). Parham's visit to New York in the spring of 1907 helped to solidify support for Glad Tidings. Through another New York contact, Mrs. Lucy Leatherman, Parham also had some influence on Thomas Barratt, the "Pentecostal Apostle to Europe." See Anderson, pp. 130–31 and Thomas Ball Barratt, *When the Fire Fell* (Larvik, Norway: Alfons Hansen and Soner, 1927), pp. 128–31.

⁶⁴ Parham's travels in 1908 carried him to California, Texas, Alabama, Mississippi, Kansas, Missouri, Oklahoma, Illinois, and New York. Parham, *Life,* pp. 203–8.

⁶⁵ The first evidence of this practice is a letter written by Parham to his supporters in Kansas and Missouri in May 1908 which noted "I am your father in the gospel." Parham, *Life,* p. 205. See also pp. 197, 433, and "Dedication." On the emphasis as founder, see "Seventh Annual Watch Night Memorial," Handbill in *PSD.*

⁶⁶ While en route to New York, Parham held services in Zion City. His presence elicited a mixed variety of approval and opposition from local Pentecostals. See T. G. A. to Miss Marie Burgess,

12 December 1908, in *Parham Scrapbook,* Apostolic Faith Church, Baxter Springs, Kansas (hereafter cited as *PSBS.* See Sources Consulted, Collections).

⁶⁷Parham, *Life,* pp. 207–8 and Shumway, "Gift of Tongues," p. 170. See also "Sure He Will Find Ark of the Covenant in Palestine at Once," Miscellaneous newsclipping; "NOTICE!," Handbill; "The Restoration of the Ark of the Covenant," Handbill; and "Not Listed, Freight Tariffs Don't Mention Rate on Arks," Miscellaneous newsclipping, all in *PSD.*

7

¹Sarah Parham's biography indicates a noticeable decline in her husband's travels for 1909, then a dramatic resurgence in activity from 1910 on. See Parham, *Life,* pp. 208–58. Significantly, in light of the split in Texas, the fourth annual Orchard reunion in 1909 was moved to Brookshire, Texas. It was held in varying locations thereafter.

²Quoted from the *Kansas City Star* in *Apostolic Faith* (Melrose-Houston) 1 (July 1905):7.

³Wayne Griswold, *Kansas, Her Resources and Developments* (Cincinnati: Robert Clarke and Co., 1871), pp. 35–36. For a similarly optimistic assessment, see *Faithful Witness* (Topeka, Kansas) 4 (July 1, 1882):3.

⁴Dolph Shaner, *John Baxter of Baxter Springs* (Souvenir ed., Eightieth Anniversary of the Baxter State Bank, 1985) and *Baxter Springs . . . A City on the Move,* (Baxter Springs, Kansas: Baxter Springs Chamber of Commerce, 1986). Though small, Baxter Springs enjoyed steady growth during the early part of the century. The 1920 census listed 3,608; the 1930 figure ws 4,541. *World Almanac and Book of Facts: 1933* (New York: New York World Telegram, 1933), p. 348. After the Great Depression and the decline of the mining industry, the town's growth stymied. The 1986 population was only 5,203.

⁵Parham, *Life,* pp. 233, 245, and 254. Also Harshfield Interview. The meeting was actually held on the weekend closest to Parham's birthday. The practice continued throughout his lifetime.

⁶Ibid., pp. 235, 248.

[7]Ibid. Before Parham's death, one historian of Kansas labeled him "a distinguished and world-famed evangelist" and described the converted brewery in Baxter Springs as a "spacious and attractive residence." Connelley, p. 1,342.

[8]Ibid., p. 247. In 1958 Parham was prominently featured in the town's centennial history. *Centennial: The Baxter Springs Story, 1858–1958* (Baxter Springs, Kansas: Souvenir program, 1958), p. 17.

[9]Conspicuously, Illinois registered only nine entries on the list with one lone addressee from Zion City. The poor showing is evidence of the tremendous decline in Parham's support there after 1907.

[10]Gail W. Schultz, comp., "Mailing List of the Apostolic Faith," (Manuscript, editorial files of the *Apostolic Faith Report*, Baxter Springs, Kansas, n.d.). The typed-list dates sometime between Parham's death in 1929 and Mrs. Parham's death in 1937, though the 110 written entries may have been added even later. Staff personnel in Baxter Springs were uncertain how long the recently discovered list had actually been used.

[11]Cf. appendix A. The estimate is fairly conservative. In 1910, the average number of persons per dwelling in the United States was 5.2; the average number of persons per family was 4.5. *World Almanac: 1915*, p. 709.

[12]A favorite crowd attraction was Parham's music program which featured congregational singing, special vocals from a traveling evangelistic team, and instrumental ensembles. Stanberry and Haire Interviews. Also "My Personal Testimony" in Bennie Stanberry, *Songs of Inspiration* (Katy, Texas: By the author, 1967) and Parham, *Life*, pp. 308, 327–28, 435–37.

[13]Geralean Harshfield, a young girl in the 1920s, recalled that her grandmother was healed in a Parham revival in Texas during this period and noted that healing services were a regular part of Parham's camp meetings. Harshfield Interview.

[14]Stanberry Interview. A similar account is found in Parham, *Life*, p. 323.

[15]Parham Interview.

[16]The claim is recorded in Connelley, p. 1,342.

[17]This information on McPherson comes from front-page coverage of her expected trip to Fayetteville, Arkansas, in 1928. Parham visited the city for a small meeting at precisely the same time but

received no mention in local papers. Ironically, Sister Aimee was stranded by floods in Enid, Oklahoma and was unable to make the trip. At the last minute, she sent a telegram which was read to the two thousand people who had gathered to hear her. See *Fayetteville Daily Democrat* (26 June 1928): 1, 6 and (28 June 1928): 1, 4.

[18] Parham, *Life,* pp. 265, 269.

[19] Parham, *Everlasting Gospel,* p. 7 and *Selected Sermons,* p. 52.

[20] *World Almanac: 1922,* p. 389. There is no evidence in Parham family records that Charles Parham ever received a sufficient net income ($1,000 in 1919) to require him to file a federal income tax return.

[21] This assessment is based on personal interviews with surviving Parham followers and also on photographs which reveal the presence of automobiles and a relatively well-dressed clientele at Apostolic Faith camp meetings. Haire, Harshfield, and Stanberry Interviews.

[22] "Texas State Convention of the Apostolic Faith Movement at Temple, Texas, April 12–26, 1914," Handbill in *PSD*. Also *Apostolic Faith* (Baxter) 1 (August 1925): 6 and 2 (August 1926): 2.

[23] *Apostolic Faith* (Baxter) 1 (July 1912): Supplement, and 2 (September 1913): 10–11. Also Blumhofer, pp. 43–44.

[24] Parham, *Voice,* pp. 23–24.

[25] Synan, *Holiness-Pentecostal Movement,* pp. 153–63. Books by Oneness Pentecostals have been much more sympathetic to Parham than those by other Pentecostals. Frank J. Ewart's *The Phenomenon of Pentecost* recognized Parham's role long before other denominational treatments. In addition, a recent Oneness history appropriately opens with this quote from Parham. See Clanton, p. 13.

[26] See chapter 2, p. 35.

[27] *Apostolic Faith* (Baxter) Special ed. (December 25, 1910): 5 and 2 (August 1926): 2. For opposition to the doctrine within holiness-Pentecostal circles, see *Live Coals* (Mercer, Missouri) 2 (January 6, 1904): 1, 4 and *Discipline of the Pentecostal Holiness Church* (Franklin Springs, Georgia: Publishing House of the Pentecostal Holiness Church, 1925), p. 8.

[28] *Way of Faith* 19 (April 22, 1909): 6.

[29] *Word and Witness* 8 (October 20, 1912): 3.

[30] On Parham's continued espousal of xenoglossic mission tongues, see *Apostolic Faith* (Baxter) 2 (November 1913): 14

and 2 (August 1926):15–16. Also Shumway, "Gift of Tongues," pp. 41–42.

[31] Ibid., Special ed. (December 25, 1910):3–4. Agnes Ozman LaBerge attended the camp meeting around 1912 and later noted that the fear of fanaticism was, in her opinion, excessive. See LaBerge, *What God Hath Wrought*, p. 51.

[32] *Apostolic Faith* (Topeka) 1 (March 22, 1899):4 and Parham, *Voice*, pp. 109–14. For an excellent summary of Parham's eschatological framework, see Anderson, pp. 81–87.

[33] Parham, *Everlasting Gospel*, p. 77. Parham claimed that he received replies to three of the letters but none of the recipients cared to comment specifically on his eschatological model. No evidence of such responses are found in the Parham family scrapbooks. It is unclear how Parham considered such warnings needful since, presumably, future events could not be altered.

[34] *Everlasting Gospel* (Baxter Springs, Kansas) 5 (April 1916): 1–2. Also Parham, *Everlasting Gospel*, pp. 19–30. The significance of the name seems to be related to Parham's early connection with Frank Sandford. Shortly after Parham's visit to Shiloh in 1900, Sandford changed the name of his journal *Tongues of Fire* to *Everlasting Gospel*. As with Parham's later move, the switch involved a greater emphasis on world events and biblical prophecy. See Hiss, pp. 273–74.

[35] Other Pentecostals published eschatological works during the years surrounding the First World War. Particularly prolific was George Floyd Taylor who chronicled his ideas in *The Second Coming of Jesus* (Franklin Springs, Georgia: Publishing House of the Pentecostal Holiness Church, 1916). Less erudite, but enjoying a wider circulation, was Aimee Semple McPherson's *The Second Coming of Christ* (Los Angeles: By the author, 1100 Glendale Boulevard, 1921). The prophetic theme has remained a popular one for Pentecostal authors up to the present day. Examples of this literature are: D. E. Boatwright, *Time Please—It is 11:30* (Cleveland, Tennessee: Church of God Publishing House, n.d.); Ralph M. Riggs, *The Story of the Future* (Springfield, Missouri: Gospel Publishing House, 1968); Clyne W. Buxton, *Expect These Things* (Old Tappan, New Jersey: Fleming H. Revell, 1973); and James D. Case, *The Beginning of the End* (Franklin Springs, Georgia: Advocate Press, 1973). A more in-depth list with some analysis can be found in Goff, "Pentecostal Millenarianism," pp. 22–24.

[36] Parham, *Everlasting Gospel*, pp. 27–28. When the well-known Socialist newspaper editor Julius A. Wayland committed suicide in 1912 in nearby Girard, Kansas, Parham included a sympathetic article in the *Apostolic Faith*. Wayland's ideals had been noble, Parham thought, but his hope of victory through political means was sadly misguided. See *Apostolic Faith* (Baxter) 1 (December 1912):8–9. On Wayland, see Ira Kipnis, *The American Socialist Movement, 1897–1912* (New York: Columbia University Press, 1952), pp. 44–47, 248–49 and Howard H. Quint, "Julius A. Wayland, Pioneer Socialist Propagandist" *Mississippi Valley Historical Review* 35 (March 1949):585–606.

[37] "Christianity vs. Socialism" and "Mass Meeting of the Unemployed," Handbills in *PSD*.

[38] Parham, *Selected Sermons*, p. 2. Although Parham on occasion expressed his own political views, he generally stayed away from pulpit electioneering. Shumway reported that he advised his followers to avoid even voting in political contests. Shumway, "Gift of Tongues," p. 166.

[39] On the strength of socialism in the Southwest where Parham drew his largest support, see James R. Green, *Grass-Roots Socialism: Radical Movements in the Southwest, 1895–1943* (Baton Rouge and London: Louisiana State University Press, 1978) and Garin Burbank, *When Farmers Voted Red: The Gospel of Socialism in the Oklahoma Countryside, 1910–1924* (Westport, Connecticut and London: Greenwood Press, 1976). The southeastern counties of Kansas were particularly fertile fields for socialism in the prewar era. In 1912, twenty-five percent of Parham's native Cherokee County voted for the Socialist Party ticket. Green, pp. 248 and 264.

[40] Parham, *Voice*, p. 59. Also *Apostolic Faith* (Topeka) 1 (June 28, 1899):8 and *Apostolic Faith* (Melrose-Houston) 1 (September 1905):15.

[41] Parham, *Life*, pp. 272–74. On pacifism among early Pentecostals, see Hollenweger, pp. 400–1.

[42] Parham to his family, Houston, Texas, 10 October 1918 and "Obituary: Francis Rolland Romack" *Baxter Daily Citizen* (22 October 1918) in *PSBS*. These materials and other letters of correspondence between Parham and Romack are found in *PSBS*, pp. 50–70. Parham registered for the draft prior to Romack's death, but he never served.

[43] *Apostolic Faith* (Baxter) 3 (January 1927):7 and (March 1927):5. Douglas Nelson's analysis of Parham's Klan connections fails to take into consideration that Parham had undergone a dramatic change not unlike Tom Watson's switch from Populist libertarian to racist demagogue. See Nelson, p. 97. On Watson, see C. Vann Woodward, *Tom Watson: Agrarian Rebel* (New York: Oxford University Press, 1963).

[44] *Apostolic Faith* (Melrose-Houston) 1 (October–November 1905):12–13. This antieducational bent was noted by contemporary writers. See Dunkan Aikman, "The Holy Rollers" *American Mercury* 15 (October 1928):180–91 and Allene M. Sumner, "The Holy Rollers on Shin Bone Ridge" *Nation* 121 (July 29, 1925):137–38.

[45] *Apostolic Faith* (Baxter) 1 (June 1925):2 and "Public Sale," Handbill in *PSD*.

[46] Ibid., 2 (November 1913):13. The allusion is to Balaam's talking donkey in Numbers 22:30.

[47] Parham was vastly better-read than most Pentecostals. On occasion he quoted from the Apocryphal book of Second Esdras. His knowledge of the angel Uriel also indicates familiarity with extracanonical works. See Parham, *Voice*, pp. 115–16 and *Selected Sermons*, p. 39. He also published tracts written by prominent Methodist ministers of the nineteenth century.

[48] Parham, *Life*, pp. 349–99. The trip received extensive coverage in the January through May 1928 issues of *Apostolic Faith* (Baxter).

[49] Ibid., pp. 399–404.

[50] Ibid., pp. 391, 405–12. Also Burnside Interview.

[51] Ibid., pp. 413–18.

[52] Ibid., pp. 415–18b. Also *New York Times* (31 January 1929):23.

Conclusion

[1] Parham, *Life*, pp. 290, 311–24.

[2] *Apostolic Faith* (Baxter) 11 (May 1935):6. Also Parham, *Life*, pp. 410–12 and Parham Interview.

[3] Ibid., pp. 3, 7.

⁴ "Brewery Into Parsonage Now Into Bible College" (December 21, 1936), Miscellaneous newsclipping in Parham Showcase, Apostolic Faith Church, Baxter Springs, Kansas.

⁵ Numbers are difficult to assess since no membership rolls were kept. However, some decline after Parham's death is indicated by the 387 names crossed off Sarah Parham's typed subscription list from the mid-1930s. Only 110 additional names were subsequently scribbled in. See Schultz, "Mailing List." Pauline Parham recalled that her husband's camp meetings in the 1930s drew as many as four thousand (Parham Interview)—a number generally consistent with the three thousand Apostolic faithful personally informed of the opening of the Bible School in 1937 ("Brewery Into Parsonage"). Nevertheless, those figures are quite small when compared to overall Pentecostal growth in the 1930s. Cf. introduction, pp. 8–10.

⁶ Parham Interview. Sarah Parham had actively defended the controversial theology. Cf. Parham, *Selected Sermons,* pp. 93–115.

⁷ Ibid. The exact cause of Robert Parham's death is not known; however, the symptoms described by his wife and his age at the time seem to indicate death by heart attack. Ironically, all of Charles Parham's minister sons died young. In a striking similarity to Robert, Claude died in 1941 at age 44, and Wilfred ca. 1948 at age 44. The other two children far outstripped their brothers in longevity. Philip died in 1963 at age 61 and Esther Marie, the only daughter, in 1975 at age 77. Letter from Kathy Arnall, Apostolic Faith Bible College, Baxter Springs, Kansas, 15 October 1986.

⁸ Interview with Jack Cornell, Superintendent of Apostolic Faith Bible College, Baxter Springs, Kansas, 31 March 1983 and 25 March 1986. Also Haire, Harshfield, and Parham Interviews.

⁹ Ibid. On reasons for founding the Full Gospel Evangelistic Association (but no mention of a split), see Alma Nehrbass, *This Is Full Gospel Evangelistic Association* (Houston: By the author, 1980), p. 4. The figures are from *Apostolic Faith* (Baxter) (April 1951): 10 ff as printed in Nichol, p. 98.

¹⁰ *Directory of Members and Churches, Full Gospel Evangelistic Association* (Houston: Full Gospel Evangelistic Association, January 1987); Parham Interview; and Telephone Interview with Mrs. Alma Nehrbass, former editor of *Full Gospel News* (Houston, Texas), 23 January 1987. The estimate was tabulated by adding an equal number of "cooperating churches" and figuring an average of seventy-five members per church.

[11] Cornell Interviews. The most recent directory lists 109 ministers, forty-seven of whom are designated "pastor." 1974 figures listed 118 ministers and one hundred churches. Cf. *Apostolic Faith Report* (Baxter Springs, Kansas) 33 (November 1986): 5–8 and J. Gordon Melton, *The Encyclopedia of American Religions* 2 vols. (Wilmington, North Carolina: McGrath Publishing Co., 1978), 1: 270. Current subscription to the *Apostolic Faith* (now *Apostolic Faith Report*) is 3,562. Interview with Karen Oakes, editor of *Apostolic Faith Report,* Baxter Springs, Kansas, 25 March 1986. The membership estimate was tabulated by figuring an average of seventy-five members per church.

[12] Jacob C. Regier, *Bible Doctrine* (Perryton, Texas: By the Author, 1963), pp. 135–40 and 160–71. This book is used as a text at Apostolic Faith Bible College. The theological differences between the Apostolic Faith churches and the Full Gospel Evangelistic Association are still evident in their most recent faith statements. Cf. *Apostolic Faith Report* 33 (November 1986): 12 and *Full Gospel News* 14 (March 1985): 16.

Sources

Collections

Apostolic Faith Report Editorial Files, Baxter Springs, Kansas.

Assemblies of God Archives, Springfield, Missouri.

Baker University United Methodist Collection, Baldwin City, Kansas.

Corum, Fred T., comp. *Like as of Fire: A Reprint of the Old Azusa Street Papers*. Wilmington, Massachusetts: By the compiler, August 1981.

Haire, Marjorie Collection, Personal possession of Mrs. Geralean Harshfield, Oklahoma City, Oklahoma.

Holy Spirit Research Center, Oral Roberts University, Tulsa, Oklahoma.

Kansas Historical Society, Topeka, Kansas.

Parham Family Scrapbook, Apostolic Faith Church, Baxter Springs, Kansas. *PSBS*.

Parham Family Scrapbook, Personal possession of Mrs. Pauline Parham, Dallas, Texas. *PSD*.

Parham Showcase, Apostolic Faith Church, Baxter Springs, Kansas.

Pentecostal Evangel Editorial Files, Springfield, Missouri.

Pentecostal Holiness Church Archives, Oklahoma City, Oklahoma.

Religious Publications from the Estate of Rev. and Mrs. Almon H. Butler, Care of Mrs. Mary Louise Butler Edwards, Fayetteville, North Carolina.

United Pentecostal Church Archives, Hazelwood, Missouri.

Interviews

Burnside, Wade W., M.D. Fayetteville, Arkansas. Interview, 31 January 1986.

Busch, Naomi. Former editor of *Apostolic Faith Report,* Baxter Springs, Kansas. Interview, 31 March 1983.

Chalfant, Charles, M.D. Fayetteville, Arkansas. Telephone Interview, 2 May 1983.

Cornell, Jack D. Superintendent, Apostolic Faith Bible College, Baxter Springs, Kansas. Interviews, 31 March 1983 and 25 March 1986.

Floyd, David Lee. Interviewed by Wayne Warner, 10 April 1981. Tape no. 3, Assemblies of God Archives, Springfield, Missouri.

Garcia, David J. District Clerk, Bexar County, San Antonio, Texas. Interview, 14 August 1985.

Haire, Marjorie. Rogers, Arkansas. Interview, 12 June 1985.

Harshfield, Geralean. Oklahoma City, Oklahoma. Interview 14 May 1985.

Nehrbass, Alma. Former editor of *Full Gospel News,* Houston, Texas. Telephone Interview, 23 January 1987.

Oakes, Karen. Editor of *Apostolic Faith Report,* Baxter Springs, Kansas. Interview, 25 March 1986.

Parham, Pauline. Dallas, Texas. Interview, 12 August 1985.

Stanberry, Algernon Benoni. Alvin, Texas. Interview, 16 August 1985.

Research Correspondence

Arnall, Kathy. Apostolic Faith Bible College, Baxter Springs, Kansas. Letter, 15 October 1986.

Black, Joanne. Commission on Archives and History, Kansas West Conference, United Methodist Church, Southwestern College, Winfield, Kansas. Letter, 26 November 1985.

Decker, Ralph W., Jr. Registrar, Southwestern College, Winfield, Kansas. Letter, 25 November 1985.

Kolling, Harold. Curator, Baker University United Methodist Collection, Baldwin City, Kansas. Letter, 10 December 1985.

Parham, Byron A. Supervisory Archivist, General Services Administration, National Archives and Records Service, Washington, D.C. Letter, 23 August 1984.

Strong, Gregory. Research Assistant, General Commission on Archives and History, United Methodist Church, Madison, New Jersey. Letter, 9 May 1986.

Zipp, Judy. Librarian, *San Antonio Express and News*, San Antonio, Texas. Letter, 29 April 1986.

Holiness and Pentecostal Periodicals

Apostolic Faith (Baxter Springs, Kansas), 1910–1916, 1925–1935.

Apostolic Faith (Goose Creek, Texas) no. 20 May 1921.

Apostolic Faith (Houston) 2 October 1908.

Apostolic Faith (Los Angeles), 1906–1908.

Apostolic Faith (Melrose, Kansas, and Houston), 1905–1906.

Apostolic Faith (Portland, Oregon), 1909–1912.

Apostolic Faith (Topeka, Kansas), 1899–1900.

Apostolic Faith Report (Baxter Springs, Kansas) March 1974; November 1979; November 1986.

Burning Bush (Waukesha, Wisconsin) 6 September 1907.

Bridegroom's Messenger (Atlanta) 1 December 1907.

Everlasting Gospel (Baxter Springs, Kansas), 1916–1917.

Faithful Witness (Topeka, Kansas), 1882–1886.

Full Gospel News (Houston) 14 March 1985.

Gospel Trumpet (Moundsville, West Virginia) 22 September 1902.

Herald of the Church (Houston) 1 June 1925.

Holiness Advocate (Goldsboro, North Carolina, and Clinton, North Carolina), 1901–1907.

Latter Rain Evangel (Chicago), 1918–1931.

Leaves of Healing (Chicago and Zion City, Illinois), 1899–1904.

Live Coals of Fire (Lincoln, Nebraska), 1899–1900.

Live Coals (Mercer, Missouri, and Royston, Georgia), 1904–1906.

Message of the Apostolic Faith (Los Angeles) 1 April 1939.

Upper Room (Los Angeles) 1, June–September 1909.

Way of Faith and Neglected Themes (Columbia, South Carolina), 1897–1930.

Word and Witness (Malvern, Arkansas, and Findlay, Ohio), 1912–1914.

Newspapers

Atchison [Kansas] *Globe,* 18 October 1906.

Chicago Blade, 5 February 1901.

Fayetteville [Arkansas] *Daily Democrat,* June–August 1928.

Galveston Nerve, 23 August 1905.

Houston Chronicle, July–September 1905.

Houston Daily Post, July–August 1905; July–August 1906.

Los Angeles Daily Times, 18 April 1906.

Kansas City Journal, January–March 1901.

Kansas City World, January–March 1901.

Kansas City Times, January–March 1901; 7 March 1904.

New York Times, April 1906; September 1906; January 1929.

St. Louis Post-Dispatch, 2, 5 August 1906.

San Antonio Daily Express, June–September 1907.

San Antonio Light, June–September 1907.

Topeka Capital, 12, 18 November 1951; 30 July 1972.

Topeka Daily Capital, January–March 1901; 7 December 1901.

Topeka Daily State Journal, July 1906.

Topeka Mail and Breeze, 22 February 1901.

Topeka State Journal, October 1900–March 1901.

Waukegan [Illinois] *Daily Gazette,* 28 September 1906.

Waukegan Daily Sun, May 1906–January 1908.

Zion [Illinois] *Herald,* July 1907.

Primary Sources

Argue, Zelma E. *What Meaneth This? The Story of Our Personal Experiences and Evangelistic Campaigns.* Alton, Illinois: By the author, 1924.

Arthur, Mary A. "Beginning History of Galena Church." Manuscript, Assemblies of God Archives, n.d.

Barratt, Thomas B. *When the Fire Fell and an Outline of My Life.* Larvik, Norway: Alfons Hansen and Soner, 1927.

Bartleman, Frank. *How Pentecost Came to Los Angeles.* Los Angeles: By the author, 1925; reprint ed. as *Azusa Street*. Plainfield, New Jersey: Logos International, 1980.

Bell, Eudorus N. "What the General Council Stands For." *Pentecostal Evangel* (January 7, 1922):8.

Blackstone W. E. *Jesus Is Coming*. Chicago: Fleming H. Revell Co., 1898; rev. ed., 1908.

Boatwright, D. E. *Time Please—It Is 11:30*. n.p., n.d. Holy Spirit Research Center, Oral Roberts University, Tulsa, OK.

Bodine, L. T. *Kansas Illustrated*. Kansas City, Missouri: Ramsey, Millett, and Hudson, 1879.

Bohm, Charles J. T. *The Second Coming of Christ and His Kingdom in Visible Glory*. Glasgow: D. Hobbs and Co., 1902.

Burch, Lawrence D. *Kansas as It Is*. Chicago: C. S. Burch and Co., 1878.

Buxton, Clyne W. *Expect These Things*. Old Tappan, New Jersey: Fleming H. Revell, 1973.

Carradine, B. *The Old Man*. Kentucky Methodist Publishing Co., 1896; reprint ed., Jamestown, North Carolina: Newby Book Room, n.d.

Case, James D. *The Beginning of the End*. Franklin Springs, Georgia: Advocate Press, 1973.

Criminal Minutes: District Court, Bexar County, Texas. File No. 18668, "State of Texas vs. J. J. Jourdan."

Directory of Members and Churches, Full Gospel Evangelistic Association. Houston: Full Gospel Evangelistic Association, January 1987.

Discipline of the Pentecostal Holiness Church. Franklin Springs, Georgia: Publishing House of the Pentecostal Holiness Church, 1925.

Freeman, Rev. and Mrs. Dallas Dolphus. *Missions On the March: Pentecostal Holiness Church in Southern Africa*. Franklin Springs, Georgia: Pentecostal Holiness Church Press, 1962.

Griswold, Wayne. *Kansas, Her Resources and Developments*. Cincinnati: Robert Clarke and Co., 1871.

Herzl, Theodor. *The Jewish State*. Translated by Sylvie D'Avigdor. 4th ed. London: Rita Searl, 1946.

Holmes, Nickels J. and Holmes, Lucy Simpson. *Life Sketches and Sermons*. Royston, Georgia: Publishing House of the Pentecostal

244   *Sources*

Holiness Church, 1920; reprint ed., Franklin Springs: Advocate Press, 1973.

Hutchinson, Clinton Carter. *Resources of Kansas*. Topeka: By the author, 1871.

LaBerge, Agnes N. O. "A History of the Pentecostal Movement From January 1, 1901." Manuscript, *Pentecostal Evangel* Editorial Files, February 1922.

———. *What God Hath Wrought*. Chicago: Herald Publishing Co., 1921.

Lawrence, Bennet F. "Reminiscences of an Eyewitness." *Weekly Evangel* (February 26, 1916):4–5; (March 4, 1916):4–5.

———. *The Apostolic Faith Restored*. St. Louis: Gospel Publishing House, 1916.

Loomis, Marjorie L. *With All My Love*. Springfield, Missouri: Gospel Publishing House, 1963.

McPherson, Aimee Semple. *The Second Coming of Christ*. Los Angeles: By the author, 1100 Glendale Boulevard, 1921.

MacPherson, Hector, Jr. "The Creation Story in the Light of Modern Astronomy." *Popular Astronomy* 19 (August 1911):426–30.

Muenzner, Franz. *Apostolic Faith! Erste Deutsche gedruckte Predigt von Franz Muenzner*. Orchard, Texas: By the author, 1905.

Nehrbass, Alma. *This Is Full Gospel Evangelistic Association*. Houston: By the author, 1980.

Parham, Charles Fox. *Kol Kare Bomidbar: A Voice Crying in the Wilderness*. Kansas City, Missouri: By the author, 1902; reprint ed., Joplin, Missouri: Joplin Printing Co., 1944.

———. *The Everlasting Gospel*. n.p., [1919–20].

———. and Sarah E. *Selected Sermons of the Late Charles F. Parham and Sarah E. Parham*. Compiled by Robert L. Parham. Baxter Springs, Kansas: By the compiler, 1941.

Pinson, Mack M. "Sketch of the Life and Ministry of Mack M. Pinson." Manuscript, Assemblies of God Archives, September 6, 1949.

Quinlan, Florence. "History of the United Methodist Church in Linwood, Kansas." Manuscript, Baker University United Methodist Collection, August 13, 1970.

Regier, Jacob C. *Bible Doctrine*. Perryton, Texas: By the author, 1963.

Riggs, Ralph M. *The Story of the Future*. Springfield, Missouri: Gospel Publishing House, 1968.

Schultz, Gail W., comp. "Mailing List of the Apostolic Faith." Manuscript, *Apostolic Faith Report* Editorial Files, [1930s].

Simpson, Albert Benjamin. *Missionary Messages*. Harrisburg, Pennsylvania: Christian Publications, n.d.

Stanberry, Bennie. *Songs of Inspriation*. Katy, Texas: By the author, 1967.

Taylor, George Floyd. *The Rainbow*. Franklin Springs, Georgia: Publishing House of the Pentecostal Holiness Church, 1924.

————. *The Second Coming of Jesus*. Franklin Springs, Georgia: Publishing House of the Pentecostal Holiness Church, 1916; reprint ed., 1950.

————. *The Spirit and the Bride*. Dunn, North Carolina: By the author, 1907.

Turner, William Henry. *Pioneering in China*. Franklin Springs, Georgia: Publishing House of the Pentecostal Holiness Church, 1928.

————. *Pentecost and Tongues*. 2nd ed. Franklin Springs, Georgia: Advocate Press, 1968.

Warner, Wayne E., ed. *Touched by the Fire*. Plainfield, New Jersey: Logos International, 1978.

Watson, George D. *The Bridegroom Saints*. Cincinnati: Office God's Revivalist, n.d.

————. *Coals of Fire*. Boston: McDonald and Gill, 1886; reprint ed., Jamestown, North Carolina: Newby Book Room, n.d.

White, Alma. *Demons and Tongues*. 4th ed. Zeraphath, New Jersey: The Pillar of Fire, 1949.

Woodworth, Maria Beulah. *Life and Experience of Maria B. Woodworth*. Dayton, Ohio: United Bretheren Publishing Hosue, 1885.

————. *The Life, Work, and Experience of Maria Beulah Woodworth*. St. Louis: By the author, 1894.

York, Dan and Dollie. *Life Events of Dan and Dollie York*. n.p., 1951. Pentecostal Holiness Archives, Oklahoma City, OK.

Zahm, Jeanna; Makings, Elinor; and Bieber Clione; comps. *Record of Affidavit of Death: Book A, Cherokee County*. Columbus, Kansas: Cherokee County Genealogy Society, n.d.

Secondary Sources

Ahlstrom, Sydney. *A Religious History of the American People.* New Haven and London: Yale University Press, 1972.

Aikman, Duncan. "The Holy Rollers." *American Mercury* 15 (October 1928):180–91.

Anderson, Robert Mapes. *Vision of the Disinherited.* New York and Oxford: Oxford University Press, 1979.

Andreas, Alfred T. *History of the State of Kansas.* Chicago: A. T. Andreas, 1883.

———. *Illustrated Historical Atlas of the State of Iowa.* Chicago: Andreas Atlas Co., 1875.

Bader, Robert Smith. "Mrs. Nation." *Kansas History* 7 (Winter 1984–85):246–62.

Barrett, David B., ed. *World Christian Encyclopedia.* Oxford: Oxford University Press, 1982.

Baxter Springs . . . A City on the Move. Baxter Springs, Kansas: Baxter Springs Chamber of Commerce, 1986.

Bloch–Hoell, Nils. *The Pentecostal Movement.* Oslo: Universitetsforlaget; London: Allen and Unwin; New York: Humanities Press, 1964.

Blumhofer, Edith Waldvogel. *The Assemblies of God: A Popular History.* Springfield, Missouri: Gospel Publishing House, 1985.

Brauser, Bradley O. *Yestermorrows.* Ponca City, Oklahoma: By the author, 1969.

Brumback, Carl. *Suddenly . . . from Heaven: A History of the Assemblies of God.* Springfield, Missouri: Gospel Publishing House, 1961; reprint ed. as *A Sound From Heaven* and *Like a River,* 1977.

Bullough, Vern L. *Homosexuality: A History.* New York and London: Garland STPM Press, 1979.

Burbank, Garin. *When Farmers Voted Red: The Gospel of Socialism in the Oklahoma Countryside, 1910–1924.* Westport, Connecticut, and London: Greenwood Press, 1976.

Burkett, Randall K. and Newman, Richard, eds. *Black Apostles: Afro-American Clergy Confront the Twentieth Century.* Boston: G. K. Hall and Co., 1978.

Campbell, Joseph Enoch. *The Pentecostal Holiness Church, 1898–1948*. Franklin Springs, Georgia: Pentecostal Holiness Church Press, 1951; reprint ed., Raleigh, North Carolina: World Outlook Publications, 1981.

Carroll, B. H., Jr., ed. *Standard History of Houston, Texas*. Knoxville, Tennessee: H. W. Crew and Co., 1912.

Centennial: The Baxter Springs Story, 1858–1958. Souvenir program, Baxter Springs, Kansas, 1958.

Chappell, Paul G. "The Divine Healing Movement in America." Ph.D. dissertation, Drew University, 1983.

Clanton, Arthur L. *United We Stand: A History of Oneness Organizations*. Hazelwood, Missouri: Pentecostal Publishing House, 1970.

Clark, Max A. X. *Latter Rain and Holy Fire: The Beginnings of the Pentecostal Movement*. n.p., n.d. Kansas Historical Society, Topeka, KS.

Cohn, Norman. *The Pursuit of the Millennium*. 2nd ed. New York: Oxford University Press, 1970.

Conn, Charles W. *Like a Mighty Army*. Cleveland, Tennessee: Church of God Publishing House, 1955.

Connelley, William E. *History of Kansas State and People*. 5 vols. Chicago and New York: American Historical Society, 1928.

Cook, Philip Lee. "Zion City, Illinois: Twentieth Century Utopia." Ph.D. dissertation, University of Colorado, 1965.

Damboriena, Prudencio. *Tongues as of Fire*. Washington, D.C., and Cleveland: Corpus Books, 1969.

Deacon, Marie. "Kansas as the 'Promised Land': The View of the Black Press, 1890–1900." M.A. thesis, University of Arkansas, 1973.

D'Epinay, Christian Lalive. "The Pentecostal 'Conquista' in Chile." *Ecumenical Review* (1968):16–32.

Dieter, Melvin Easterday. *The Holiness Revival of the Nineteenth Century*. Metuchen, New Jersey, and London: Scarecrow Press, 1980.

Driscoll, Charles B. "Major Prophets of Holy Kansas." *American Mercury* 8 (May 1926):18–26.

Duffy, John. *The Healers: A History of American Medicine*. Urbana: University of Illinois Press, 1979.

Durasoff, Steve. *Bright Wind of the Spirit.* Englewood Cliffs, New Jersey: Prentice-Hall, 1972.

Ewart, Frank J. *The Phenomenon of Pentecost.* St. Louis: Pentecostal Publishing House, 1947.

———. *The Phenomenon of Pentecost.* rev. ed. Hazelwood, Missouri: Word Aflame Press, 1975.

Farnsworth, Elmer Dean, ed. *The Story of Southwestern.* Winfield, Kansas: Anderson Press, 1925.

Flower, J. Roswell. "Birth of the Pentecostal Movement." *Pentecostal Evangel* no. 1907 (November 26, 1950): 3, 12–13.

———. "Historical Review of the Pentecostal Movement." Address at the 1955 Pentecostal World Conference. *Assemblies of God Heritage* 5 (Fall 1985): 10–12, 16.

Frodsham, Stanley H. *With Signs Following.* 3rd ed. Springfield, Missouri: Gospel Publishing House, 1946.

Gaustad, Edwin S., ed. *The Rise of Adventism.* New York: Harper and Row, Publishers, 1974.

Gee, Donald. *The Pentecostal Movement.* London: Elim Publishing Co., 1949.

Gerlach, Luther P. and Hine, Virginia H. *People, Power, Change: Movements of Social Transformation.* Indianapolis: Bobbs-Merrill Educational Publishing Co., 1970.

Gibson, Arrell M. "Lead Mining in Southwest Missouri After 1865." *Missouri Historical Review* 53 (July 1959): 315–28.

Goff, James R., Jr. "Charles F. Parham and His Role in the Development of the Pentecostal Movement: A Reevaluation." *Kansas History* 7 (Autumn 1984): 226–37.

———. "Pentecostal Millenarianism: The Development of Premillennial Orthodoxy, 1909–1943." *Ozark Historical Review* 12 (Spring 1983): 14–24.

Golder, Morris E. *History of the Pentecostal Assemblies of the World.* Indianapolis: By the author, 1973.

Goss, Ethel E. *The Winds of God: The Story of the Early Pentecostal Days (1901–1914) in the Life of Howard A. Goss.* New York: Comet Press Books, 1958.

———. *The Winds of God: The Story of the Early Pentecostal Days (1901–1914) in the Life of Howard A. Goss.* rev. ed. by

Ruth Nortje Goss. Hazelwood, Missouri: Word Aflame Press, 1977.

Gottschalk, Stephen. *The Emergence of Christian Science in American Religious Life.* Berkeley: University of California Press, 1973.

Gray, David E. "Lean Not Thou on the Arm of Flesh." *Shawnee County Historical Society Bulletin* 57 (November 1980): 143–50.

Green, James R. *Grass-Roots Socialism: Radical Movements in the Southwest, 1895–1943.* Baton Rouge and London: Louisiana State University Press, 1978.

Grob, Gerald N. *Edward Jarvis and the Medical World of Nineteenth-Century America.* Knoxville: University of Tennessee Press, 1978.

Handy, Robert T. *A Christian America.* New York: Oxford University Press, 1971.

———. *A History of the Churches in the United States and Canada.* New York: Oxford University Press, 1977.

Harper, Michael. *As at the Beginning: The Twentieth Century Pentecostal Revival.* Plainfield, New Jersey: Logos International, 1965.

Harrell, David Edwin, Jr. *All Things Are Possible: The Healing and Charismatic Revivals in Modern America.* Bloomington and London: Indiana University Press, 1975.

Harris, Ralph W. *Spoken by the Spirit.* Springfield, Missouri: Gospel Publishing House, 1973.

Harrison, Irvine John. "A History of the Assemblies of God." Th.D. dissertation, Berkeley Baptist Divinity School, 1954.

Harrison, J. F. C. *The Second Coming: Popular Millenarianism, 1780–1850.* New Brunswick, New Jersey: Rutger's University Press, 1979.

Hatch, Nathan O. *The Sacred Cause of Liberty.* New Haven and London: Yale University Press, 1977.

Hicks, John D. *The Populist Revolt.* Minneapolis: University of Minnesota Press, 1931.

Hiss, William Charles. "Shiloh, Frank W. Sandford and the Kingdom, 1893–1948." Ph.D. dissertation, Tufts University, 1978.

Historical Account of the Apostolic Faith. Portland, Oregon: Apostolic Faith Publishing House, 1965.

Hobsbawm, E. J. *Primitive Rebels: Studies in Archaic Forms of Social Movement in the Nineteenth and Twentieth Centuries.* 2nd ed. New York: Frederick A. Praeger, Publisher, 1963.

Hollenweger, Walter J. *The Pentecostals.* Minneapolis: Augsburg Publishing House, 1972.

Hoover, Mario G. "Origin and Structural Development of the Assemblies of God." M.A. thesis, Southwest Missouri State College, 1968.

Hudson, Winthrop S. *Religion in America.* 2nd ed. New York: Charles Scribner's Sons, 1973.

Hughes, Ray H. "A Traditional Pentecostal Looks at the New Pentecostals." *Christianity Today* 18 (June 7, 1974): 6–10.

Hunter, Harold. "Spirit-Baptism and the 1896 Revival in Cherokee County, North Carolina." *Pneuma* 5 (Fall 1983): 1–17.

In Loving Memory: Marie Estelle Brown. New York: Glad Tidings Tabernacle, 1971.

Jones, Charles Edwin. *Perfectionist Persuasion: The Holiness Movement and American Methodism, 1867–1936.* Metuchen, New Jersey: Scarecrow Press, 1974.

Jorstad, Erling. *The Holy Spirit in Today's Church: A Handbook of the New Pentecostalism.* Nashville and New York: Abingdon Press, 1973.

Kantzer, Kenneth S. "The Charismatics Among Us." *Christianity Today* 24 (February 22, 1980): 25–29.

Kendrick, Klaude. *The Promise Fulfilled: A History of the Modern Pentecostal Movement.* Springfield, Missouri: Gospel Publishing House, 1961.

Kenyon, Howard Nelson. "An Analysis of Racial Separation Within the Early Pentecostal Movement." M.A. thesis, Baylor University, 1978.

King, Joseph Hillery. "History of the Fire-Baptized Holiness Church." Manuscript, Pentecostal Holiness Archives, 1921.

Kipnis, Ira. *The American Socialist Movement, 1897–1912.* New York: Columbia University Press, 1952.

Knight, Herbert V. *Ministry Aflame.* Amherst, Wisconsin: Palmer Publications, 1972.

Laqueur, Walter. *A History of Zionism.* New York: Holt, Rinehart, and Winston, 1972.

Lindsay, Gordon. *They Saw It Happen!* Dallas: Christ For the Nations, 1972.

Lovett, Leonard. "Black Holiness-Pentecostalism: Implications For Ethics and Social Transformation." Ph.D. dissertation, Emory University, 1978.

McCullough, David. *Mornings on Horseback.* New York: Simon and Schuster, 1981.

McLoughlin, William G., Jr. *Modern Revivalism: Charles Grandison Finney to Billy Graham.* New York: Ronald Press Co., 1959.

Marsden, George M. *Fundamentalism and American Culture: The Shaping of Twentieth Century Evangelicalism, 1870–1925.* New York and Oxford: Oxford University Press, 1980.

Martin, John Rutledge, "Sexuality and Science: Victorian and Post-Victorian Scientific Ideas on Sexuality." Ph.D. dissertation, Duke University, 1978.

Mechem, Kirke, ed. *The Annals of Kansas: 1886–1925.* 2 vols. Topeka: Kansas State Historical Society, 1954–56.

Melton, J. Gordon. *The Encyclopedia of American Religions.* 2 vols. Wilmington, North Carolina: McGrath Publishing Co., 1978.

Menzies, William W. *Annointed to Serve: The Story of the Assemblies of God.* Springfield, Missouri: Gospel Publishing House, 1971.

Merricks, William S. *Edward Irving: The Forgotten Giant.* East Peoria, Illinois: Scribe's Chamber Publications, 1983.

Meyers, Jeffrey. *Homosexuality and Literature, 1890–1930.* Montreal: McGill-Queens's University Press, 1977.

Mitchell, Robert Bryant. *Heritage and Horizons: The History of Open Bible Standard Churches.* Des Moines, Iowa: Open Bible Publishers, 1982.

Montgomery, G. H. "The Origin and Development of the Pentecostal Movement." *Pentecostal Holiness Advocate* (March 14, 1946): 3–5, 10.

Moorhead, James H. *American Apocalypse: Yankee Protestants and the Civil War, 1860–1869.* New Haven and London: Yale University Press, 1978.

Morris, W. Eddie. *The Vine and Branches: Historic Events of the Holiness and Pentecostal Movement.* Franklin Springs, Georgia: Advocate Press, 1981.

Murphy, Lyle P. "Beginning at Topeka." *Calvary Review* 13 (Spring 1974):2–5, 8–10.

Nelson, Douglas J. "For Such a Time as This: The Story of Bishop William J. Seymour and the Azusa Street Revival." Ph.D. dissertation, University of Birmingham, England, 1981.

———. "The Black Face of Church Renewal: A Brief Essay Examining the Meaning of the Pentecostal-Charismatic Church Renewal Movement, 1901–1985." Private manuscript, 1985. Assemblies of God Archives, Springfield, MO.

Nagel, Paul C. *Missouri: A Bicentennial History.* New York: W. W. Norton and Co., 1977.

Nichol, John Thomas. *Pentecostalism.* New York: Harper and Row, Publishers, 1966.

Orr, J. Edwin. *The Flaming Tongue.* Chicago: Moody Press, 1975.

Ostling, Richard N. "Counting Every Soul on Earth." *Time,* May 3, 1982, pp. 66–67.

Parham, Sarah E. *The Life of Charles F. Parham.* Joplin, Missouri: Tri-State Printing Co., 1930; reprint ed., Birmingham, Alabama: Commercial Printing Co., 1977.

Parker, William. *Homosexuality: A Selective Bibliography of Over 3,000 Items.* Metuchen, New Jersey: Scarecrow Press, 1971.

Paul, George Harold. "The Religious Frontier in Oklahoma: Dan T. Muse and the Pentecostal Holiness Church." Ph.D. dissertation, University of Oklahoma, 1965.

Quebedeaux, Richard. *The New Charismatics: The Origins, Development, and Significance of Neo-Pentecostalism.* Garden City, New York: Doubleday and Co., 1976.

Rausch, David A. *Zionism Within Early American Fundamentalism: 1878–1918.* New York and Toronto: Edwin Mellen Press, 1979.

Reeder, Hilda. *A Brief History of the Foreign Missionary Department of the Pentecostal Assemblies of the World.* Indianapolis: Pentecostal Assemblies of the World, 1951.

Ripley, John W. "Erastus Stone's Dream Castle—Birthplace of Pentecostalism." *Shawnee County Historical Bulletin* 52 (June 1975):42–53.

Ryrie, Charles C. *Dispensationalism Today.* Chicago: Moody Press, 1965.

Sage, Leland L. *A History of Iowa.* Ames: Iowa State University Press, 1974.

Samarin, William J. *Tongues of Men and Angels: The Religious Language of Pentecostalism.* New York and London: Macmillan Co., 1972.

Sandeen, Ernest R. *The Roots of Fundamentalism: British and American Millenarianism, 1800–1930.* Chicago: University of Chicago Press, 1970; reprint ed., Grand Rapids, Michigan: Baker Book House, 1970.

Shaner, Dolph. *John Baxter of Baxter Springs.* Souvenir ed., Eightieth Anniversary of the Baxter State Bank, 1985.

Sherrill, John L. *They Speak With Other Tongues.* New York: Pillar Books, 1964.

Shopshire, James Maynard. "A Socio-Historical Characterization of the Black Pentecostal Movement in America." Ph.D. dissertation, Northwestern University, 1975.

Shumway, Charles William. "A Critical History of Glossolalia." Ph.D. dissertation, Boston University, 1919.

———. "A Study of 'The Gift of Tongues.'" A. B. thesis, University of Southern California, 1914.

Shoemaker, Floyd C. "Cedar County." *Missouri Historical Review* 53 (July 1959): 329–36.

Smith, Timothy L. *Called Unto Holiness.* Kansas City, Missouri: Nazarene Publishing House, 1962.

———. *Revivalism and Social Reform: American Protestantism on the Eve of the Civil War.* Gloucester, Massachusetts: Peter Smith, 1976.

Spillman, Patricia R. "The Kansan Ethos in the Last Three Decades of the Nineteenth Century." *Emporia State Research Studies* 29 (Summer 1980): 5–47.

Stolee, H. J. *Pentecostalism: The Problem of the Modern Tongues Movement.* Minneapolis: Augsburg Publishing House, 1936; reprint ed. as *Speaking in Tongues,* 1963.

Stotts, George R. "Mary Woodworth-Etter: A Forgotten Feminine Figure in the Late Nineteenth and Early Twentieth Century Charismatic Revival." Paper presented at the American Academy of Religion, Washington, D.C., 26 October 1974.

Sweet, William Warren. *The Story of Religion in America.* rev. ed. New York: Harper and Bros., 1950.

254   *Sources*

Synan, Vinson. *Aspects of Pentecostal-Charismatic Origins*. Plainfield, New Jersey: Logos International, 1975.

———. *In the Latter Days: The Outpouring of the Holy Spirit in the Twentieth Century*. Ann Arbor, Michigan: Servant Books, 1984.

———. *The Holiness-Pentecostal Movement in the United States*. Grand Rapids, Michigan: William B. Eerdman's, 1971.

Taylor, George Floyd. "Our Church History." Manuscript, Pentecostal Holiness Archives, 1921.

Teeple, Howard M. *The Noah's Ark Nonsense*. Evanston, Illinois: Religion and Ethics Institute, 1978.

Tinney, James S. "Black Origins of the Pentecostal Movement." *Christianity Today* 16 (October 8, 1971):4–6.

Van Dusen, Henry P. "The Third Force in Christendom." *Life*, (June 9, 1958):113–24.

Vital, David. *The Origins of Zionism*. Oxford: Clarendon Press, 1975.

Wacker, Grant. "Into Canaan's Fair Land: Brokenness and Healing in the Pentecostal Tradition" in Ronald Numbers and Darryl Amundsen, eds. *To Care and To Cure: Health and Healing in the Faith Traditions*. New York: Macmillan Co., forthcoming.

———. "Marching to Zion: Religion in a Modern Utopian Community." *Church History* 54 (December 1985):496–511.

———. "The Functions of Faith in Primitive Pentecostalism." *Harvard Theological Review* 77 (1984):353–75.

———. "The Holy Spirit and the Spirit of the Age of American Protestantism, 1880–1910." *Journal of American History* 72 (June 1985):45–62.

Wagner, Peter. "The Greatest Church Growth Is Beyond Our Shores." *Christianity Today* 28 (May 18, 1984):25–31.

Waldvogel, Edith Lydia. "The 'Overcoming Life': A Study in the Reformed Evangelical Origins of Pentecostalism." Ph.D. dissertation, Harvard University, 1977.

Washington, Joseph R., Jr. *Black Sects and Cults*. New York: University Press of America, 1984.

Weber, Timothy P. *Living in the Shadow of the Second Coming*. New York and Oxford: Oxford University Press, 1979.

Wheelock, Donald Ray. "Spirit Baptism in American Pentecostal Thought." Ph.D. dissertation, Emory University, 1983.

Whittaker, Colin. "The Korean Pentecost." *Dedication* 9:20–22. Oral Roberts University Holy Spirit Research Center. No date.

Wiebe, Robert H. *The Search For Order: 1877–1920.* New York: Hill and Wang, 1967.

Willems, Emilio. *Followers of the New Faith.* Nashville: Vanderbilt University Press, 1966.

———. "Religious Mass Movements and Social Change in Brazil" in Baklanoff, E. N., ed. *New Perspectives of Brazil.* Nashville: Vanderbilt University Press, 1966.

Williams, Walter, ed. *The State of Missouri.* Columbia, Missouri: E. W. Stephens, 1904.

Wolkoff, Regina Lois. "The Ethics of Sex: Individuality and the Social Order in Early Twentieth Century American Sexual Advice Literature." Ph.D. dissertation, University of Michigan, 1974.

Wood, Dillard L. and Preskitt, William H., Jr. *Baptized With Fire: A History of the Pentecostal Fire-Baptized Holiness Church.* Franklin Springs, Georgia: Advocate Press, 1982.

Zornow, William Frank. *Kansas: A History of the Jayhawk State.* Norman: University of Oklahoma Press, 1957.

Index